UNIVERSITY OF NORTH CAROLINA AT CHAPEL HILL
DEPARTMENT OF ROMANCE LANGUAGES

NORTH CAROLINA STUDIES
IN THE ROMANCE LANGUAGES AND LITERATURES

Founder: URBAN TIGNER HOLMES
Editor: STIRLING HAIG

Distributed by:

UNIVERSITY OF NORTH CAROLINA PRESS
CHAPEL HILL
North Carolina 27514
U.S.A.

NORTH CAROLINA STUDIES IN THE
ROMANCE LANGUAGES AND LITERATURES

Number 225

MARTORELL'S *TIRANT LO BLANCH:*

A PROGRAM FOR MILITARY AND SOCIAL REFORM
IN FIFTEENTH-CENTURY CHRISTENDOM

MARTORELL'S *TIRANT LO BLANCH:*
A PROGRAM FOR MILITARY AND SOCIAL REFORM IN FIFTEENTH-CENTURY CHRISTENDOM

BY
EDWARD T. AYLWARD

CHAPEL HILL

NORTH CAROLINA STUDIES IN THE ROMANCE
LANGUAGES AND LITERATURES
U.N.C. DEPARTMENT OF ROMANCE LANGUAGES

1985

Library of Congress Cataloging in Publication Data

Alward, E. T.
  Martorell's Tirant lo Blanch.

  (North Carolina studies in the Romance languages and literatures; 225)
  Bibliography: p.
  1. Martorell, Joanot, d. 1468.   Tirant lo Blanch. I. Title.   II. Series.

PC3937.M4A86 1985   849'.933   85-2916

© 1985. Department of Romance Languages. The University of North Carolina at Chapel Hill.

ISBN 0-8078-9229-7

DEPÓSITO LEGAL: V. 551 - 1985   I.S.B.N. 84-599-0535-7
ARTES GRÁFICAS SOLER, S. A. - LA OLIVERETA, 28 - 46018 VALENCIA - 1985

CONTENTS

	Page
INTRODUCTION	11
I. TWO FERRANTES IN ONE: THE DEDICATION OF "TIRANT LO BLANCH" AS A REFLECTION OF MARTORELL'S DESIGN FOR THE NOVEL	23
II. TIRANT LO BLANCH: THE IDEAL CHRISTIAN COMMANDER	44
III. TIRANT LO BLANCH: A NEW KIND OF COURTLY LOVER	88
IV. ON QUAINT CHIVALRIC RITUALS: VOWS AND PERSONAL CHALLENGES	118
V. MORE THAN A NOVEL OF CHIVALRY: MARTORELL'S PLAN FOR "TIRANT LO BLANCH"	181
VI. SOME LITERARY CONSIDERATIONS: "TIRANT LO BLANCH," PRECURSOR OF THE MODERN NOVEL?	201
BIBLIOGRAPHY	217

This book is dedicated to the memory of My Father and My Mother, Edward and Mary.

INTRODUCTION

I have long believed that Joanot Martorell and Martí Joan de Galba's *Tirant lo Blanch* (1490)[1] is one of Hispanic literature's most misunderstood and least appreciated great novels. The enormous diversity of *TB*'s literary material makes it practically impossible to categorize. Consequently, Martorell's masterpiece has been largely misunderstood and underestimated by scholars over the centuries, and with certain exceptions — most notably, Miguel de Cervantes — the critics have treated it harshly. Only in the late 1940s did Hispanists begin to awaken to the considerable literary qualities of this unique Catalan work of fiction. The watershed year of 1969 marked the beginning of a new tide of appreciative criticism with the appearance of Mario Vargas Llosa's eloquent defense of *TB*, an essay in which he accurately categorizes Martorell's work as a masterful composite of several different narrative forms: he calls it at once a novel of chivalry, a fantastic tale, an historical novel, a military manual, a study of fifteenth-century customs and manners, as well as a penetrating and erotic psychological novel — yet none of these exclusively.[2]

My own study and analysis of *TB*, which began in 1971 with the preparation of my doctoral dissertation,[3] has led me to conclude

---

[1] Since the colophon of the 1490 edition of *Tirant lo Blanch* (referred to hereafter as *TB*) attributes only the fourth part — whatever that may consist of — to Galba, I will treat Martorell as the principal author and designer of the novel's structure and theme.

[2] "Carta de batalla por *Tirant lo Blanc*," *Revista de Occidente*, 70 (Jan. 1969), 1-21; also found as part of the prologue to the J. F. Vidal Jové translation into Castilian, *Tirant lo Blanc*, 2 vols. (Madrid: Alianza, 1969), pp. 9-41.

[3] "The Influence of *Tirant lo Blanch* on the *Quijote*," Diss. Princeton 1974.

that Martorell's novel is basically a two-pronged attack on what he considered to be the major social and political maladies of his time, the mid-1400s. On the one hand we have a pragmatic and tightly-reasoned response to and remedy for the decline in military might among the Christian kingdoms of the Mediterranean region, a downward slide which culminated in the fall of Constantinople to the Turks in 1453. The loss of the Byzantine capital to the Moslems was the cause of great consternation among European Christians in general and was especially distressing to Martorell's own sovereign, Alfonso V of Aragon (1416-58), whose foreign policy was directed from his court at Naples and was consequently heavily dependent upon Christian control of the Balkans and the Eastern Mediterranean. Alfonso, whose sobriquet was "the Magnanimous," was anything but that regarding the Turkish aggression in that area during the mid-1400s; he gave, for example, serious consideration to a scheme to forge a new alliance of Christian states whose armies would jointly undertake a new Crusade to wrest control of the Byzantine capital from the Turks, but he died before those plans could be put into effect. Thus deprived of his sponsorship, the project was destined to be stillborn. Martorell's book, then, can be viewed as an artistic (i.e., fantastic) extension of Alfonso's aborted foreign policy, including his grandiose design for the recapture of Constantinople.

On the other hand, the novel contains an equally high-charged, emotional response to a parallel decline in social and sexual mores that had taken place in contemporary Christian society. Martorell was principally concerned about the noxious effects of certain decadent courtship customs that had their origins in the idealistic traditions of Courtly Love but had been allowed to linger past the point of usefulness; he was especially vehement about a number of serious social problems that had sprung from the custom of clandestine marriage (i.e., the exchange of secret wedding vows that were supposed to be ratified later in a formal ceremony). This frivolous and casual approach to the serious business of courtship and marriage was fraught with abuse and Martorell viewed it as proof positive that the entire social institution of courtship was badly in need of reform.

The result is a novel with a Janus-like countenance: one face to serve as an apology for the Christian military orders, with an accompanying telescoped history of the martial arts; on the other side to forge a subtle and satirical exposé of some of the absurdities that had evolved from the antiquated precepts of Courtly Love.[4]

Martorell's novel opens with a prologue that is nothing more than an unabashed encomium for the military establishment, a discourse worthy of Don Quixote himself. In part it reads

> Mereixedors són d'honor, glòria e de fama e contínua bona memòria los hòmens virtuosos, e singularment aquells qui per la república no han recusat sotsmetre llurs persones a mort, perquè la vida d'aquells fos perpetual per glòria. E llegim que honor sens exercici de molts actes virtuosos no pot ésser adquirida; e felicitat no pot ésser atesa sens mijà de virtuts. Los cavallers animosos volgueren morir en les batalles ans que fugir vergonyosament. La santa dona Judic ab ànimo viril gosà matar Holofernes per delliurar la ciutat de l'opressió d'aquell. E tants llibres són estats fets e compilats de gestes e històries antigues, que no seria suficient l'enteniment humà compendre e retenir aquelles.
>
> Antigament, l'orde militar era tengut en tanta reverència, que no era decorat d'honor de milícia sinó lo fort, animós, prudent e molt expert en l'exercici de les armes. Fortitud corporal e ardiment se vol exercir ab saviesa: com, per la prudència e indústria dels batallants, diverses vegades los pocs han obtesa victòria dels molts, la saviesa e astúcia dels cavallers ha bastat aterrar les forces dels enemics. E per ço foren per los antics ordenades justes e torneigs, nodrint los infants de poca edat en l'exercici militar, perquè en les batalles fossen forts e animosos, e no haguessen terror de la vista dels enemics. La dignitat militar deu ésser molt decorada, perquè sens aquella los regnes e ciutats no es porien sostenir en pau, segons que diu lo gloriós Sant Lluc en lo seu *Evangeli*. Mereixedor és, doncs, lo virtuós e valent cavaller d'honor e glòria, e la fama d'aquell no deu preterir per longitud de molts dies. E com entre los altres insignes cavallers de gloriosa recordació sia estat aquell valentíssim cavaller Tirant lo Blanc, del qual fa especial commemoració lo present llibre, per ço d'aquell, e de les sues grandíssimes virtuts e cavalleries, se fa singu-

---

[4] For a full treatment of Martorell's attitude toward clandestine marriage and Courtly Love, see Justina Ruiz de Conde, *El amor y el matrimonio secreto en los libros de caballerías* (Madrid: Aguilar, 1948), pp. 101-70.

lar e expressa menció individual, segons reciten les següents històries.

(*TB*, 115-16)[5]

It continues with a symbolic, condensed history of several centuries' worth of technological advances in the evolution of military strategies and armaments — all within the lifetime of a single protagonist. We observe a growing reliance by the hero upon evermore sophisticated offensive and defensive weaponry and tactics, plus an increased resort to cunning and deception in the tactical deployment of men and materiel. Tirant launches his chivalric career as an Ivanhoe-like knight-errant, but eventually schools himself in the effective use of gunpowder and artillery, as well as the special arts of naval combat.

---

[5] "Virtuous men are deserving of honor, glory and fame, and should constantly be thought of kindly; this is particularly true in the case of those who have not refused to subject themselves to death on behalf of the republic, for it is right that their lives be perpetuated in glory. And one reads that honor cannot be acquired without performing many virtuous acts; and happiness cannot be attained except by means of virtues. The brave knights chose to die in battle rather than flee in disgrace. With manly courage Judith dared to slay Holofernes to free her city from his oppression. And so many books have been written and compiled about epic poems and old stories that the human mind would not be capable of understanding or keeping track of them all.

"In ancient times the military orders were held in such reverence that only strong, brave and prudent men who were also experts in the use of arms were accorded military honors. Physical strength and cunning must be exercised wisely; frequently, because of the warriors' prudence and ingenuity, the few have defeated the many, wisdom and cleverness have been sufficient to rout the enemy. And that is why the ancients sponsored jousts and tournaments, thereby encouraging young men to excel in the martial arts, with the full intention that they should become brave, strong and fearless when meeting the enemy in battle. Military honor must be respected, for without it there would be no peace in the kingdoms and towns, as the glorious St. Luke states in his gospel. And so the virtuous and brave knight is deserving of honor and glory, but his fame will not endure for more than a few days. And so that the most valiant knight Tirant lo Blanch, who is honored in this book, may be placed alongside the other distinguished knights of glorious memory, special mention is made here of him and his extraordinary virtues and chivalric deeds, as is related in the following stories."

All citations from the Catalan original of *TB* are taken from Martín de Riquer's edition, *Tirant lo Blanc i altres escrits de Joanot Martorell* (Barcelona: Ariel, 1979). Page references will be found in the text, immediately following the citation; the English translation will appear in the respective footnote, as here.

Toward the close of the novel, Martorell's hero emerges as the complete fifteenth-century Christian commander of both infantry and marine forces that the author proposes will be required to wrest the Byzantine capital from the Infidel and make the Mediterranean safe again for Christians.

At Ch. 100 the matter of romantic love — Courtly and otherwise — begins to intrude itself upon the narrative; amorous adventures continue to be injected with increasing frequency and intensity from that point on. Just as we attend the hero's military education in the battle scenes, so too do we observe Tirant in the bedchambers of the Greek Court learning how to woo and win the heart of the fair Princess Carmesina. At first Tirant attempts to accomplish this according to the hoary precepts of Courtly Love that had been established centuries before by the Provençal poets and later embellished by courtly tradition. This elaborate mating game is counterbalanced and eventually replaced by a program of sexual aggressiveness orchestrated by the charming and astute damsel Plaerdemavida (Placerdemivida in Castilian), who urges Tirant to forsake the unrealistic regimen proclaimed by the old literary theorists in favor of a more realistic (i.e., passionate and sensual) kind of courtship that will lead more quickly to marriage and carnal union — although not necessarily in that order. The conflict of the highly artificial and ritualistic Courtly Love vs. the natural and spontaneous "modern" variety championed by Plaerdemavida is the main theme of the "romantic" half of *TB*'s plot. As Justina Ruiz de Conde has shown, the choice is between illicit Courtly Love and the Sacrament of Matrimony.[6] Despite a rather ironic approach to the subject, Martorell is clearly an ardent supporter of the married state.

At the conclusion of the novel Martorell's view can be clearly seen: he rejects the archaic values portrayed in most of the romances of chivalry and proposes instead a new, more "modern" role for the ideal military figure, one which demands a willingness and ability

---

[6] Ruiz de Conde, pp. 149-52. We should bear in mind that Courtly Love was originally designed to accommodate extra-marital affairs alone, which of course made it illicit by its very nature and therefore in polar opposition to the Holy Matrimony, a sacrament of the Church. In *TB* Martorell shows how these two opposites can be reconciled if the sacramental institution subsumes the rituals and conventions that had sprung up around Courtly Love.

to avail himself of the latest in military strategy and technology, plus an instinct for diplomacy and political infighting. Martorell advocates the development of a new kind of *soldado cortesano* — not unlike the future Garcilaso de la Vega — who will be a seasoned warrior as much at home at the royal court or in the political arena as he is on the battlefield.

On the social plane, Martorell condemns the inadequacies of and the potential abuses inherent in the idealized conventions of Courtly Love, particularly with regard to the problems faced by lovers of unequal social rank. On a more practical level, he especially attacks the popular practice of clandestine marriage (of which his sister Damiata was a victim, and against which the Catholic Church was reluctant to move until the close of the Council of Trent in 1563, a century after Martorell's book was written). The author proposes the cultivation of open courtship and betrothal as the most realistic and sensible means of dealing with romantic relationships and complicating human passions, especially in the case of lovers from different social classes.

Martorell makes his point regarding courtship in a most ironic manner. Early on Tirant and Carmesina exchange secret marriage vows; several years pass before they are able to consummate the union, and only at the very end of the story do they become formally betrothed. This betrothal, following as it does the exchange of vows and physical consummation, would have constituted a valid and binding marriage in the eyes of the fifteenth-century Catholic Church.[7] However, before the hero can achieve his longtime ambition to be joined in matrimony with the Princess and thereby gain for himself a claim to the Imperial Crown, Martorell has his hero fall ill and succumb in a strangely unheroic fashion.

Tirant's death is doubly ironic, first because it is rather pedestrian in nature (he is done in by an attack of appendicitis or some such malady manifested by a sharp pain in the side), and secondly because it underscores the fact that his artificial and contrived courtship of Carmesina has been a needless botch from the very beginning. Had he not wasted so much valuable time observing silly formalities and rituals demanded by the absurd conventions of Courtly Love, his marriage to Carmesina could have been celebrated

---

[7] Ruiz de Conde, pp. 20 and 156.

at a much earlier time and their shared moments of carnal bliss would have been several times more numerous. Martorell's point of view on this matter is summed up quite effectively in the sage advice he has Estefania offer the Princess in Chapter 138:

> En tot lo món no trobareu cavaller qui ab ell se puga egualar. E vostre pare no desija altra cosa en aquest món sinó que us ves casada. ¿A qui podeu vós pendre millor que aquest jove dispost, valentíssim en les armes, lliberal, animós, savi e destre en totes coses més que tot altre? ¿Per què Déu no em féu a mi filla de l'Emperador, e que vós fósseu Estefania e jo Carmesina? Jo us assegur, res que fos en la mia persona no li fóra denegat, e si ell m'alçava la falda del meu brial, jo li alçaria la mia camisa que ell no ves, e el contentaria en gran part.
> ... ...
> Aquest és lo que vostra altesa ha mester, que us sàpia guardar de mal a vós e tot l'Imperi, e el sàpia defendre e augmentar així com fa. Aquest és aquell qui us farà cercar tots los racons de la cambra, adés tota nua, adés en camisa.
>
> *(TB, 450)* [8]

The same sentiments are repeated later (Chs. 253-54) in a lighter vein by Plaerdemavida, who is Martorell's principal instrument for expressing the need for reform in the conventions of courtship. Keeping in mind that Plaerdemavida's prediction of dire consequences nearly comes true, observe her witty censure of Carmesina's insistence upon a strictly conventional courtship and her reluctance to express her true feelings to her suitor:

> Encara vendrà temps que vós lo plorareu a ell e als seus, e us arrapareu los ulls e la cara, e maleireu lo dia e la nit e

---

[8] "You will not find any other knight in any part of the world who can be compared to him. And your father desires nothing else in the world but to see you married. Whom can you choose who will be better suited than this young man who is so handsome, extremely valiant in the use of arms, so generous, so lively, and wiser and more adept in all things than all the others? Why doesn't God make me the Emperor's daughter, that is, that you be Estefania and I be you, Carmesina? I assure you that I would deny him no favor; and if he raised my skirt, I would then raise my undergarments and he would be satisfied to the fullest.... This is the man Your Highness needs, capable of saving you and the entire Empire from evil, able to defend and expand the Empire just as he is doing now. This is the man who will pursue you into all the corners of your room, whether you be stark naked or wearing a shirt."

encara la vostra vida. Car jo sé que Tirant, lo jorn que porà cavalcar, veent la gran descontentació de vostra altesa, se n'irà en la sua terra, e tots los altres per amor d'ell, e vós restareu així com sou mereixedora, e tot l'Imperi se perdrà. E com sereu morta e vendreu davant lo juí de Nostre Senyor, demanar-vos ha compte de la vida vostra en estil de semblants paraules.

—"Per mi fon manat fos fet home a imatge e semblança mia, e de la costella de l'home fos feta companya a l'home; e més, diguí: creixeu e muntiplicau lo món e ompliu la terra. Digues tu, Carmesina, jo qui t'havia llevat lo teu germà perquè fosses senyora de l'Imperi, posant-te en aquella singular dignitat mundanal, ¿quin compte me dóues del que t'he acomanat? Has pres marit? ¿Has deixat fills perquè puguen defendre la fe catòlica e aumentar la crestiandat?" Què respondreu vós? —dix Plaerdemavida—. ¡Ai senyora, i com vos veig enfrescada, que resposta bona no hi poreu dar! Però la vostra resposta serà tal com vos diré: "Oh Senyor, ple de misericòrdia e de pietat! ¡Perdonau-me, Senyor, per la clemència vostra!" E l'àngel custodi vos farà dir aquestes paraules: "Veritat és, Senyor, que jo amava un cavaller qui en armes era molt virtuós, lo qual la vostra sacratíssima Majestat nos havia tramès per lliberar de les mans dels infels lo vostre poble crestià; jo amava aquest, e li tenia gran devoció e desijava'l per marit, e com enamorat complaïa'l tot lo que ell volia ab tota honestat; e tenia una donzella en servir meu, qui es nomenava Plaerdemavida, e donava'm tostemps bons consells, e jo no els volia pendre; e posà'l-me una nit en lo llit, jo com a inocenta cridí, e com me fui regoneguda callí e estiguí segura; e una viuda, qui sentí cridar, donà de grans crits, que tot lo palau féu avolotar, de què se seguí cas de molta dolor e congoixa per a molts per la mia temor. Aprés me pregaven que jo consentís a l'apetit del cavaller, e jamés ho consentí." En semblant cas respondrà Sant Pere, per ço com té les claus de paradís: "Senyor, aquesta no és digna d'estar en la nostra beneita glòria per ço com no ha volguts servar los vostres sants manaments." Llançar-vos han dins en l'infern, e en companya vostra la Viuda Reposada. E com jo passaré d'aquesta present vida, en paradís serà feta gran festa de mi, e dar-me han cadira en l'eterna glòria en la més alta jerarquia, e com a filla obedient seré coronada entre los altres sants.

(TB, 741-42)[9]

---

[9] "There will come days when you will cry for him and his friends, and you will scratch your eyes and face and curse the day and night and even

INTRODUCTION   19

Tirant's untimely death serves to make Plaerdemavida's constant urging of prompt consummation throughout the novel seem all the more sensible in retrospect, as even Tirant and Carmesina come to realize just before the end. [10]

If we look for an over-all scheme for Martorell's book, it would be that the author creates a hero who is extremely aggressive in war, constantly moving away from stodgy traditional models in order to embrace the latest in military tactics, strategies and technology. In

---

your life. For I know that Tirant, as soon as he is able to ride, having noted Your Highness' displeasure, will return to his own country and the rest will follow him because of their great love for him, and you will get what you truly deserve, and the whole Empire will be lost. And when you are dead and you come before Our Lord for judgment, he will ask you to make an account of your life with words such as these.

" 'I ordered man to be created in My own image and that his companion should be created from his rib; and therefore I said: Go forth and multiply and inhabit the Earth. Tell me, Carmesina, I Who have taken away your brother so that you might become the First Lady of the Empire and be elevated to such great worldly dignity, what can you tell Me about the task I have entrusted to you? Have you married? Have you given birth to any children who will defend the Catholic faith and increase the ranks of the faithful?' How will you reply? — says Plaerdemavida—. Oh, my lady, I can see that you are speechless and will not be able to utter a satisfactory retort. But your answer will be something like this: 'Oh, Lord, You are so compassionate and merciful. Forgive me, Lord, out of clemency.' And the Guardian Angel will force you to speak these words: 'It is true, Lord, that I once loved a knight who was very skillful in the use of arms, the one Your Most Blessed Majesty had sent us to deliver your Christian people from the Infidel; I loved him and was wholly devoted to him and I wanted him for my husband, and because I was so in love I pleased him in every way he desired and in a most honorable fashion; and I had a maid to serve me who was called Plaerdemavida, and she always gave me good counsel, but I would not heed her advice; and one night he came and laid me on a bed, and I cried out because of my innocence, but as soon as I realized what was happening I kept quiet and lay still; and a widow who heard me scream began to shout so loudly that the entire palace was aroused, from which there immediately followed a great deal of pain and anguish among the others about me and my fears. They then beseeched me to consent to the knight's carnal desires, but I would never consent.' In a case such as this St. Peter, since he holds the keys to Paradise, will reply: 'Lord, this woman is not worthy to enter into Eternal Glory because she has refused to fulfill Your Holy Commandments.' They will then throw you into Hell along with the Viuda Reposada. And when I pass from this life they will have a great feast in Paradise for me, and they will offer me a seat in the highest echelon of everlasting glory, and I will be crowned among the other saints for being an obedient daughter."

[10] See Ruiz de Conde, p. 109.

short, the hero succeeds on the battlefield because he is, above all else, a realist and progressive thinker. In matters of the heart, however, he is a chronic vacillator. At first he embraces the idealistic, artificial literary models of the Provençal poets and the heroes of the chivalric romances. In his amorous adventures Tirant is initially a most unimaginative and timid lover who realizes his shortcomings and bemoans his curious fate, as we note in Ch. 283, when he observes: "que en les batalles me fas ésser victoriós e triümfant, e en amar só lo més malfadat home que jamés naixqués" (*TB*, 805). [11] Eventually, under the tutelage of Plaerdemavida, he moves toward a more realistic and practical strategy which will enable him in the second half of the novel to enjoy considerably more success in his courtship of the Princess.

In each of the main divisions of his novel Martorell makes the same basic point, once positively and one time in a negative fashion: the successful man will be the realist who is willing to adapt his behavior to the constantly-changing circumstances that surround him; he will always be open to fresh ideas and dare to break with the tired, unproductive (and occasionally *counter*productive) traditions of earlier generations.

At this point a few words ought to be said about some of the particular aspects of *TB* that will be examined in the present study. I will draw attention to Martorell's deft ironic touch in describing the various ceremonies and rituals connected with the two major themes. His meticulous portrayal of pomp and ceremony, whether in love or in war, is always faithful and complete. At selected times, however, he stoops to the level of burlesque (cf. Cervantes), but always with the same sharp attention to detail. In one chapter I will examine some of the more intentionally ridiculous rituals described in Martorell's novel, things like vows, letters of challenge, and various dueling customs. We will see that there is much more subtle criticism to be found in these sections than has generally been recognized heretofore by critics.

In another section I will study Martorell's peculiar narrative technique: his ability to telescope several centuries of evolution and

---

[11] "for in battle you [Dame Fortune] make me a triumphant warrior, but in affairs of the heart I am the most wretched man who was ever born."

advancement in military technology and battlefield tactics into the lifetime of one man. I will also examine how he ingeniously manages to combine historical fact with imaginative embellishment so as to produce a composite hero who symbolizes the very real achievements of several different European military figures of the late Middle Ages. I will show that the same skillful technique is used in Martorell's Dedication to create a rather clever hoax that appears to have gone unnoticed up to now.

In another chapter I will deal with Cervantes' reaction to *TB*: the Priest's unusual comment on the novel in Chapter Six of the 1605 *Quixote*. The matter of the enigmatic "echar a galeras" remark has been discussed *ad nauseam* by the critics; I prefer to concentrate on the three or four specific references Cervantes makes to episodes and characters from Martorell's novel. I will show that the selection is perhaps not a casual one, that a number of elements cited can be related to some similar item or event in Ariosto's *Orlando Furioso*. The chapter concludes with a speculation about the peculiar narrative qualities Cervantes would have recognized in the *Furioso* and in *TB* to render them worthy of imitation in his own masterpiece.

I should not let go unmentioned the many debts of gratitude I owe to those persons and institutions that have contributed to the successful completion of this project. My sincerest thanks go to the library of the University of Valencia (and to its Directora, D.ª María del Pilar Gómez Gómez), to the Biblioteca de Catalunya in Barcelona, to the Biblioteca Nacional Española in Madrid, and to the library of the Hispanic Society of America in New York for allowing me to have access to their respective collections of materials related to *Tirant lo Blanch*. I also wish to express my gratitude to the University of South Carolina's Office of Sponsored Programs and Research for a grant that enabled me to conduct research at the various libraries mentioned above, and to the Carolina Venture Fund for the assistance it provided in defraying the costs of publication.

My thanks also to Professor Kathleen McNerney of West Virginia University, who was kind enough to share with me the fruits of her own research on *TB*. Finally I should thank my good friend and colleague, Charles J. Simmons, for his invaluable contribution in the gathering of materials necessary for the completion of this project; to my wife, Virginia, for her assistance with the proofreading of the typescript and the galley proofs; to my typist, Carolyn A. Davis; and to my graduate assistants, Laia Nadal, Agnès Subirós, and Javier Vico for their help in preparing the bibliography and rendering English translations of the sections of the Catalan text that appear in this study.

Columbia, S.C.   21 May 1984

Chapter I

TWO FERRANTES IN ONE: THE DEDICATION OF
TIRANT LO BLANCH AS A REFLECTION OF
MARTORELL'S DESIGN FOR THE NOVEL

A rare phenomenon in Medieval European fiction is a novel or romance whose Dedication reflects the same creative process that was used to compose the work itself. As I shall demonstrate here, *Tirant lo Blanch* is precisely such a *rara avis*: its Dedication, penned in the mid-1460s by its principal author Joanot Martorell, can be seen to mirror his very peculiar novelistic technique — and to reflect as well the political turmoil within the Kingdom of Aragon during that period.

Let us begin by considering the general plan of Martorell's book and the very curious nature of its hero. Joseph A. Vaeth, in one of the earliest studies on *TB*, described the novel as "a composite work, made up of elements gathered here and there, logically connected and fashioned into a consistent whole which impresses the reader with a feeling of reality, because it is based, in the main, on actual experiences and happenings in life."[1] Several trustworthy critics, among them Bohigas, Gili Gaya, Marinesco, and Riquer,[2] have

---

[1] Joseph A. Vaeth, *Tirant lo Blanch: A Study of Its Authorship, Principal Sources and Historical Setting*, Columbia University Studies in Romance Philology and Literature, Vol. 23 (1918; rpt. New York: AMS Press, 1966), p. 139.

[2] Pere Bohigas, *Tractats de cavalleria* (Barcelona: Colección "Els Nostres Clàssics," 1947), 43-77; Samuel Gili Gaya, "Noves recerques sobre *Tirant lo Blanch*," *Estudis Romànics*, 1 (1947-48), 135-47; Constantin Marinesco, "Du nouveau sur *Tirant lo Blanch*," *Estudis Romànics*, 4 (1953-54), 137-203. The contributions of these and many other critics to our present

contributed significantly to the current consensus that Tirant is actually a composite hero modeled after a number of verifiable historical personages whose famous exploits were undoubtedly known to Martorell and celebrated by him in his literary masterpiece.

The first and most obvious historical figure to appear in the novel is William (or Guy) of Warwick, a legendary Anglo-Norman hero — not unlike the Castilian Cid — whose exploits were celebrated in a thirteenth-century epic poem and a subsequent fifteenth-century French prose version. The immediate source of Martorell's adaptation appears to be an incomplete Catalan version of the Warwick legend that is preserved within MS. 7811 at Madrid's Biblioteca Nacional.[3] Bohigas, Gili Gaya and Riquer have maintained that Martorell is the author of this text and that he later expanded it to form the first part of *TB*. Inasmuch as MS. 7811 also contains copies of several letters written by and to Joanot Martorell, such a hypothesis about his authorship of the "Guillem de Varoic" fragment is not implausible. But neither is it conclusive. Martorell, a demonstrable plagiarist as we shall see, might simply have availed himself of this or some other anonymous account of Warwick's exploits for the preliminary chapters of his novel. The only thing that can be shown is that portions of the first thirty-nine chapters of *TB* — but especially the material in Chs. 1-27 in anticipation of Tirant's initial appearance — *could* have been derived from the "Guillem de Varoic" fragment of MS. 7811, or from some similar document.[4]

---

knowledge about the sources of *TB* are masterfully summarized and analyzed by Martín de Riquer in his Introduction to the 1511 Castilian translation of Martorell's novel: *Tirante el Blanco*, Clásicos Castellanos, vols. 188-92 (Madrid: Espasa-Calpe, 1974), I, vii-cix. Subsequent references to Riquer's Introduction and Notes in the 1974 edition will be found in footnotes bearing the Castilian title, e.g., *Tirante el Blanco*, I, 225, n. 3.

[3] The original Warwick fragment, called "Guillem de Varoic," is included as Appendix II within Martín de Riquer's *Tirant lo Blanc i altres escrits de Joanot Martorell* (Barcelona: Ariel, 1979), pp. 1235-49.

[4] Martorell, had he been familiar with the longer thirteenth-century version of the Warwick legend, might conceivably have used it also as the inspiration and primary source for Tirant's adventures in Constantinople, but this cannot be proved. In the longer version Warwick is summoned to the Byzantine capital to save the Greeks from defeat at the hands of the Sultan of Babylon. The Emperor offers to reward Warwick with the hand of his daughter in marriage, but the English hero remains constant in his love for his wife and respectfully declines the offer. See *Tirante el Blanco*, I, lxv.

A second historical model for Martorell's hero is the Burgundian warrior Geoffroy de Thoisy, who achieved a great deal of notoriety as a result of his heroism in helping to lift the Egyptian siege of the island of Rhodes (10 August-18 September 1444). Word-of-mouth assured his place in history after this escapade and his heroic deeds were later chronicled by Jehan de Wavrin in his *Anciennes croniques d'Engleterre*. The striking similarity between the historical Geoffroy de Thoisy's adventures at Rhodes on that occasion and those of the fictional Tirant in breaking a similar siege of that island in Chs. 98-106 would appear to be more than casual.[5]

For a more local model of heroic behavior Martorell would have had to search no farther than the leader of a famous fourteenth-century Catalan expedition to the Balkans to aid the Byzantine Emperor. The commander of this force was a warrior named Roger de Flor (who was not a Catalan, ironically) and his achievements appear to have served as the model for most of Tirant's naval exploits as well as for the various court intrigues the fictional hero encounters in Constantinople. Roger de Flor was the subject of Ramon Muntaner's famous *Crónica*, a first-hand account — by one of the actual participants — of the adventures of the celebrated mercenary force that sailed from Sicily to the Byzantine capital in 1302 to aid the Greek Emperor against his Turkish enemies. This is precisely the mission Tirant undertakes in Martorell's novel. But above and beyond the general similarity of their respective expeditions, several other specific parallels can be drawn between the adventures of the historical Roger and the fictional Tirant:

a) Both are summoned to Constantinople as mercenaries in the service of the Byzantine ruler, and for their efforts are rewarded with the title "Caesar of the Empire" — again, not a casual correspondence.

b) Both are vexed by difficult relations with and considerable resistance from a coterie of jealous Greek nobles who deeply resent the presence in their homeland of foreign soldiers of fortune who seize the lion's share of the glory. As a historical footnote we should keep in mind that the resentfulness of the Greeks eventually resulted in a massacre at Adrianople that claimed the life of Roger de Flor

---

[5] See Marinesco, 139-64.

and thousands of his followers; Tirant manages to survive the treacherous plots of his Greek enemies (e.g., the nefarious Duke of Macedonia who epitomizes the jealousy of the Greek nobles), but only because Martorell had in mind a very different kind of demise for his hero.

c) Both men discover romance in Constantinople: Roger de Flor is ultimately rewarded by the Emperor with the hand in marriage of his niece; Tirant, for his part, comes to be betrothed to the Emperor's daughter, who incidentally happens to be the sole heir to the Imperial throne.

d) Both confront and defeat a Moslem adversary bearing the title "Gran Caraman."

e) They both die prematurely at or near the city of Adrianople, Flor the victim of an assassination plot (as I mentioned earlier), Tirant brought down by a fatal attack of appendicitis or some similar ailment. [6]

A fourth model for Martorell's hero is the Hungarian Janos Hunyadi, who was indeed a major factor in checking the advance of the Turks in Eastern Europe during the fifteenth century. He defeated them on the Danube in 1448 and then again at Belgrade eight years later. Marinesco convincingly proposes Hunyadi as the source and inspiration for both Tirant's name and his heraldic emblem, the raven. Because Hunyadi hailed from the region of Wallachia, contemporary texts often appended the word "Valachus" or "Balachus" to his given name; in the West this was often transformed into "Blanc," "Blanch," or "Bianco," with a corresponding image of whiteness that had no foundation in the original. French chronicles refer to him as "le chevalier Blanc"; in Barcelona and Valencia he was called "lo Blanch" and "lo comte Blanch." As for the emblem of the raven, it was indeed Hunyadi's coat of arms; in Ch. 125 of Martorell's novel Tirant orders the very same symbol to be painted on his battle flag. [7] Notwithstanding all of the above, the Hungarian hero's major function appears to have been to provide the inspiration for the rather strange circumstances that surround

---

[6] *Tirante el Blanco*, I, lxv-lxvi.
[7] Marinesco, 164-77; see also *Tirante el Blanco*, I, lxvi-lxvii.

Tirant's death. Although it is probably true that Hunyadi's victory at Belgrade is reflected in Tirant's final triumph over the Turks at the close of the novel, Hunyadi's death from the plague only three weeks thereafter (11 August 1456) is an even more likely source of inspiration for Tirant's ironically unheroic passing in the final chapters of Martorell's book.

Another veteran of the Danubian and Balkan skirmishes who may have served as a model for Tirant is the Castilian (possibly Galician) soldier Pedro Vázquez de Saavedra. Vázquez's fame is derived from his adventures as a young knight in England ca. 1440 (shortly after Martorell himself had resided there) and later in Cologne and at the Burgundian court of Philip the Good. He achieved even greater renown as a result of his participation in battles against the Turks on the Black Sea and the Danube.[8] Still another possibility is the Valencian corsair Jaume de Vilaragut, who was a personal friend of Martorell and who has been proposed by Marinesco and Riquer as the author's probable source of information about the terrain of the Eastern Mediterranean region and some of the naval tactics described in the novel.[9] Finally there are the figures of Peter II of Aragon, Louis IX of France, and the Aragonese monarch Jaime I, all of whom have been suggested by Vaeth (p. 158), but not convincingly.

Regardless of how many or which of the historical personages mentioned above may actually have served as an inspiration for Martorell, the evidence is clear that Tirant's character is a curious combination of characteristics taken from a number of renowned military figures of the late Middle Ages, augmented by a great deal of imaginative embellishment provided by the author.

A second aspect of Martorell's peculiar style that merits consideration here is his proclivity for plagiarism. Examples abound of instances in which *TB*'s author borrows freely from other sources — no literary sin in the 1400s — to enhance his own composition. I call attention to Martorell's plagiaristic tendencies here only because I intend to show that they are an integral part of the Valencian writer's style, not to censure him or denigrate his achievement.

---

[8] *Tirante el Blanco*, I, lxvii-lxviii.
[9] *Tirante el Blanco*, I, lxi-lxii; Marinesco, 150-51.

The first and most obvious case of borrowing occurs with the Warwick legend that dominates the first thirty-nine chapters of the book. Little needs to be added to what already has been said about the "Guillem de Varoic" fragment (MS. 7811, Biblioteca Nacional) and its relationship to Martorell's novel. Whether the Catalan version of the Warwick lengend was penned by Martorell or some other writer is immaterial; the entire first section of the novel's narrative is clearly not of Martorell's own invention, but rather taken from a foreign source.

The second major work from which passages were lifted for *TB* is Ramon Llull's *Libre de l'orde de cavalleria,* which provides the general content — and occasionally an entire passage — of the hermit Varoic's counsel to the young squire Tirant in Chs. 28-39. [10] With regard to the section devoted to the founding and organization of England's Order of the Garter (Chs. 85-97), Martorell's source is unknown, but Riquer offers an interesting speculation about a possible source document and how Martorell might have come in contact with it. [11]

Another occasion when Martorell borrows freely from others is noted in the many rhetorical letters and oral discourses that are scattered throughout the pages of *TB*. From time to time Martorell reproduces, almost verbatim, actual passages and key phrases taken

---

[10] *Tirante el Blanco,* I, 94, notes 5 and 21. Riquer explains here that the content of the hermit's instructions on the meaning and importance of the military profession are taken from Llull's work but that the actual title of the instructional manual mentioned in Chapters 28 and 32 *(Arbre de Batalles)* corresponds to that of another famous book on the subject, the *Arbre de batailles* of Honoré Bouvet, or Bonet; the chivalric doctrine presented by Bouvet in his treatise, however, is not represented in these chapters of *TB*. Martorell appears to have blended Llull's philosophy with Bouvet's title.

[11] *Tirante el Blanco,* I, lix, n. 9. Riquer proposes a *second* voyage made by Martorell to England in the year 1450 (he had previously journeyed there in 1438 to make arrangements for his anticipated duel with Joan de Monpalau); during this second visit Martorell is supposed to have had access to a beautiful manuscript that was presented to Margaret of Anjou upon her marriage (ca. 1444-45) to Henry VI of England by John Talbot. This document, which is today preserved in the British Museum (Old Royal 15. E. VI.), contains copies of the French prose version of *Guy of Warwick,* Bouvet's *Arbre de batailles,* and a French translation of the statutes of the Order of the Garter — all of which play a role in Martorell's novel.

from the correspondence of real historical figures, documents preserved — in a sixteenth-century hand, not the original — in the very same MS. 7811 that houses the "Guillem de Varoic" fragment. The most notable examples of this sort of borrowing are the following:

> a) a letter from the Sultan of Babilonia to the King of Cyprus (27 July 1435), in which he announces his decision not to wage war on the Grand Master of Rhodes; entire passages from this document appear in Ch. 135 of *TB* in a letter from the Sultan of Babilonia and/or Cairo to Tirant, in which he grants the Christian commander's request for a six-month truce; [12]
> b) a letter from Joanot de la Serra to Bernat de Vilarig (30 December 1452), challenging him to a duel; the opening lines of this epistle (e.g., "Si us erre lo nom ab aquest títol de cavaller" — "If I erred in calling you a gentleman") re-appear in Ch. 154 of Martorell's book in the haughty reply of the malicious Duke of Macedonia to the Marquis of St. George; a smaller borrowing from another of Serra's letters to Vilarig (15 January 1453) appears in Ch. 149 when the King of Egypt addresses a council of Moorish nobles. [13]

The invaluable MS. 7811 yields still another document that eventually found its way — with some variations and corruptions — into Martorell's work. I am referring to the Catalan translation of a letter written (in Latin) by the Italian poet Petrarch to Niccolò Acciaiuoli; it is found immediately preceding the "Guillem de Varoic" codex in the Madrid manuscript. Martorell uses it in Ch. 143 when the Moorish ambassador Abdal·la Salomó counsels Tirant about the vicissitudes of life. It is one of the longest examples of literary piracy to be found in Martorell's book. [14]

The statement of King Escariano of Ethiopia in praise of certain famous women of antiquity (Ch. 309) can be shown to be taken from Book IV of the Catalan poet Bernat Metge's *Lo somni* (1399). There is considerable disfiguration in some of the names — for a number of reasons that Riquer mentions — but the text is very close

---

[12] *Tirante el Blanco*, II, 220, n. 13; 221, ns. 8 and 10. See also Gili Gaya, 139.

[13] *Tirante el Blanco*, II, 334, n. 15; 305, n. 6.

[14] *Tirante el Blanco*, II, 261, n. 10.

to Metge's original.[15] Similarly, Tirant's reply to Queen Maragdina in Ch. 323 includes one passage that has been taken literally from a letter written by the Catalan author Joan Roiç de Corella to the Prince of Viana.[16] The same Roiç de Corella also provides Martorell with two of the more moving passages of the book: the description of Princess Carmesina's tearful confrontation with Tirant's enbalmed corpse as it lies in state (Ch. 473), and later the verses that are sculpted over the tomb of the two lovers in Nantes (Ch. 485). In each case the material in question has been lifted from Roiç de Corella's *Història de Leànder y Hero*.[17]

Other striking similarities have been noted between passages or episodes in *TB* and works by other authors. The resemblance may be too slight to justify a charge of plagiarism, but there are undeniable correspondences between parts of Martorell's novel and certain other identifiable texts. Among the more notable examples are: the *Doctrina moral* of the Mallorcan writer Nicolau de Pachs, which appears to be the basis for Carmesina's discourse in Ch. 181; Boccaccio's *Decameron*, which is reflected in certain short narratives that appear in Chs. 265, 299 and 350; an imitation of Dante's second sonnet from the *Vita nuova* that appears in Ch. 400; and finally the *Travels* of Sir John Mandeville, a lengthy passage from which is incorporated as part of the adventure of the knight Espercius on the island of Cos (Ch. 410).[18]

And so it is obvious that Martorell's technique in composing *TB* often involved borrowing freely and without attribution (as was the custom of the times) from the literary works of other writers. Having noted this, let us now turn our attention to Martorell's Dedication and observe how the same combination of historical fact, fanciful embellishment, and a generous amount of literary piracy is used to create a rather clever hoax.

---

[15] *Tirante el Blanco*, IV, 37, n. 21. See also Luis Nicolau d'Olwer, "Sobre les fonts catalanes del *Tirant lo Blanch*," *Revista de bibliografía catalana*, 5 (1905), 27-35.

[16] *Tirante el Blanco*, IV, 92, n. 8. See also F. de B. Moll, "Rudiments de versificació en el *Tirant lo Blanch*," *Bolletí del Diccionari de la llengua catalana*, 16 (1934), 181.

[17] *Tirante el Blanco*, V, 196, n. 21; 233, n. 18. See also Riquer's *Nuevas contribuciones a las fuentes del "Tirant lo Blanch"* (Barcelona: Biblioteca Central, 1949), pp. 18-20.

[18] See Riquer's notes on the following pages of *Tirante el Blanco*: III, 53-56, 275, 366; IV, 168, 283; V, 35-37.

The Dedication to Don Ferrando of Portugal

It has long been recognized that Joanot Martorell's Dedication to the Portuguese prince was not an original composition.[19] It was lifted, at times verbatim, from a letter of dedication composed by Enrique de Villena to the Aragonese nobleman Pero Pardo at the opening of the former's *Doze trabajos de Hércules*; the original Catalan version (now lost) was penned in April 1417, then translated into Castilian in September of the same year.[20] I have reproduced below the Castilian text of Villena's dedication as published by Margherita de Morreale in 1958; for the sake of clarity, the sections that were later taken by Martorell either directly or indirectly (paraphrases, slight alterations of form, substitution of synonyms, etc.) are printed in italics:

> Muy honorable e *virtuoso* cavallero, *ya sea por vulgada fama fuese informado de vuestras virtudes, mucho mayormente agora he avido conosçimiento de aquellas por querer comunicarme e desvelar vuestros* loables *deseos.* Talante aviendo de saber *los fechos de los antiguos e gloriosos cavalleros de los quales los poetas e istoriales han en sus obras comendado, perpetuando* las *recordaciones de aquellos, singularmente* los trabajos del // fuerte ercules, que por su virtud fue entre los gentiles deificado, *rogandome los allegase* e juntos en un tractado *poner quisiese en lengua catalana* por informacion vuestra, *opinando vos yo* oviese leido los istoriales que desto han tractado e poetas con ello guarnesçieron sus ficçiones, *fue a mi plazible* vuestra loadera inclinaçion e la satisfaçion cargosa, *considerando mis insufiçiençia* e discreçion, si quiera la poquedat

---

[19] *Tirante el Blanco*, I, lxxi; Riquer refers also to his earlier *Nuevas contribuciones...*, 8-10. For a full discussion of the matter, see also Luis Nicolau d'Olwer, "*Tirant lo Blanc*: Examen de algunas cuestiones," *Nueva Revista de Filología Hispánica*, 15 (1961), 131-54.

[20] Pero Pardo came to reside in Valencia during the 1430s; it is therefore probable that Martorell met him during that period and/or had access to Villena's original Catalan dedication. From this document Martorell might easily have made a copy, from which he could later have taken those portions that suited his purpose in composing the Dedication for *TB*. (See Nicolau d'Olwer, "Examen...", 131-33.) It is probable that Martorell penned his Dedication to Ferrante of Portugal some time between 1460 (the date mentioned in the text itself) and 1468, the best estimate as to the year of the author's death (*Tirante el Blanco*, I, xxix).

de istorias por mi vistas, non algo menos *las curiales e familiares ocupaçiones que* non dan lugar, e sobre todo *las adversidades de la movible fortuna, non consistiendo el mio reposar pensamiento.* Enpero confiando en el bien soberano que es dador de todos los bienes e ayuda a los buenos deseos, supliendo el fallesçimiento de los deseantes, e trae los buenos propositos a devidas fines, e que *vos por* vuestras amistança e bondat *soportarades los fallesçimientos asi en estilo como en orden en el presente por mi puestos tractado, por inadvertencia e mas verdaderamente inorançia, atrevime* en buscar, cojer e ordenar los dichos trabajos, en tal guisa que non se perdiese tan buen deseo somido en la mar de potençia nin peligrase por las ondas del tiempo, antes fuese en acto deduzido por viento suave paçifico de eloquencia a platicable puerto. E si por mi segunt es dicho menguadamente fuese tractado, por otros mas sufiçientes vista la materia ser pudiese de mejor vestida forma, *rogandovos açebtedes la presente obra, acatando* las materia e *afecçion mia, non aviendo respecto a la rudidat de la ordenaçion e escuridat de sentençias, e la comuniquedes en logar que faga fruto* e de que tomen enxenplo, acresçimiento de virtudes e purgamiento de viçios, si sera espejo actual a los gloriosos cavalleros *en armada cavalleria, moviendo el coraçon de aquellos en non dubdar los asperos fechos de las armas e a prender* grandes e *onrrados partidos, enderesçandose a sostener el bien comun, por cuya razon caualleria fue fallada. E non menos a la caualleria moral dara lunbre e presentara señales de buenas costumbres, desfaziendo la texedura de los viçios e domando la feroçi//dat de los monstruosos actos, en tanto que la materia presente* mas es satira que tragica, ya sea tragicos la ayan deduzida, aviendome por escusado si mas aina non he acabado el tratado aqueste por lo que en mis escusaçiones de suso dixe. E quisiera en mayores cosas e quiero quanto buenamente pueda complazer la nobleza vuestra, la qual dios conserve en su gracia e faga non solamente seguir las proezas de los antiguos, mas aun que seades exenplar de virtudes a los presentes e venideros cavalleros que actual e moralmente buscan enxenplo. [21]

---

[21] Enrique de Villena, *Los doze trabajos de Hércules,* ed. Margherita de Morreale (Madrid: Biblioteca Selecta de Clásicos Españoles, 1958), pp. 5-7. Because this selection is written in Castilian — albeit very old Castilian — it is assumed that the reader will not require an English translation. Catalan texts, however, will continue to be translated into English in footnotes.

Martorell is somewhat particular about the portions of Villena's text he will borrow. He is especially interested in Villena's manner of praising his subject — a rather conventional gambit, to be sure, but a necessary one. Let us examine each of the points Martorell takes from his model.

a) The author begins by making a fawning reference to the fame and virtuous nature of his patron/subject; he confesses to some previous knowledge of the subject's reputation, but remarks that his appreciation of the true worth of the man was increased upon receipt of a personal request from his patron to compose the present work.

b) The author then pauses, in a rare burst of immodesty, to remind the reader that he has been commissioned to perform the task because he is considered well versed in the epic accomplishments of ancient knights and other military heroes of the past whose exploits have been celebrated by poets and historians. The assignment, we are reminded with a great deal of false humility, has been to compile a complete historical account of the life and works of a particular heroic figure (Hercules in the case of Villena, Tirant for Martorell), which is to be presented in the native language of the patron (Catalan and Portuguese, respectively).

c) Next we have the assertion that this assignment was undertaken with great pleasure; however, this is immediately followed by the standard disclaimer and protestation of the writer regarding his own shortcomings ("insufiçiençia"), as well as the existence of certain pressing matters (of a business and familial nature, one supposes), petty daily annoyances, etc., that have hindered and complicated the swift completion of the task ("las curiales e familiares ocupaçiones").

d) At this point the author, exhibiting a true medieval surge of faith in the Divine Plan of Things, declares that he trusted in the Creator's desire to bring all worthy projects to their rightful fruition, and also in the patron's willingness to overlook or forgive the inevitable blemishes ("fallesçimientos") in style and organization within the text — flaws attributable to the compiler's ignorance or carelessness. He concludes with a plea that the work be accepted as a token of his affection for the patron, despite some coarseness of style or language. [Up to this point the concentration has been on certain rhetorical devices that Villena has used to good effect. This material resembles very closely the kind of bombast — spoken and written — found in many of the passages Martorell purloined from a variety of sources and sprinkled through the text of *TB*. As we move to the final section of the Dedication, we note that Martorell takes from Villena's letter a statement about the general didactic intent of his work: to glorify the military establishment. But even here the tone continues to be rhetorical.]

e) Ultimately the author expresses his hope that the present work may prove fruitful in inspiring others not to be discouraged or shrink from the harsh realities of military service, but rather to dedicate themselves to a noble and honorable calling: the maintenance of the Common Good, which was the original purpose for the founding of the military orders. Furthermore, there is the knight's obligation to set the moral tone for the rest of human society and serve as a shining example of virtuous and temperate behavior to others ("E non menos... los monstruosos actos").

At this point one might wonder why Martorell chose not to copy or paraphrase Villena's final sentence ("E quisiera... enxenplo"), in which he begs his patron to strive to serve as an example for all present and future knights. It is a perfectly fine closing line that might easily and profitably have been appended to Martorell's own conclusion. I believe the reason for this omission has to do with the nature of the real Prince Ferrante of Portugal as contrasted with the literary version of that personage presented here in the Dedication. This matter will be discussed at a later point in this chapter.

Let us now study the text of Martorell's Dedication to Ferrante, stressing those portions of the Catalan document (italicized here) that are original with Martorell.

Molt excellent, virtuós e *gloriós Príncep, Rei expectant:* Jatsia per vulgada fama fos informat de vostres virtuts, molt majorment ara he hagut notícia d'aquelles, per vostra senyoria voler-me comunicar e disvetlar vostres virtuosíssims desigs sobre los fets dels antics *virtuosos* e *en fama molt* gloriosos cavallers dels quals los poetes e historials han en ses obres comendat perpetuant *llurs* recordacions e *virtuosos actes*. E singularment *los molt insignes actes de cavalleria d'aquell tan famós cavaller, que, com lo sol resplandeix entre los altres planetes, així resplandeix aquest en singularitat de cavalleria entre els altres cavallers del món, apellat Tirant lo Blanc,* qui per sa virtut *conquistà molts regnes e províncies donant-los a altres cavallers, no volent-ne sinó la sola honor de cavalleria. E més avant conquistà tot l'imperi grec, cobrant-lo dels turcs qui aquell havien subjugat a llur domini dels crestians grecs.*

E com la dita història e actes del dit Tirant sien en llengua anglesa, e a vostra il·lustre senyoria sia estat grat volerme pregar la giràs en llengua *portuguesa,* opinant, *per jo ésser estat algun temps en l'illa d'Anglaterra, degués millor saber aquella llengua que altri;* les quals pregàries són estades a mi molt acceptables manaments; *com ja jo sia per mon orde obligat manifestar los actes virtuosos dels cavallers passats, majorment com en lo dit tractat sia molt estesament lo més de tot lo dret e orde d'armes e de cavalleria;* e jatsia, considerada ma insuficiència e les curials e familiars ocupacions qui obsten, e les adversitats de la noïble fortuna qui no donen repòs a la mia pensa, *d'aquest treball justament excusar me pogués,* emperò, confiant en lo sobiran Bé, donador de tots los béns, qui ajuda als bons desigs suplint lo defalliment dels desijants, e porta los bons propòsits a degudes fins, e *vostra senyoria* qui per sa virtut comportarà los defalliments, així en estil com en orde, en lo present tractat per mi posats per inadvertència, e pus verdaderament ignorància, m'atreviré *expondre, no solament de llengua anglesa en portuguesa, mas encara de portuguesa en vulgar valenciana, per ço que la nació d'on jo só natural se'n puixa alegrar e molt ajudar per los tants e tan insignes actes com hi són;* suplicant *vostra virtuosíssima senyoria* accepteu *com de servidor afectat* la present obra —*car si defalliments alguns hi són, certament, senyor, n'és en part causa la dita llengua anglesa, de la qual en algunes partides és impossible poder bé girar los vocables*—, atenent a l'afecció *e desig que continuament tinc de servir vostra redubtable senyoria,* no havent esguard a la ruditat de l'ordinació e diferència de sentències, *a fi que per vostra virtut* la comuniqueu *entre els servidors e altres* perquè en pugueu traure lo fruit que es pertany, movent los coratges d'aquells a no dubtar los aspres fets de les armes, e pendre honorosos partits endreçant-se a mantenir lo bé comú per qui milícia fon trobada.

No res menys a la cavalleria moral donarà llum e representarà los escenacles de bons costums, abolint la textura dels vicis e la ferocitat dels monstruosos actes. E perquè en la present obra *altri no puixa ésser increpat si defalliment algú trobat hi serà, jo, Joanot Martorell, cavaller, sols vull portar lo càrrec, e no altri ab mi; com per mi sols sia estada ventilada a servei del molt il·lustre Príncep e senyor Rei expectant Don Ferrando de Portugal la present obra, e començada a dos de giner de l'any mil quatre-cents e seixanta.*

(TB, 113-14) [22]

---

[22] "Most excellent, virtuous and glorious Prince and Expectant King: Although your widely acknowledged reputation has already made me aware of your virtues, I have been accorded even further knowledge of them since Your Lordship has seen fit to communicate and reveal your most worthy desires concerning the accomplishments of those ancient knights who were morally excellent and exalted in reputation, and about whom poets and historians have written thereby perpetuating their memory and the deeds they performed. And of special interest are the most distinguished chivalric acts of that celebrated knight who, like the sun among the other planets, shines in most singular chivalric splendor among the other knights of the world; he is called Tirant lo Blanc, the one who conquered so many kingdoms and provinces by his own merits and then offered them to other knights because he desired only the honors that could be bestowed by the chivalric code. Subsequently he conquered the entire Greek Empire, recovering it from the Turks who had subjugated the Greek Christians.

"And because the story and deeds of this Tirant are recorded in English, Your Illustrious Lordship has been pleased to ask me to translate it into Portuguese, because you believed that I was better acquainted with the English language than any other person as a result of my having spent some time in England; and I have willingly received your request as a command that I will gladly obey; and because I am a knight, I am obliged to publicize the meritorious acts of the knights of old, especially since the aforesaid treatise is one in which you can find an extensive treatment of all things relative to the laws that govern the military orders and chivalry in general. Given my personal shortcomings as well as the professional and family matters that so often intrude, not to mention the setbacks of fickle Fortune which refuse to give my mind any rest whatsoever, I could easily excuse myself from performing this task, but I shall not. I trust in the Supreme God, giver of all good things who assists our good intentions by providing compensation for the weaknesses of those who have righteous aims, and thereby enables them to achieve their goals. And Your Lordship, who in his goodness will excuse these failings both in style and in orderliness, will recognize that I have committed these errors inadvertently, or more precisely, out of ignorance; I shall therefore dare to translate this treatise not only from English into Portuguese, but also from the Portuguese into popular Valencian so that my own people can take pleasure in and derive great benefit from so many and such distinguished acts as are to be found within. I beg Your Most Gracious Lordship to accept the present work as submitted by a loyal servant — for if there are shortcomings, certainly, Your Lordship, it is partly owing to the nature of the English language whose terms are sometimes impossible to translate correctly. And considering my constant affection and desire to serve Your Redoubtable

The question of plagiarism — and the consequent substitution of Tirant's name for that of Hercules — is no longer of interest, since it has already been discussed in the previous section. On the other hand, we are definitely concerned with the historical reference implicit in the Dedication: the figure of Ferrante of Portugal and his implied relationship, real or imaginary, with author/ "historian" Joanot Martorell. Other questions of interest are Martorell's assertions regarding his sole responsibility for the book, the date of its composition, and the various foreign languages that figured in the creative process. Martorell's claims in the Dedication merit close scrutiny.

His declaration that Ferrante was "singularment" interested in the adventures and career of the celebrated Tirant lo Blanch, conqueror of sundry kingdoms, is superficially credible as the inspiration and principal motivating factor behind Martorell's work. But this is nothing more than a well-known and hackneyed literary convention of the romances of chivalry, a transparent ruse that no sophisticated reader would take at face value. Martorell's aim here is to give maximum credibility to his work. Although the Portuguese prince is real, the subject of the novel is not; therefore, the author makes clever use of his Dedication to link these two disparate figures in such a way as to convince the undiscerning reader that Tirant is as real as the historical prince who is supposed to have expressed so much interest in the hero's exploits. (Martorell

---

Lordship, I have disregarded the roughness in the arrangement and the diversity of its sentence forms to enable you to communicate its contents, by virtue of your position and power, to your subjects and to others so that they may enjoy the fruit that is appropriate for them, inspiring them not to be fearful of the more unpleasant aspects of military life and to take part in honorable exploits to safeguard the public good, which is the reason for which the military establishment was created.

"Furthermore, this treatise will cast a light upon the moral aspects of knighthood and will present examples of noble customs, thereby doing away with the effect of the various vices and the ferocity of monstruous acts. And so that in the present work no other person may be reprimanded for the presence of any weakness in it, I, Joanot Martorell, a gentleman and a knight, wish to assume complete responsibility for the work, without the collaboration of anyone else; I am the sole author of this work, which was performed in the service of the Most Illustrious Prince and Lord, Expectant King Don Ferrante of Portugal, a task begun on the second day of January 1460."

is careful never to mention the true reason/inspiration for his book: the fall of Constantinople to the Turks in 1453.)

Historical fact is again mixed with fantasy in Martorell's second avowal: that he translated Tirant's biography from an English source-document into Portuguese for Ferrante, then again from Portuguese to the Valencian dialect of Catalan, his native tongue. This statement has been discounted by practically every scholar who has ever worked with *TB*, most notably by Vaeth and Riquer. But even so, there is some small historical basis for the incredible claim Martorell makes. There are documents which show that Joanot Martorell actually did reside in England in the years 1438-39, at which time he would have had access to an English version of the *Guy de Warwick* romance, the foundation of the first thirty-nine chapters of *TB*.[23] With the exception of these chapters and the material pertaining to the Order of the Garter (Chs. 85-97), no other portion of Martorell's novel can be said to be based on any English source. As for the claim for a Portuguese version of *TB*, none is known to have existed at any time.

And so Martorell's claim in the Dedication is at best only partially plausible. An English source for a small section of the novel? Possibly accurate. A Portuguese translation? Hardly likely and certainly not supported by any physical evidence. The most likely explanation is that the Dedication is a hoax and that the entire novel was composed originally and completely in the Valencian idiom of the 1490 edition.

Martorell's third claim is that he is the sole author of *TB*, with total responsibility for the work's content, design and incidental defects. We note that he has cited 2 January 1460 as the date on which he began to compose the novel. Ample evidence of plagiarism has already been supplied here to discredit Martorell's assertion of sole authorship; more acceptable to modern literary criticism might be a claim for "principal editorship" for the Valencian writer. None-

---

[23] *Tirante el Blanco*, I, lv. The documents referred to are copies of actual letters of challenge *(lletres de batalla)* exchanged by Martorell and Joan de Monpalau, two of which were written by Martorell from the English court of Henry VI, dated 22 March 1438 and 13 February 1439. Copies of these letters, as well as of so many important documents related to *TB*, are preserved in Madrid's Biblioteca Nacional in MS. 7811. See *Tirante el Blanco*, I, xvii-xxii.

theless, at the time when Martorell penned his Dedication — between 1460 and 1464/65, according to Riquer [24] — an assertion of total responsibility for the text might indeed have been accurate. However, by the time the book reached publication in 1490, some twenty-two years after Martorell's death, the collaboration of Joan Marti de Galba in preparing the manuscript for the printer had rendered Martorell's claim inoperable. As for the date of 2 January 1460 as the beginning of Martorell's creative effort, not even the erudite Riquer can find any internal or external evidence to contradict the author's statement, so we must accept that claim as irrefutable.

Ultimately we must confront Martorell's most incredible assertion: his claim to a friendship — or an acquaintanceship, at the very least — with Prince Ferrante of Portugal. But before considering that issue, I would like to address the matter of the identity of the Portuguese prince and the likelihood — or unlikelihood — that he could reasonably have been referred to as a "rei expectant" in the mid-1460s.

Ferrante (1433-70) was the younger brother of Alonso V of Portugal, who ruled his nation from 1438 to 1481. Until the year 1451 Ferrante might have been considered a legitimate expectant heir to the throne in his native land, but with the birth of a son to Alfonso and his queen in that year Ferrante's claim evaporated. We must look elsewhere to justify the epithet Martorell assigns him in the Dedication.

Coincidentally, Ferrante was related to still another Alfonso V who ruled on the Eastern shore of the Iberian Peninsula at the same time, the Aragonese monarch who bore the sobriquet "El Magnànimo." This Aragonese Alfonso died in 1458 without a legitimate heir and the Iberian throne passed to his brother Juan while an illegitimate son inherited the lesser and newly acquired Kingdom of Naples. The name of this bastard son? Ferrante, whose identity might easily be confused — intentionally or otherwise — with that of his Portuguese cousin. I will have more to say about this at a later point.

To complicate matters even further, the Portuguese Ferrante at one time had been considered one of the possible successors to the

---

[24] *Tirante el Blanco*, I, lxxvii.

Neapolitan throne, but his aspirations were dashed by Alfonso el Magnanimo's announcement in the mid-1450s of his intention to divide his realm between his brother and his illegitimate son. The disposition of Alfonso's various titles continued to be a thorny issue in the Mediterranean region even after his death. His son was obliged to defend his claim to the Italian possessions against a powerful French claimant and did not succeed in taking final control there until 1464.[25] Meanwhile back in Aragon, Catalan dissatisfaction with the reign of Juan II and his shabby treatment of his son, Charles of Viana — who had a strong claim of his own to the Aragonese crown — led to a long civil war (1462-72) that featured an unsuccessful attempt by the Catalans in Barcelona to secede from the kingdom and establish their own monarchy.

Recorded history places the Portuguese Ferrante at the scene of a number of military expeditions in the Mediterranean region during the 1450s and 1460s. By August 1464 he was stationed in Barcelona at the side of his heirless cousin Don Pedro el Condestable who, following the sudden and mysterious death of Charles of Viana in 1461, was about to be proclaimed "rey dels catalans" in September of 1464 by the dissident Catalan faction. The civil strife continued up to and beyond the death of Don Pedro in 1466, but Ferrante, Pedro's closest relative, had already left Barcelona as of 11 March 1465. The Portuguese prince continued to take part in military adventures in Africa and the Mediterranean region up to the time of his death in 1470 at the age of thirty-seven.[26]

In summary then, Ferrante was eliminated fairly early (1451) from any claim to the Portuguese throne, and then only a few years later he was declared out of the running for the Neapolitan crown as well. By 1464-65, the time when Martorell is generally presumed to have been at work composing his Dedication, Ferrante could be considered a "rei expectant" only among the dissident Catalans — and even then only with the exercise of a great deal of optimism and imagination: he might conceivably have been considered a successor to the childless Pedro el Condestable by virtue of their family ties, but even then his aspirations would have been most

---

[25] *Tirante el Blanco*, I, lxxv-lxxvi; Nicolau d'Olwer, "Examen..." 131-33.
[26] In 1468, for example, Ferrante is named as one of the commanders in the expedition that took and destroyed the city of Anapé.

tenuous in view of the fact that Pedro's "rule" in Barcelona was never confirmed as a political reality in the eyes of the other European kingdoms. All in all, Ferrante's prospects hardly justified Martorell's choice of epithet. On the other hand, the Portuguese prince does appear to have been a rather bellicose individual and one who relished combat and the military life in a way that would have made him an otherwise ideal subject for the dedication of a work such as *TB*.

Did Martorell actually know the Portuguese Ferrante, as he claims? In his Introduction to *Tirante el Blanco* (I, xxv) Riquer reports the existence of documentation that confirms Martorell's presence in Portugal shortly before September 1443 on a business matter. If he had met Ferrante at that time, the Portuguese prince would then have been only a boy of ten. Unfortunately for Riquer's thesis, there is absolutely no evidence to support any claim for personal contact between these two figures on that occasion. And as for Ferrante's residence in Barcelona in 1464-65, again there is nothing to confirm a meeting of the two men there nor of any correspondence between them. Martorell, it must be remembered, was based to the south in Valencia where the supporters of Juan II were in the majority. We cannot be certain that author Martorell and subject Ferrante actually shared the same political convictions regarding the Catalan insurrection. It is therefore unclear as to whether Martorell's reference to the Portuguese prince and his royal aspirations was made seriously or with sarcastic intent. As any reader of *TB* can attest, the author's penchant for sarcasm and irony is quite strong, so if the Dedication had been written in the mid-1460s — as is most likely — the moribund state of the Catalan cause, Pedro el Condestable's health, and Ferrante's royal aspirations at that particular moment would have provided the mordant Martorell with the perfect pretext for a satirical broadside.

It is Riquer's thesis that Martorell and Ferrante did indeed meet in Portugal in 1443, at which time the Portuguese prince, still theoretically expectant of a crown, requested his Valencian guest to translate the Warwick story — which Martorell had obtained/copied during his earlier stay in England — into Portuguese. And it was at this time that Martorell composed the Dedication to the prince. Much later, upon expanding the Warwick fragment to the full-length *TB*, the Valencian writer decided to keep most of what he had previously written (and borrowed from Villena's *Carta*); he then simply made a few minor alterations and substitutions in the old Dedication to make it fit the new work.[27]

Such a scenario might be convincing if it were not for the final sentence of *TB*'s Dedication, in which Martorell clearly links his dedication of the work to Ferrante with the 2 January 1460 date for beginning the novel. His reference to the wandering Portuguese prince as a "rei expectant" is clearly intentional, not a mere oversight. Whether or not there ever existed a 1443 Dedication to Ferrante is moot. What appears to have happened is that at some time after 1460, probably between 1464 and 1468 [when Martorell died], the novelist decided to dedicate his pseudo-historical work to a fairly well-known Lusitanian vagabond prince who for years had been wandering about the Mediterranean region harboring vague expectations of ascending to the Aragonese or Neapolitan throne. (For this to occur in Barcelona, for example, it would have been necessary for Don Pedro to defeat Juan II's Aragonese forces, ascend to the Catalan throne, then die childless, leaving Ferrante to inherit the crown as Pedro's closest relative.)

If the Dedication were written with a tinge of sarcasm for ironic effect — as I believe it was — there would be no mystery as to why Martorell elected not to reproduce the final sentence of Villena's *Carta*, since it calls upon his rather risible subject to set a personal example for others. Such a notable omission in so heavily plagiarized a document as Martorell's Dedication convinces me that the entire piece has been written with tongue in cheek and was never intended to be taken seriously, which unfortunately is what Riquer and others seem all-too-prepared to do. But yet another possibility suggests itself, an extension of something I alluded to only vaguely earlier: perhaps the "subject" of Martorell's Dedication is not one but *two* Ferrantes, a combined image of the Portuguese and Aragonese princes with the same name who at various times aspired to the Neapolitan throne. Such a composite figure would have been a perfect reflection of Tirant himself, a fictional fusion of perhaps half a dozen or more historical heroes.

In sum, then, the Dedication of *TB*, like the novel itself, is actually a clever hoax that Martorell has constructed around a

---

[27] *Tirante el Blanco*, I, lxxiii-lxxiv.

skeleton of historical fact, then skillfully overlaid with a coating of plausible but purely synthetic flesh. We must remember to keep in mind at all times Joanot Martorell's ironic temperament and the kind of novel it produced: a heavily plagiarized "history" about a totally fictitious military hero whose character is actually an amalgam of several famous historical figures. I propose that Martorell then extended his peculiar novelistic technique to his Dedication, still another plagiarized document in which a hybrid subject is forged from the images of two distinct historical princes who happened to bear the same name.

CHAPTER II

TIRANT LO BLANCH:
THE IDEAL CHRISTIAN COMMANDER

As I indicated in the Introduction to this study, Joanot Martorell's novel — more than half of it — is principally devoted to a complete examination of the military as a social institution, especially regarding the value system and personality traits of the male-dominated warrior class.[1] Martorell traces the history of the military establishment, roughly from the twelfth through the fifteenth centuries; the treatment is stylized, however, since the evolution of military customs, tactics and weaponry during these centuries is condensed into the brief lifetime of the hero. Great emphasis is placed on ceremony and symbolic elements, e.g., Tirant's induction into knighthood (Chs. 58-59), the customs and ceremonies of England's Order of the Garter (Chs. 85-97), and the peculiar rites of the

---

[1] The conflict between the austere — almost barbaric — values of the male warriors vs. the more compassionate — civilized, if you will — point of view of the female in medieval society is clearly brought out in Chs. 20-22. In response to the King of England's call for the conscription of all healthy males between the ages of 11 and 70, the Countess of Warwick confronts the monarch with a moving plea to exempt her son. Her tearful supplication that he mercifully spare her only child from the dangers of military combat is roundly rejected by the King, who then admonishes her to take proper pride in her son's military prowess and bask in his future glory, just as she did in that of his famous father. The debate closes in Ch. 22 with the Countess' moving expression of grief at the imminent departure of her son, but the English monarch holds firm in his decision. Ultimately, even the young man whose fate is being decided refuses to support his mother's position. This episode demonstrates clearly that the female system of values, though eloquently presented, must ultimately yield to the more uncompromising male code of military conduct.

knighthood ceremony for those who insist upon being invested by a woman, which requires the donning of one gold and one silver spur instead of the usual two gold (Ch. 189).

The key to understanding the military elements in *TB* is Martorell's Prologue, in which he frankly states that his goal is to restore the decadent military orders to their former unassailable prestige and effectiveness. The Prologue, which I cited in my Introduction, is nothing more than an apology for the military orders and a piece of political propaganda designed to strengthen the clout of the warrior caste by showcasing chivalry as a necessary force in medieval society. These sentiments spill over into the very first sentence of the opening chapter:

> En tan alt grau excelleix lo militar estament, que deuria ésser molt reverit si los cavallers observavan aquell segons la fi per què fonc instituït e ordenat. [2] (*TB*, 117)

As the novel develops we see more clearly the particular measures Martorell wished to suggest: the reinforcement of the noblest chivalric virtues and long-standing traditions that continued to have significance in the 1400s; the replacement of old, hollow values that had become outmoded and virtually useless for the fifteenth-century military situation. [3] Still another important aspect of Tirant's military character, one which is not alluded to in the Prologue but which plays a very significant part in the novel, is the hero's integration of Christian spiritual virtues with his military ones. The generous, honest, forthright Tirant stands out in contrast with the general mendacity and treachery of his Turkish/Moorish adversaries. Certain enemy chieftains may approach the level of Tirant in military prowess, but he almost always stands high above them in moral and ethical perfection. In short, *TB* is addressed to the fif-

---

[2] "The military estate stands out above all others to such a degree that it ought to be venerated, [and would be] if only the knights themselves would look upon it and consider the purpose for which it was created and made part of the social order."

[3] It should be recalled that Tirant does precisely what Don Quijote fails to do: adapt to changing circumstances and new social and political realities. Cervantes may indeed have taken Martorell's hero as the perfect model of chivalric virtue — Amadis notwithstanding — against which he hoped to contrast his own endearingly fallible and anachronistic protagonist.

teenth-century Christian community as a reasoned (but imaginative) response to the Turkish capture of Constantinople in 1453 and the Moslem advances in the Balkans and Eastern Mediterranean regions during the mid-1400s. It is a call to arms, a plea for swift, decisive action by the Christian nations to check the Moslem threat.

Tirant as Knight Errant

In the early part of the novel (Chs. 28-97 — at the English Court) Tirant is presented as a typical medieval knight of the twelfth or thirteenth century, roughly. When we first meet him, he is a young squire with aspirations of becoming a knight but a shortage of knowledge about the profession. He is subsequently tutored by the hermit Guy of Warwick in the meaning and obligations of knighthood (Chs. 28-29) before embarking for England where he eventually achieves his goal in a ceremony that is described with painstaking care by Martorell (Chs. 58-59). The author provides us with a full treatment of ceremonies and rituals surrounding the chivalric orders, plus detailed descriptions of various forms of individual combat in a variety of duels and tournaments — most of them of a serious nature, but occasionally with ridiculous intent.

Tirant's initial hand-to-hand encounters are presented in a rather straightforward manner: his first combat is on horseback, a joust with lances (Ch. 59); the second takes place on foot with a hatchet, sword and dagger for weapons (Chs. 59-60). Both of these battles — Tirant's apprenticeship, so to speak — end in death for his opponent, but even this unpleasant result is not considered something negative or worthy of censure.

The next two of the hero's battles contain a number of ridiculous elements. His nearly disastrous duel with the Lord of Vilesermes (Chs. 60-67) is ludicrous on two counts: first of all, because it is fought over a trifle of etiquette; secondly, because the combatants dress in long nightshirts and wear garlands of flowers on their heads as they proceed to slice each other to pieces with sharp, double-edged knives, using only papier-maché shields for defense. The tooth-to-tooth battle of Tirant and the Prince of Wales' mastiff is likewise laughably foolhardy (Ch. 68); Tirant's refusal to use any weapon against the vicious beast is simply a *reductio ad absurdum* of the hallowed chivalric practice of maintaining a literal and absolute equality of offensive and defensive arms between any two combatants.

Likewise, Tirant's four consecutive victories over the Kings of Poland and Friesland and the Dukes of Burgundy and Bavaria (Chs. 68-73) are notable for their rigorous formality. Four distinct kinds of combat are required by the four challengers. Special stipulations are made regarding virtually every aspect of each duel, and as a result these chapters provide the reader with a wealth of information about the many different kinds of jousting and individual combat that were popular in previous centuries in the royal courts and among the military orders. Tirant's victories here also serve to emphasize Martorell's point that cleverness and conditioning can often overcome superior physical strength.

Similarly, Tirant's triumph over a pair of giants, the brothers Kirieleison and Tomàs de Muntalbà (Chs. 77-80 and 80-84, respectively), serves principally as an excuse for Martorell to demonstrate his extensive knowledge concerning the dueling customs of the French (i.e., Burgundian) Court, which are insisted upon by the challengers. Once again, Tirant's stamina and *ingenio* — not to mention his expertise in every type of combat with every kind of weapon — carry him to victory over an adversary with a distinct physical advantage.

The final battle of Martorell's hero in England (actually, Scotland in this case) is hardly described at all, the reason being that Martorell has no interest in portraying any new combat techniques, but prefers instead to point out a legal technicality regarding the grounds on which a solemn promise may be broken. A knight named Vilafermosa (a Scottish cavalier with a very Latin name), secures from Tirant a firm promise to duel as soon as the latter's wounds — acquired in the course of his previous battles with the two kings and two dukes — have healed (Ch. 74). But before Tirant can keep his word and do battle with him (Ch. 84), the two Muntalbà brothers intervene with their charges of treachery against the hero, accusations which demand immediate satisfaction (Chs. 77-84). The battle itself occupies only two short paragraphs within Ch. 84 and is halted by the Scottish Queen before any damage can be done. What remains is the question of whether a charge of treachery (*tració*) takes precedence over a previous commitment made in good faith. The question is posed but never satisfactorily resolved by Martorell, who apparently was unable to reach a firm decision in his own mind.

Soon thereafter Tirant departs England to return home to Brittany, at which point new adventures begin which require the hero to alter his style of combat. The episode of the Egyptian siege of Rhodes (Chs. 98-108) introduces the use of the crossbow, not only in the account of the Genoese plot to sabotage the crossbows of the island's defenders (Chs. 98-99), but also in Tirant's skillful employment of that weapon in Ch. 106 when he kills eight Moors and captures ten others by cleverly combining the crossbow's deadly accuracy with the swift mobility of fighting on horseback. Martorell uses this episode to demonstrate the tactical advantage of the new crossbow over the traditional lance-and-sword method of combat which the hapless Moorish footsoldiers attempt to employ against the mounted hero who is able to attack and kill from a reasonably safe distance and then ride swiftly out of range of their inferior and antiquated weapons.[4]

Again we observe the old having to yield to the new in Ch. 153 when Tirant negotiates with the King of Egypt the terms of a forthcoming battle between their respective armies. Martorell's hero insists upon imposing one of the formalities of the chivalric code governing individual combat to a battlefield situation: he informs the Moorish commander that because the Moors have suffered two consecutive defeats in which they lost their flag, the rules of chivalry require them to present themselves for the next battle without a flag (although small pennants will be permitted). Tirant

---

[4] Tirant's actions in this chapter embody a curious combination of technological advances in the art of war. For example, the crossbow's popularity soared after it was proved to be extremely effective against the Moslem cavalry's archers during the Crusades. Tirant here manages to combine the best features of both modes — the quickness of the mounted warrior plus the long-range firepower of the crossbow — with maximum effectiveness. At one point the crossbow's devastating efficiency became so terrifying that the Lateran Council of 1139 banned its use — but only against other Christians. Moslems were still fair game, apparently.

Curiously enough, Martorell makes little or no reference to the crossbow after this point; his panoramic and historical point of view causes him to place greater emphasis on later and more sophisticated technological and tactical discoveries in the later chapters of his book.

goes on to stipulate that if the King of Egypt does not conform, he (Tirant) will impose the usual penalty: he will paint the King's portrait on a large shield and drag it from a horse's tail through as many cities as he can. Such a penalty is consistent with the code of conduct we observed in England, but the reader cannot help but sense that the transfer of this code to a situation involving entire armies is somewhat outdated and impractical.

The same feeling that the old order passeth and that even the most worthy of customs will eventually lose their significance is rekindled in Ch. 189 when Tirant — now in Constantinople — competes in his final joust. The disintegration of this once-noble tradition begins to be evident when Diafebus, Tirant's right-hand man who is competing anonymously in strange colors, continually pulls up his lance when he and Tirant charge each other. Diafebus' refusal to do battle annoys Tirant considerably. In a later joust with a knight called El Gran Noble, Tirant succeeds in unhorsing his opponent but suffers in return a tremendous blow that kills his horse and forces him to break his fall by putting his right hand on the ground. The judges award the victory to Tirant, but impose a slight penalty because his hand has touched the ground: he will henceforth be compelled to do battle without ornaments or trappings of any sort; furthermore, he must compete without his right spur and his right gauntlet. Tirant, shamed and outraged by their verdict, vows never to joust again, except against a king or the son of a king.

Martorell uses Tirant's pique here to show that jousting, at one time a favorite exercise of the protagonist, no longer can be said to play a significant role in his development as a soldier. Tirant realizes that he must now move on to modern, more complex forms of combat if he is to develop as a field commander. His skills in hand-to-hand battle never diminish in the novel, but the joust and all other ancient forms of tournament competition disappear after Ch. 189.

Let us now examine some of the peculiar values and rituals of the chivalric code that are highlighted in these early chapters. First of all, there is the notion of Death before Dishonor. In Ch. 60, for example, the Lord of Muntalt (Tirant's second opponent in England) opts for a quick death rather than suffer the indignity of asking Tirant for mercy in front of his colleagues. Similarly, in the Tirant-Vilesermes feud neither combatant is willing to concede the slightest point for fear of dishonor; the result is a senseless death for one of them and a nearly fatal injury for the other. In contrast to these cases we have that of Tomàs de Muntalbà, who, having been defeated by the wily Tirant, gladly renounces his previous accusations against the hero in return for his life. Muntalbà's dishonorable choice is immediately punished by a ceremony of expulsion (including the pouring of hot water over his head) from his military order (Chs. 82-84). The disbarred knight eventually becomes a Franciscan friar and lives out his days peacefully in a monastery.

A second aspect of the chivalric code that is portrayed in the early chapters is the insistence upon strict equality of arms between adversaries. I have already commented on the application of this principle to the celebrated battle of Tirant and the Prince of Wales's mastiff (Ch. 68); on this occasion the hero's refusal to use a steel weapon against a fierce animal is intended to seem rather ridiculous and foolhardy. In an earlier chapter, however, the same principle is applied seriously. Warwick, though wounded, refuses the offer of a horse in the middle of a battle because he feels that it would give him an unfair advantage over the enemy soldiers who must fight on foot (Ch. 25). This pattern is consistent in Martorell's book: a principle, tradition, rule, or custom that is presented in a positive light in an early chapter will eventually be shown to have become debased, perverted, mis-applied, inappropriate, inoperable, wrongheaded or simply archaic in a later period.

The matter of equal arms is again brought up in the last of the four consecutive duels Tirant is obliged to fight against the foreign kings and dukes. His fourth opponent resorts to the illegitimate trick of wearing cardboard leg armor doctored to resemble steel (to give him greater foot speed).[5] Another variation on the same theme occurs in the very next chapter (Ch. 74) when the challenger Vilafermosa offers young Tirant the advantage of an extra piece of equipment — except a sword — during their projected duel. Tirant takes umbrage at the offer, with good reason: such an offer was customary only in the case of a seasoned warrior who wished

---

[5] See Riquer's note, *Tirante el Blanco*, I, 234.

to lessen his natural advantage when battling a novice or a much older opponent.[6] As might be expected, the offer is summarily refused.

Still another quaint ritual presented here deals with the formal penalties that were customarily imposed on a disgraced knight by the chivalric code. I have already mentioned the indelicate manner in which Tomàs de Muntalbà was drummed out of the military establishment in Chs. 82-84. There is also a ritual for cases in which a knight refuses to accept a lawfully issued challenge. In Ch. 77 Kirieleison de Muntalbà specifies the action he will take if Tirant refuses to respond to his request to do battle: he will paint Tirant's coat of arms backwards, have him hanged upside down as a traitor, and publicize Tirant's treachery in all the great royal courts of Europe. This sort of punishment, which appears appropriate (if somewhat bizarre) in the setting of the English court, becomes strangely unrealistic later when Tirant threatens the King of Egypt with a similar punishment in Ch. 153 regarding the matter of flags vs. pennants, as I remarked earlier.

Other instances in which Martorell catalogues penalties to be imposed include Ch. 92, in which he informs the reader how the Order of the Garter proceeds against absent or deceased members who have disgraced the Order: they take vengeance upon a statue or some other effigy made of the malefactor, first baptizing it, then drumming it out of the Order. It is even possible that they will sentence the effigy to perpetual imprisonment. Finally there are the stiff penalties imposed by the Greek Emperor in Constantinople (Ch. 146) upon the Greek nobles who have aided and abetted the Turkish forces against the Christian cause. They are stripped of their nobility and all connection with their noble ancestors, then solemnly defrocked of their knighthood in a ceremony not unlike those mentioned earlier for knights found guilty of having disgraced their order.

The final point about the chivalric code that is made in these early episodes is the unacceptability of deceit as a tool for the knight-errant. A knight's word was his bond and no deception of

---

[6] Riquer explains that Martorell himself made such an offer in London to Perot Mercader in a letter dated 13 February 1439 *(Tirante el Blanco,* I, 237, n. 8).

any kind was permitted. In matters of one-to-one combat, taking advantage deceitfully (e.g., by using lightweight cardboard armor disguised as steel, as we noted in Ch. 73) was considered extremely bad form and punishable by severe penalties. Once Tirant arrives in Constantinople he learns that the question of tactical deception needs to be reexamined in light of the new technology available and newly developed battlefield strategies; measures heretofore totally unacceptable for narrow jousting and tournament competitions may now prove to be extremely beneficial, and perhaps even necessary in a broad battlefield situation, which is the subject of the next section of this study.

TIRANT AS COMMANDER OF LAND AND NAVAL FORCES

Immediately upon leaving England, Tirant becomes aware of the need for *indústria,* the use of clever but honorable tricks of the trade to compensate for perceived deficiencies in firepower or numerical strength. Martorell's hero takes advantage of any leverage he can find — technological or psychological — to turn the tide of battle in his favor. Since Tirant's development as a military commander is presented in a linear fashion by author Martorell, let us observe the lessons he learns and the schemes he concocts in chronological order.

The instructional aspects of *TB* actually begin some time before the hero makes his initial appearance. In Ch. 10 the wily hermit Guillem de Varoic (Guy of Warwick) counsels the English king in the manufacture of delayed-reaction firebombs that can be extinguished only with oil or pine resin — not with water. Four chapters later the hermit instructs the monarch as to how he may deceive the Moorish ambassadors into believing that the English have more soldiers in the city than actually exist; he proposes that they dress all the women in head and chest armor and station them along the route to be taken by the Moorish dignitaries. This same kind of deception is used later by Tirant in hanging lighted lanterns high on masts, yardarms and poles of a variety of small naval vessels at sundown so that the awaiting Turks, upon counting the number of lanterns visible in the dim twilight, would mistake twelve warships and sixty-two fishing vessels for a fleet of seventy-four fighting ships (Ch. 164). We find it still again during Tirant's adventure in Barbary (Ch. 343), when he arranges for the enemy to observe a procession of white-clad "soldiers" — 40,000 in number — who appear to arrive to reinforce Tirant's besieged army. What the opposing forces do not realize is that the "reinforcements" consist entirely of women, children, and old men dressed in white sheets, blankets, shirts, etc., to make them appear to be soldiers in dress uniform.

Varoic strikes again in Ch. 24 with an old trick called "iron thistles": it consists of luring the Moors into the city through a narrow passageway that has been covered with star-shaped copper (not iron) thorns that when trod upon will stifle the charge of man or beast.[7] The enemy is enticed by an additional piece of trickery: the English troops pretend to be in a state of unpreparedness and disarray when the Moslems attack, then conveniently "retreat" to an area that can be approached only through the booby-trapped corridor. The deception results in total English victory, of course.

A subsequent Genoese plot to capture Rhodes provides Martorell with the opportunity to demonstrate two more examples of military cunning. First there is the clever plan to replace part of the firing mechanism of the defenders' crossbows with soft substances like soap or cheese that will render them inoperable when the Genoese assault is launched (Ch. 98).[8] Secondly, there is the design for a collapsible crossbow that the Genoese attempt to smuggle inside the fortress under their flowing robes (Ch. 99).[9]

Through the first ninety-nine chapters Tirant's role regarding tactical maneuvers is purely passive; in Ch. 100, under the tutelage of the wily sailor Cataquefaràs ("Watch what you will do," literally), he begins to apply his newly-acquired knowledge to actual situations. In this particular episode Tirant employs three different defensive strategies to ward off an attack by 15 Moorish vessels: 1) he hangs heavy fishing nets high on the riggings to catch and deflect the hail of missiles fired by the Moslem attackers; 2) he orders the crew's mattresses to be nailed to the side of the ship to cushion it from the blows of the enemy's cannonade; 3) boiling

---

[7] *Tirante el Blanco*, I, 75, n. 7.
[8] *Tirante el Blanco*, I, 297, n. 1.
[9] *Tirante el Blanco*, I, 304, n. 15.

oil and tar are readied for use against any infidel attacker who may attempt to board the Christian vessel during the siege.

Martorell follows the same general format in having Tirant successfully break the Genoese blockade of Rhodes in Ch. 104. The hero avails himself of the expertise of two French sailors in plotting a strategy that will allow his ship to slip quickly past the swarming attackers and into the port with the desperately needed provisions. He begins by approaching from the East, which deceives the Genoese into believing he is a Turkish ally; he delays his move until he has a very strong wind at his back; then, just as he nears the blockade, he unfurls all of his sails in a bold tacking maneuver that carries his vessel at full speed through the blockade before the Genoese in turn can react and pursue. Rather than risk the crew's safety with a normal, slow docking maneuver, Tirant continues at full speed into the harbor and deliberately runs his ship aground on a sandbar, from which point he can unload his cargo without fear of attack from the Genoese because of his proximity to the port and its friendly defenders.

Only two chapters later Tirant allows another sailor to put into effect an ingenious plan to set fire to the flagship of the Genoese fleet. The minute detail with which this fascinating adventure is narrated is one of the triumphs of Martorell's book, as Dámaso Alonso has clearly shown.[10] One can imagine the consternation aboard the flagship as the Genoese sailors spy a flaming barge making its way relentlessly toward their vessel, seemingly propelled by ghostly forces (it is actually being towed from the shore by the arms of a hundred sailors using an unseen underwater pulley system).

Tirant's encounter with the Turks at Pelidas (Ch. 133) gives further proof of the Christian commander's increasing wiliness as he keeps the enemy off-balance and in a constant state of confusion. It is here that camouflage is first employed by seven of Tirant's scouts as they lie in ambush at an oasis to capture four Moorish guards. As a preliminary to a night attack on the enemy camp, Tirant sows panic and confusion among the Moors by turning loose a herd of rutting mares in a place where their scent is certain

---

[10] "*Tirante el Blanc*, novela moderna", *Revista Valenciana de Filología*, 1 (1951), 179-215.

to be picked up by the enemy stallions. The consequent stampede causes chaos in the Turkish camp; this is the signal for the Christian attack, which naturally results in a complete victory for Tirant.

Martorell's hero again outwits his Turkish adversaries at the river near Malveí (Chs. 140-41), where he controls a stone bridge and the Moors a wooden one. For three days the Christian commander plays a cat-and-mouse game with the numerically superior Moslem forces. He lures the enemy to one side or the other of the river, then immediately crosses the stone bridge to safety on the other side if the situation seems disadvantageous. The Turks eventually tire of the game and decide to divide their forces into two groups of equal size and attack the Christians on *both* sides of the river simultaneously — which is precisely what Tirant has been hoping they will do. In a maneuver not unlike the burning of the Genoese flagship in Ch. 106, Tirant's agents secretly move downstream and set fire to the wooden bridge behind the enemy, leaving the Turks permanently weakened on both sides of the river; Tirant quickly exploits this momentary advantage and scores still another incredible victory over a superior force, in this case a perfect application of the divide-and-conquer theory.

In Ch. 149 Tirant initiates the practice of intelligence-gathering through the use of a double agent, Ciprès de Paternò, a Christian-born Cipriot who later converted to Islam but finally embraced Christianity again. Ciprès de Paternò is the prototype of the double agent: he moves freely between the Turkish and Christian camps and pretends to be funneling information to the Turks while secretly serving only the Christian cause.[11] As a precaution, the alert Tirant never fails to confirm the information received from Ciprès de Paternò by comparing it against the data received from other sources, such as Turkish prisoners. The same sort of espionage is used again in Tirant's African adventure, when the sly Albanian takes on the role of the double agent, but the Albanian's personal character is less positively drawn than that of Ciprès, as I shall show in another section of this study.[12]

---

[11] A possible historical model for this character is mentioned by Riquer, *Tirante el Blanco*, II, 309, n. 3.

[12] Tirant recruits the Albanian in Ch. 311 because the latter has free entry to the fortress at Mount Tuber, where Escariano has taken refuge from Tirant's pursuing forces. The scheme by which the Albanian wins

Martorell's attention shifts back to battlefield strategy in Ch. 157 when Tirant's forces employ trickery to lure the Turks into still another trap. With Diafebus' squadron hidden in ambush behind a large rock formation, Tirant's forces feign retreat (while remaining in tight formation) so as to entice the Turks to full pursuit. The Moslems gladly oblige them and proceed to throw down their shields, lances, and crossbows in order to lighten themselves for quicker pursuit. When the Christians, in tight formation and still fully armed, suddenly wheel about and attack, the Turks are caught ill-equipped for the strong resistance they encounter. Unfortunately, the impatient Diafebus leads his troops out of hiding before the most propitious moment and Tirant's victory on this occasion is less than total.

When the action returns to the sea, Tirant makes full use of additional advice he receives from a captured Genoese sailor named Galançó. The captive counsels Tirant to lighten his ships for greater maneuverability when doing battle with the more numerous Turkish vessels; he also suggests that the Christian commander send two of his galleys to search for the expected fleet of the Grand Caramany (a Moslem noble). One of these ships will return with a report on the size and location of the enemy armada; the other is to shadow the Grand Caramany's flagship from a safe distance. Galançó's advice on both occasions proves invaluable to Tirant's success as a naval commander.

Even after he is shipwrecked on the North African coast and finds himself in the role of a Moorish chieftain's prisoner, Tirant continues to grow in knowledge and military expertise. When called upon to aid the chieftain in an important campaign, Tirant makes three outstanding contributions (Ch. 304). His first accomplishment is to concoct a special unguent — which Martorell informs us is

---

Escariano's confidence is much more elaborate than the one involvingCiprès de Paternò earlier. The Albanian willingly submits to a public whipping and to having his earlobes cut by Tirant's men in order to deceive the Ethiopian leader. The crafty *albanés* eventually betrays the ingenuous Escariano into Tirant's hands, but he accomplishes his mission in such a bloodthirsty and treacherous manner as to cause Tirant to dismiss him shortly thereafter. The episode of the Albanian spy is an unmistakable comment on the unpleasant and occasionally dishonorable aspects of having to rely on espionage and trickery to achieve a military goal.

composed of whale bile, mercury, nitrate, and sulphuric acid, among other ingredients — designed to rust out any metal within three hours of application. Disguised as a shepherd, Tirant works his way into the enemy camp and succeeds in anointing 37 cannons with his corrosive mixture. When fired, these weapons quickly break down and the enemy defenders of the castle are thereupon left without any large artillery to ward off an attack. The next phase of this plan involves destroying one of the arches of the stone bridge across the river that separates the two armies; he replaces it with a wooden drawbridge controlled by his forces. This allows Tirant and his followers to dictate the location and general conditions of all skirmishes that follow. Having established this control, he puts into operation the third part of his strategem: he stages a diversionary attack at the bridge to engage the entire enemy force while he makes his way unseen to the besieged castle of the King of Tlemcen, where he rescues the king's party and leads them to safety back at the capital city.

At a later point in the war between Tlemcen and Ethiopia, Tirant is called upon to shore up the defenses of another city under siege, Asinac (Ch. 309). He proceeds to construct a series of barricades outside the city to fortify it against bombardment and attack; furthermore, he orders a system of underground passageways constructed in the weaker zones to facilitate escape to the orchards outside in case of attack. Tirant develops even more sophisticated defensive strategies to break the siege of Tlemcen (Ch. 339). Here he employs *contraminas*, brass basins placed in dwellings along the city's walls; vibrations from these delicate instruments will indicate the location of tunneling activities from the outside. When such a tunnel is finally detected, Tirant and his men pounce upon the enemy soldiers as they emerge from the tunnel, then fire a cannon into the tunnel to finish off scores of invaders who are following close behind.

In the same chapter Tirant avails himself of another plebeian advisor, just as he did previously with the sailors Caraquefaràs and Galançó. A Genoese galley slave named Almedíxer (who was shipwrecked along with the hero in Ch. 299) comes forth with a plan to drive away from the city gates the many cattle and horses that the Moorish attackers have placed there to impede traffic into or out of the town. Almedíxer concocts a foul-smelling brew that he ignites at strategic spots outside the gates to stampede the herd in the direction of the Moorish camp. The resultant confusion and disarray among the enemy forces is the signal for a well-timed attack by Tirant's ally Escariano from a nearby forest, and the siege is broken (Ch. 340).

The situation is reversed in Ch. 394 at Caraman, when it is Tirant's turn to play the role of the frustrated besieger. Unable to bring the resisting inhabitants to their knees even after a full year of bombardment, Martorell's hero ultimately must resort to the same tunneling strategy he thwarted earlier at Tlemcen. In concert with an all-out assault at ten different points in the city's defenses, a thousand of Tirant's troops finally penetrate one of the city's walls and succeed in opening three of the gates from the inside. The result, unsurprisingly, is the last of Tirant's string of impressive victories in North Africa.

The hero's development as a military virtuoso also includes some experimentation with the techniques of guerrilla warfare to supplement the more conventional strategies. At one point Tirant launches a surprise attack from a wooded area on an unsuspecting Moorish camp, then retreats to the safety of Tlemcen's walls (Ch. 334). Tirant finishes the enemy off with still another well-coordinated assault from the woods by Escariano's troops, but only after rendering the Moors vulnerable to attack by stampeding — as described above — a herd of horses and cattle through their camp with the aid of Almedíxer's pungent mixture (Ch. 340). Finally, Martorell's hero leads a daring raid on the Moorish camp to rescue the Marquis of Luçana, carrying out the assignment and burning the camp to the ground with a force of only 500 men (Ch. 343).

The final stage of Tirant's development during the African campaign (preparatory to his triumphant return to the Byzantine theater) takes place at Caraman. In a fierce battle just outside the city (Chs. 386-87), Tirant divides his army into seven squadrons, each of the first six commanded by a trusted lieutenant, the seventh by the Christian commander himself. The pace is at first slow; he sends the first squadron, then the second, to engage the Moorish forces. When the tide appears to be turning against him, Tirant hastens to send the third through sixth waves into the fray. He leads his own squad into battle only as a last resort. The battle itself is fiercely fought but the victory is not decisive — Tirant must ultimately resort to a year-long siege capped by the tunneling maneuver mentioned earlier to bring the city under his control. Martorell uses this episode to show just how adept his protagonist has become in the rather sophisticated art of commanding large land forces prior to his return to Constantinople. Riquer points out one other interesting novelty in this battle: it marks the first use of a helmet in battle; all previous employment of such headgear was restricted to jousts and tournaments. [13]

Tirant's greatest military triumph — and the culmination of his gradual education as a Christian commander — takes place back at the Byzantine front when, in a combined land and naval assault, the Christian hero cleverly outmaneuvers his Turkish adversaries and forces them to sue for peace (Ch. 418). He sets sail with his armada from the port of Troy and approaches the besieged city of Constantinople under the cover of darkness. The Christian fleet launches a surprise pre-dawn attack that catches the Moslem forces completely off-guard, with the result that the Turkish navy is completely routed. As the enemy swarms to the beach in anticipation of an attempted landing, Tirant orders his ships to reverse their course and return to Troy. But after nightfall he doubles back again unseen and lands his troops on the shore behind the enemy lines. By the time the Turks realize what Tirant has done, he has seized a strategic bridge and cut off their only possible avenue of retreat. With their ships destroyed and having no hope of escape by land, the two Turkish leaders must immediately agree to Tirant's terms for peace.

It might be interesting to speculate here as to whether this account of Tirant's final triumph over the Turks might not also represent author Martorell's personal plan for the recapture of the Byzantine capital. The author appears to have made an intensive study of the topography of the area in and around Constantinople and designed what he obviously feels would be the perfect battle plan for re-taking the city. From a purely literary standpoint, however, we can only concern ourselves with the events as they are related. In that light, the final victory at Constantinople is simply the culmination of Tirant's fictional military career and a logical extension of his previous professional conduct. But in one sense

---

[13] *Tirante el Blanco*, IV, 255, n. 20.

the final stages of Tirant's career represent a radical departure from the strict chivalric code that governed his earlier performance as a knight-errant. His increased reliance on technology in the later years is immediately apparent; equally so is his willingness to resort to deception (including espionage) as an instrument of war. Tirant's cunning and shiftiness in the field are developed gradually — almost imperceptibly — in the course of many battles on the Greek and North African fronts. Martorell's hero ultimately exchanges the role of a solitary warrior who seeks to defeat a single adversary by depending primarily upon his personal valor, his excellent physical conditioning, his versatility and expertise in all the popular forms of combat, etc., for that of a sophisticated field commander who relies principally on solid administrative techniques and clever strategic maneuvers to overcome what is generally a numerically superior enemy force.

MARTORELL ON THE TRAINING OF WARRIORS

With regard to the preparation of young men for a military career, Martorell's novel again approaches the subject as a contrast between the old and the new traditions, occasionally as a clash between the barbarian pagan practices and the more civilized Christian training. Unfortunately, it is not always clear what Martorell's attitude might be toward the material he presents. On the one hand, the primitive practices he describes at various points appear unnecessarily cruel and barbaric; on the other, the reader cannot help but sense a certain awe and admiration in the tone Martorell adopts when recounting the old-fashioned training methods used by the ancient Christian warriors and some contemporary Moslem fanatics. Let us examine some of the more notable examples.

The first illustration of primitive training practices occurs in Ch. 3 when the Count of Warwick announces to his wife his plan to abandon her and their infant son to make a pilgrimage to Jerusalem. The Countess, understandably upset at the news but powerless to alter her fate, decides to prepare her three-month-old son for the difficult life that awaits him with only a mother to raise and protect him. She grabs him by the hair of his head and slaps him across the face, an act which certainly seems cruel by today's standards (and probably by those of Martorell's time), but which fazes the Count not at all. He, after all, will have his turn at the boy several years later (Ch. 25) when he personally dubs him a knight. On that occasion, immediately following the ceremony, Warwick insists that the new cavalier, who is by then only eleven or twelve years of age, kill his first Moor. An extraordinarily large Moorish prisoner is brought out and bound for slaughter; the new knight is then invited to hack away at the helpless figure with his sword until he succeeds in dispatching him. This done, the father seizes the boy — again by the hair — and throws him atop the bleeding victim, rubbing his face in the gore until his eyes, nose, etc., are covered with blood. Next he obliges the lad to place his hands into the wounds he has inflicted until he is entirely drenched in the oozing red substance. The ceremony concludes with a statement to the effect that afterwards the boy became a brave knight and virtuous person, so renowned that no other could be found to equal him in much of the world.[14]

Tirant himself is used to demonstrate the need of warriors to be physically fit and expertly trained in the use of a wide variety of arms when he accepts the simultaneous challenges of four noblemen who insist that each of the four duels be fought with different weapons and under distinct battle conditions (Chs. 72-73). Martorell's hero emerges victorious because of his dexterity and expertise in the use of the lance, sword, dagger, axe, etc., and proves himself equally adept at fighting on foot or on horseback. It is specifically mentioned that he wins the final battle because of his superior conditioning and long-windedness.

Martorell's final reference to training techniques is the most interesting — and perhaps the most puzzling — of them all. In Ch. 239 the Emperor announces that the Turks have been joined recently by fresh support troops from several Moslem kingdoms, among them 40,000 troops from the providence of Enedast (Evedasi in the 1511 Castilian version). The warriors from Enedast are renowned for their cruelty, bravery, and expertise with every sort of weapon. Their male children are raised to be warriors: at the

---

[14] "Aprés isqué molt valent cavaller e virtuós de sa persona: tant valgué en son temps, que en una gran part del món no s'hi trobà cavaller que tant valgués." (*TB*, 158-59)

age of ten they are taught to ride and to fence; following this they serve an apprenticeship with a blacksmith to learn how to wield heavy weapons and to increase their arm strength; next they are instructed in wrestling and the javelin throw, then move on to similar courses utilizing a variety of other weapons; the final phase is a term at a school for butchers where they are taught to quarter steers and overcome any aversion to bloodshed they might have. This butcher's technique carries over easily into combat where they have been known to quarter any luckless enemy soldier who falls into their hands. Finally, the Enedastian warriors are obliged to drink ox or sheep's blood twice a year, a ritual which they believe steels them even further for the cruel and rigorous life they will lead. With such training it is no wonder that they are the best and most feared of all the pagan mercenaries, each one said to be the equal of four Christian soldiers.

The reader cannot help but notice a certain ambivalence on the part of Martorell in presenting this information. It is obvious that he considers the Enedastians little more than savages, but even so he appears to approve of the various apprenticeships that constitute a warrior's training in that pagan society. This is, of course, the same impersonal treatment he gave to the earlier episodes of the Count and Countess of Warwick and the preparation of their son for knighthood during a more primitive Christian epoch. Neither the author nor his characters offer any comment whatsoever on the astonishing practices that are described; Martorell presents the information in a matter-of-fact manner and without the slightest indication of personal approval or disapproval. This even-handed treatment of the theme is ultimately unsatisfying to the critical reader. What sort of training does Martorell actually propose for fifteenth-century Christian soldiers? Unfortunately, the unemotional attitude of the author toward these primitive practices is not counterbalanced in the novel — as it is in so many other cases — by episodes that detail Tirant's own approach to the matter. There are no chapters devoted to a description of how Martorell's hero trains his troops. Tournament competition (e.g., jousting) is Tirant's personal conditioning program, but he abandons that activity after Ch. 189, so it hardly seems likely that Martorell is proposing in his novel that the Christian nations resurrect that ancient rite as a viable training method for the 1400s. One can only speculate as to whether Martorell intended to include sections that would describe innovative techniques for steeling Christian troops for the rigors of combat against the fanatical and cruel Moslem forces. If he did, he failed to include them in his manuscript — and Galba appears to have added nothing concerning the subject.

Martorell's curious posture regarding this theme brings us back to Tirant's strange combat experiences with Vilesermes and the Prince of Wales's mastiff in Chs. 67 and 68. One wonders what exactly was the point Martorell wished to make 1) by having two men duel with deadly blades while wearing nothing but nightshirts and paper armor, or 2) by presenting an adventure in which a foolhardy knight eagerly consents to fight tooth-to-tooth with a fierce canine. Ridiculous combat? Absolutely, but intentionally presented as such, presumably for satirical purposes. What does Martorell suggest to replace these absurd rituals? Nothing, unfortunately.

In short, author Martorell does a magnificent job of burlesquing old, silly, or barbaric customs, but he does not always contribute a viable alternative for the reader's consideration — all of which makes for a supremely interesting but occasionally unsatisfying novel.

TIRANT AS A LEADER OF MEN

The warrior Tirant is not required to demonstrate any leadership qualities until he arrives at the Greek court in Constantinople in Ch. 117. From that point on, however, he proves to be an exemplary commander who anticipates and prepares for all eventualities, is attentive to detail, and demonstrates a remarkable capacity for prudence and patience in dealing with both superiors and subordinates. Let us examine some of the particular instances in which Martorell's hero displays the various qualities that a military commander ought to have.

Tirant's first opportunity to shine as a field marshal occurs at Pelidas in Ch. 133; here he demonstrates his enormous capacity for keen judgment and his careful attention to detail. While on the road to Pelidas he orders his camp to be guarded at night by two shifts of armed sentries who will partrol on horseback; each squad — one on duty until midnight, one after that hour — is to consist of two thousand men. At the same time Tirant orders another group of sentries to monitor the roads for any sign of enemy troop movements that might indicate a surprise attack. To set an example for his men, the commander himself participates in the first watch, keeping constantly on the move between locations to supervise the operation. Martorell informs us that Tirant is at all times dressed for battle and removes his armor only to change shirts.

Reveille is sounded two hours before dawn; the day begins with the celebration of the Mass, after which the Commander personally oversees the preparations for breaking camp at sunrise. Upon arriving at the besieged city, Tirant wisely chooses to enter at night so that the Turks will have no idea of the number of reinforcements he brings. Once inside he urges the citizen-defenders to maintain a constant state of readiness for battle, with their horses shod and their saddles freshly tanned. He personally scouts the enemy camp in search of some weakness he may exploit; this eventually results in a daring night raid that drives the Turks to seek refuge on a nearby mountain. Faced with the decision as to whether to pursue the fleeing enemy troops, Tirant prudently opts *not* to engage the Turks while the latter hold the high ground; instead, he pitches his camp at the base of the mountain and waits for them to bring the battle to him.

As for Tirant's relations with his fellow officers and the enlisted men in general, he is most considerate. When pitching camp, for example, Tirant refuses to dismount until all troops have been settled in their quarters. He later moves from tent to tent to invite his subordinate officers — Greek dukes, counts and marquises, for the most part — to dine with him. (He has enlisted three of the finest French cooks to prepare the meals for his troops.) Martorell notes that Tirant's soldiers are as well provisioned in the field as they would be back in Constantinople.

Another important leadership skill is the ability to motivate the troops and incite them to fight more fiercely when the situation seems hopeless. Tirant's ability as an orator is most evident on two occasions when all appears lost: in Ch. 141 at Malveí when the Turks have the Christians outnumbered and backed into an indefensible position, and at Caraman in North Africa (Ch. 387) when the newly Christianized forces meet stiff Moorish resistance. In both cases Tirant's rhetorical skills save the day as he appeals to their chivalric sense of honor and the fire of their Christian faith as sources of spiritual strength upon which they may draw for inspiration in making the maximum effort required. But when the occasion demands it, Tirant's tongue can also serve as a biting lash — as even his closest friend, Diafebus, learns in Ch. 157 when Tirant publicly rebukes him for failing to follow his orders to the letter, thereby costing Tirant a total victory at Sant Jordi.

In many other ways Tirant is shown to be the ideal military leader. As any good commander would do in the wake of a tremendous victory (cf. the Cid), Tirant sends to the Greek Emperor all of the booty and Turkish prisoners taken at Sant Jordi (Ch. 159). In a subsequent battle at a town that is offering great resistance, Tirant spurs his troops on to greater effort by personally leading the assault against the city's wall, scaling a ladder in the face of many hostile archers armed with highly lethal crossbows (Ch. 161).

Still another requisite for leadership is the ability to cultivate certain intangible fighting qualities among the enlisted men. Tirant reveals a secret test for combat readiness and fighting "heart" in Ch. 164 when he advises one of his junior officers to sound a false battle alarm from time to time in order to observe the condition of the troops as they fall into formation. A simple check of the tightness of a soldier's spurs (for horsemen) or his linen trunks (for footsoldiers) will reveal those who are careful to keep themselves in constant readiness, he asserts.

From these early examples of Tirant's performance we can gauge his tremendous capacity for leadership. This is not to say that Martorell's hero is without flaws. On the contrary, the author's plan calls for Tirant's unbridled courage to turn occasionally into reckless temerity, as in Ch. 238 when he foolishly attempts to return to the front in spite of a serious injury (a broken leg) that he has sustained in a fall back at Constantinople. The same injury is the pretext for the hero's protracted absence from the front during his convalescence at the Imperial palace, a period when he becomes so distracted by romantic intrigues involving the Princess Carmesina that he eventually loses his desire to fight. This momentary lapse is ultimately corrected with the aid of a clever Jewess who succeeds in bringing Tirant back to his senses (Ch. 292) so that he can rededicate himself to his original military objective.

Tirant's campaign against the Turks in defense of the Byzantine Empire suffers a major setback when he unexpectedly becomes shipwrecked on the Barbary coast, but Martorell's hero remains steadfast in his resolve to return to the Balkan front; meanwhile, he continues to develop as a military strategist and leader of men during his African exile. The ultimate compliment to Tirant's leadership is paid by the defeated and dying King of Tunis in Ch. 345 when he commends the Christian commander's cleverness and generalship in defeating a numerically superior Moslem force with genius and tactical skill ("ab aptea e indústria"). In particular he cites the confidence Tirant has instilled in his troops, an element which enables them to remain calm under adverse conditions and hold their ground when others might panic and run. He also praises Tirant's selection of experienced lieutenants, hardened veterans fifty to sixty years of age, and the fact that Tirant is a born leader as well as his own best advisor.[15]

---

[15] The complete text of his remarks — plus the English translation thereof — is as follows:

> —La noblea e virtut és ja coneguda d'aquell famós cavaller Tirant lo Blanc, e d'aquesta hora avant, tots los reis e cavallers de la Barberia se deuen humiliar a ell, car jo el veig en sobirana esperança de pujar en imperi esdevenidor, com a la sua gran indústria e alta cavalleria la fortuna li ve tan pròspera que no seria negú qui d'ell pogués traure lo cabal. Emperò, aquesta victòria que ara de nosaltres ha aconseguida no la deu atribuir a les llurs forces, com en la batalla més poderosos érem nosaltres que no ells, ni jamés nos fórem deixats de combatre, sinó per lo frau e decepció que ens ha fet de les dones. Car en la primera batalla, encara que ens fallís rei, no ens fallí la virtut, e fórem vencedors; mas en esta segona, perquè és estada molt dolorosa e per poc saber nos som perduts. Per causa d'açò me vull deixar de viure, e oferir lo meu cos a deshonrada sepultura, puix tan poc he sabut de la guerra, car veig que per pietat no són estats deixats los fills a les mares, ne los marits a les mullers. E per no veure tanta crueldat, ab bones obres vull acabar la glòria de la mia vida ans que venir en més extrema desaventura, e per experiència veig que los nostres fets no poden haver llonga durada, per ço com la gent de Tirant és molt ben ordenada, e com entren en batalla se pot ben dir que són mestres de cavalleria. E Tirant no dóna càrrec a negú que sia capità en la batalla, sinó a hòmens qui passen cinquanta o seixanta anys, e no és negú de tota la sua gent que sol li passàs per l'enteniment de fugir, ans tots tenen per certa la victòria, puix tenen a Tirant per capità, e no és negú qui pose l'esperança en los peus, sinó en los braços i en les mans. E

THE IDEAL CHRISTIAN COMMANDER

One virtue that Martorell's hero must acquire in the course of the novel is patience. Tirant is initially given to making an occasional rash vow or promise, for example the ill-considered utterance

> tot lo contrari d'açò fa la nostra gent, e per causa d'açò som tots vençuts e vituperats, car aquest sap vençre les forts batalles, dures e aspres ab aptea e indústria, e sap consellar a si mateix e instruir als altres, e ha sabut cremar lo nostre camp, e ab dones ha vençuda tan gran multitud de morisma, e portats a total destrucció, car la vista d'elles féu perdre tot lo nostre esforç, que no gosaren tornar en lo nostre camp, on les tendes eren cremades, ans ab gran dejecció nostra se mudaren en altre lloc. E dic-te, Capità gloriós, que jamés fui vençut en batalla ne corromput per avarícia.
>
> (*TB*, 941-42)

"The nobility and virtue of that famous knight, Tirant lo Blanch, is already well known, and from this moment on every king and knight in Barbary must bow down before him; for as I see it, he has a real hope of establishing a future empire here, given his great industriousness and the tremendous chivalric talents that cause Fortune to favor him to such an extent that no one will ever be able to outwit him. But he cannot attribute his victory over us here to his numerical strength, since we were much more powerful than his forces and would never have stopped battling if it weren't for the fraud and deceit he used against us by employing women. For in the first battle, even though we did not have a leader, we were deserving and triumphant; but in this second skirmish we have lost because it was a hard-fought encounter and because we have not fought wisely. And because of that I want now to die and offer my body for dishonorable burial, for I have shown so little expertise in matters of war, and I realize that out of piety children have been separated from their mothers and husbands from their wives. And so, in order not to witness so much cruelty, I wish to end my life in glory with good works rather than fall into a greater misfortune; and I realize from experience that our deeds cannot endure for very much longer, since Tirant's forces are very well trained and when they join battle it can truly be said that they are masters in the chivalric arts. And Tirant does not appoint anyone to a leadership position in battle who is not at least fifty or sixty years of age, and there is no one among his troops who would dare run from battle; instead, they are confident of victory because their captain is Tirant and they do not rely upon their feet, but rather on their arms and their hands. And our soldiers are precisely the opposite, and because of this we are defeated and cursed; he knows how to win the hard and tough battles with ability and cleverness, and he can serve as his own best counsel as well as train others; and he has found a way to burn our camp to the ground, and he has defeated and totally destroyed so many Moors by using women [as a decoy], for we lost all our fighting spirit when we saw them and did not dare to return to our camp where our tents were being consumed by flames; instead, we shamefully moved our camp to another location. And I want to tell you, Glorious Captain, that I have never been defeated in any battle nor corrupted at any time by greed."

he makes in Ch. 341 after the Moors have treacherously broken the truce and ambushed a Christian convoy. Such is Tirant's outrage at the enemy's perfidy that he vows never again to grant such a temporary peace to any adversary, and threatens that if any of the other Christian leaders should grant one, he will refuse to honor it and will immediately withdraw from the campaign. An emotional appeal from his friend and comrade Escariano eventually moves Tirant to retract his threat to abandon his allies in their time of need (Ch. 343). The real test of his patience — and his word — comes in Ch. 349 when the Moors once again request a truce; Tirant rejects their plea in accordance with his vow, but four of the other Christian lieutenants grant the requested ceasefire so that both armies may bury their dead and heal their wounded. But then the Moors attempt to move secretly to the safety of the mountains during the night shortly before the expiration of the truce; Tirant, who had previously demonstrated great restraint in allowing the Moors to retreat to their camp after the previous battle, avails himself of this opportunity as a pretext for pouncing on them and exacting a punishing toll in casualties and booty. The Moors immediately claim a technical violation of the treaty and threaten to denounce the Christian commander to the world as a treacherous breaker of solemn promises. Given the choice of either 1) claiming that his previous vow rendered him exempt from the provisions of the treaty (and risking a consequent loss of esteem among some of his followers), or 2) simply honoring the agreement made by his comrades and making restitution to the aggrieved Moors, Tirant prudently opts for the second course of action.

This display of patience and emotional restraint represents a completely new facet of Tirant's personality and is intended by Martorell to represent a transition to a more mature and reflective stage in the protagonist's development. The Christian commander's new maturity is immediately contrasted with the volatile and intemperate behavior of his cohort Lord Agramunt, who in the very same chapter (349) vows that every inhabitant of the city of Montàgata — male and female alike, young and old — will pass under his sword. This vow is not made without some provocation — Agramunt is seriously wounded by a missile fired from within the city's walls — but he utters it rashly and in the heat of anger. Subsequent events in the story eventually render the fulfillment of his vow practically impossible and politically embarrassing. A clever solution that will allow Agramunt technically to fulfill his vow yet avoid senseless bloodshed is eventually proposed by Plaerdemavida in Ch. 372; however, it requires Agramunt to go to rather ridiculous lengths to extricate himself from this moral dilemma. More will be said about the significance of Agramunt's silly vow in a later chapter; for the moment I merely wish to point out how careful Martorell is to place this episode where it will reinforce by contrast the developing emotional maturity of Tirant.

In the final portion of his novel — the triumph of Tirant in the Barbary States and his eventual return to Constantinople to complete the rescue of the Greek Empire from the clutches of the Turkish invaders — Martorell takes pains to show that military prowess presupposes a complementary talent for diplomatic leadership. Tirant's success as a military commander inevitably requires him to display similar virtues on the diplomatic/political front in order to consolidate the fruits of his hard-won military victories. The confirmation of the political side of Tirant's leadership qualities is found in his use of ambassadors and other diplomatic messengers in the final stages of his North African campaign.

When faced with stiff resistance by the inhabitants of Caraman, Tirant sends to them a Spaniard named Rocafort as his personal representative to convince them to surrender and thereby avoid an unnecessary slaughter (Chs. 384-86). Although this initial attempt at diplomacy fails — Tirant is obliged to take the city by force — Martorell's hero resorts to diplomatic channels with increasing frequency from this point on. For example, the newly named lord of Montàgata, a knight named Melquisedec, is dispatched with a shipload of wheat for the besieged city of Constantinople and permission to serve as Tirant's ambassador to the Emperor and ultimately bring back news of the Empire and his beloved Carmesina (Chs. 383; 388-93; 395-97; 401). At the same time Tirant commissions another knight named Espèrcius to recruit on the island of Mallorca and in the Italian city-states of Pisa, Genoa, and Venice as many large sailing vessels as possible in order to outfit a merchant marine that will carry food and other supplies to Constantinople (Ch. 387). He is instructed to promise them a year's salary if they will report to a certain Tunisian port where they will receive Tirant's orders. The same Espèrcius later functions as Tirant's ambassador to the King of Sicily to enlist his aid for the final battle in the reconquest of the Byzantine Empire (Chs. 401; 405-06).

Tirant's aptitude for selecting excellent representatives extends likewise to his choice of messengers, wherein special talents are matched to specific assignments. Upon returning to the Byzantine front at a port near Troy (Ch. 414), Martorell's hero learns that all land and sea routes to the capital are controlled by the Turks and their Moorish allies. In order to notify the Emperor that his forces are at Troy (some hundred miles distant), Tirant entrusts a recently converted Tunisian Moor named Sinegerus with the delivery of the message. The Christian leader correctly guesses that his messenger will be captured by the enemy, but that a Moorish-speaking agent will easily be able to convince them of his innocence and be allowed to proceed to Constantinople. The plan works perfectly and Sinegerus' message offers great consolation to the hard-pressed Greeks. Similarly, in Ch. 420 when Tirant has completely surrounded the Turkish and Moorish forces outside the capital and wishes to communicate this information to the Emperor, his choice is a Greek called Carillo, who is a native of Constantinople and knows routes that will enable him to arrive there undetected by the enemy.

A considerable part of Tirant's success as a leader is his ability to delegate authority wisely. Just as he chose six excellent lieutenants earlier at Caraman (Chs. 386-87), at Constantinople he entrusts the entire naval part of the operation to the Marquis of Luçana/Liçana, an experienced admiral who can be trusted to make sound naval decisions and leave Tirant free to take charge of the land-based offensive (Ch. 423).[16]

Still another reason for the success of Martorell's hero in commanding such large numbers of men is his concern for the welfare and morale of those in his charge. I have already alluded to the merchant marine he commissions in Africa to supplement his fighting armada. Tirant's instructions to Liçana when he appoints him

---

[16] The Marquis of Luçana makes his initial appearance in Ch. 340 when he is introduced as one who serves the King of France; the spelling remains the same in Ch. 343 when he is rescued from the Moorish camp in the course of Tirant's daring night raid. In Ch. 386, however, when the Marquis is named to lead one of Tirant's squadrons at Caraman, the spelling is changed to Liçana, the form it keeps for the remainder of the book.

as his admiral specifically mention liberal payments to the chartered ships. He authorizes the payment of a bonus of 1000 ducats per man if they will agree to deliver food and supplies to allied forces under siege at Sinòpoli and Pera. More will be said concerning Tirant's extreme generosity in the next section of this study. Suffice it to say here that Martorell's protagonist can count on the loyalty of his subordinates because he makes a great effort to ensure that they are always well fed and amply rewarded for their services.

Finally, I would like to mention one of the most important leadership qualities exhibited by Martorell's hero: the willingness to allow his nominal superiors (i.e., political figures) and his subordinates to participate in the decision-making process. When the Turks and their allies propose a three-month peace (during which time they promise to withdraw from all the Greek territory they have conquered), Tirant refuses to reply without first consulting his council of advisors (Ch. 427). This democratic gesture is perhaps not of supreme importance on the field of battle, but it does serve to minimize the growth of dissension within the chain of command. Similarly, when the Sultan's proposal is finally presented to the Emperor (Ch. 445), Tirant insists that the Emperor and his Council make the decision to accept or reject it. Here we note that the hero — Martorell's model for the perfect Christian commander — declines to take part in the political (i.e., policy-making) decision; he simply reaffirms his commitment to carry out the decisions made by the rightful civilian authority. Martorell wishes to demonstrate here that Tirant has a clear understanding of the limited and subordinate role the military establishment must play within a well-ordered society.

TIRANT THE MERCIFUL, TIRANT THE GENEROUS

One of the lessons Martorell attempts to teach in his novel is that merciful gestures are not incompatible with the many other virtues of a strong military leader. But in order to appreciate the mercifulness of Tirant, the reader must compare the hero's character with that of several other warrior figures that appear in Martorell's book. Once again, we note the inevitable striking contrast between the sophisticated, "modern" Tirant and the rather crude and primitive Varoic (Guy of Warwick), who in Ch. 25 condemns 22,000 trapped Moors to a fiery death by refusing their desperate offer to surrender. Those who attempt to flee the burning castle are butchered on the spot or driven back into the flames with lances. As we shall soon observe, even Tirant has his harsh moments, but Martorell's hero is designed with a clear-cut understanding of when, how, and with whom mercy should be shown.

At Miralpeix (Ch. 133) and later at Malveí (Ch. 142) Tirant extends the maximum clemency to the defeated Turks when they deliver themselves into his hands. He sees that they are well fed and given the proper medical attention; furthermore, he goes out of his way to transport them back to the Emperor in Constantinople, the place from which they may possibly be ransomed at a later date.[17] Tirant's compassionate side is also seen during the Barbary adventure when the wounded but gallant King of Tunis is captured by Tirant's men, only to succumb shortly thereafter. The Christian commander orders the Moor's remains to be given a magnificent wake (to be covered with a gold cloth and guarded by a hundred armed knights) and invites the dead sovereign's followers to retrieve the body (Ch. 345). In so honoring a fallen adversary, Tirant casts himself in an honorable light as well.

As the hero sweeps across North Africa, taking city after city, we are constantly apprised of Tirant's mercifulness toward those who surrender to him without resistance: neither their person nor their property is damaged or violated in any way, and many liber-

---

[17] Many of the prisoners taken at Pelidas, Miralpeix and Malveí are in fact Christian renegades who opted to aid the Moslem cause against the Christian Emperor. These special cases receive rather harsh treatment back at the Greek capital. The most perfidious are condemned as traitors, stripped of their titles of nobility, and drummed out of the military orders with considerably ceremony. They are hung upside down to die, after which their remains are refused Christian burial and simply thrown out into a field to be defiled and eventually devoured by dogs and wild beasts. Diafebus and Carmesina successfully appeal for clemency in the case of the squire who served the evil Duke of Macedonia; they point out that the man served only as a messenger for the Duke and took no part in any of his master's treachery. Prisoners who are not ransomed by family and friends are then sold as slaves or bartered for arms, horses or food. Some are allowed to volunteer for service in the Imperial army; those who will not swear allegiance to the Emperor are condemned to chains and a term at hard labor (Ch. 146).

ties are granted them — particularly the freedom of worship. Even so, Martorell tells us, because of Tirant's great liberality many of the defeated Moors soon convert to Christianity of their own volition (Ch. 384). The same general pattern is followed even when there is fierce resistance, as at Caraman (Ch. 395, where Tirant is revered for his "molta humanitat") and following Tirant's final great victory over the Turks outside Constantinople. In the latter case, Tirant personally escorts the Sultan and the Grand Turk to the capital as his prisoners; they are graciously received by the Emperor and feted as if they were visiting dignitaries rather than hostages (Chs. 446-49). By the end of the novel Martorell's hero has become the most gracious of victors.

However, on those few occasions when Tirant's treatment of his enemies is less than merciful, there is always good reason for his harshness. For example, in Ch. 157 there is an extremely ferocious encounter between Tirant's forces and those of the Kings of Egypt and Capadocia. The two Moorish sovereigns make a special attempt to kill Tirant during the battle, and the Christian commander barely escapes with his life. Ultimately, Tirant and the King of Capadocia square off and the Christian hero delivers a mortal blow to the Moor's head, leaving him helpless on the ground with his life slipping away. As Martorell's hero prepares to sever the King's head, a horseman pleads for mercy for the fallen monarch. Tirant's reply summarizes the chivalric ethic: cruelty is to be repaid with cruelty, and this particular individual has personally tried several times to slay me; he will receive the very same treatment he would give me if the situation were reversed. With that he severs the defeated man's head.

Later in the same chapter at the conclusion of the day's hostilities, Tirant is invited by the Marquis of Sant Jordi to slit the throat of the King of Egypt, whom the Marquis is holding prisoner. At this point, however, Tirant replies that under no circumstances would he murder a man who had surrendered. The vehemence that Martorell's hero otherwise displays on the battlefield is put completely aside when he deals with prisoners. Lest we miss the point, Martorell immediately contrasts Tirant's merciful attitude toward helpless captives with the vengefulness of the Marquis, who forthwith carries out the sentence he had originally suggested.

The same refusal to take vengeance on those unable to defend themselves is observed again in Ch. 316 in Africa, when the Cabdillo seeks to avenge the death of the King of Tlemcen by executing King Escariano and Queen Maragdina. Tirant is obliged to remind his ally that the code of chivalry forbids cruelty toward and the taking of vengeance on a captive; furthermore, he declares that Escariano killed the King of Tlemcen in a just war (which removes guilt) and that Queen Maragdina is exempt from such treatment by virtue of her sex, which at all cost ought to be defended — not offended — by virtuous knights (with one exception: adultery — the single unpardonable sin a woman can commit according to the chivalric code).

Martorell's hero is equally generous with his subordinates and cohorts. At one point (Ch. 124) the Emperor presents his commander with a gift of eighty-three horses; Tirant selflessly orders Diafebus to reserve for himself the steed of his choice, then see to it that the remaining stallions are distributed among the rest of his subordinate officers. He keeps nothing for himself. At Pelidas (Ch. 133) the Christian commander promises a generous reward to his scouts if they succeed in bringing back four Moorish guards for interrogation. When they accomplish the task, he rewards them even more generously than he had originally promised. Still another case of the Captain's magnanimity is the gift of a beautiful charger and its trappings that he bestows upon the Grand Noble in recognition of the latter's brilliant performance in a jousting tournament when he nearly succeeded in unhorsing Tirant (Ch. 189).

TIRANT THE PRUDENT JUDGE AND ADMINISTRATOR

If one is to judge by the content of Joanot Martorell's personal correspondence and his only novel, it is obvious that the Valencian writer was disdainful of what he considered effeminate jurists and lawyers and the ineffectual judicial system of fifteenth-century Valencia. In addition to representing a new, idealized breed of Christian warrior, Tirant also serves as a model judicial figure who knows how to dispense justice quickly, objectively, and with a certain manly vigor.[18]

---

[18] See Riquer's comment on Martorell and his opinion of jurists in his Introduction to *Tirante el Blanco*, I, pp. xiv and lxxxviii.

Martorell's negative portrayal of the tribunals and their corrupt officials begins in Ch. 41 during the hero's residence at the English court when the King's cousin, the Duke of Lancaster, takes it upon himself to mediate a silly dispute between the blacksmiths and the linen weavers over which group will precede the other in the annual St. John's Day procession. The jurists not only are unable to resolve the dispute, but they actually serve to obfuscate matters almost beyond resolution with their sophistry and convoluted arguments on behalf of one or the other litigant. Lancaster expedites the case by publicly executing three jurists from each camp. The King gives immediate approval of his cousin's actions against them for enriching themselves at the public's expense by accepting bribes from the disputants.

Lancaster goes on to propose a totally new and different system of justice for England, one which will consist of only two jurists for the entire kingdom. These judges will be required to resolve all cases brought before them within ten to fifteen days, and any court officer found guilty of enriching himself unethically will perish on the gibbet in the same disgraceful manner — suspended by the ankles — as his six unlucky predecessors.

The subsequent ideal comportment of Tirant when he is thrust into a judicial role is an essential part of Martorell's notion of good, swift justice. The hero's first taste of the judicial office occurs at Constantinople when the Emperor insists that the new commander occupy his Imperial chair in the Hall of Justice (Chs. 123-24). Tirant's function at this point is merely to re-establish the former judicial system that had been suspended after the Empire came under attack by the Sultan of Cairo and the Grand Turk. He begins to function in earnest as a jurist at Miralpeix (Ch. 133) when he is called upon to obviate a crime spree that they fear may break out in the midst of all the confusion about the Turkish invasion. He resorts to the same type of clever deception that he uses from time to time as a field commander to intimidate the enemy. The local gendarmes are instructed to build six or seven gallows outside the city and to hang from each one the corpse of some recently killed soldier. Tirant next sees to it that rumors are spread concerning the reason for these "executions": one for rape, another for stealing from the Church, a third for refusing to pay for food that he took, etc. Upon returning to his camp he has the town crier read a proclamation that imposes a death sentence for each of the crimes supposedly committed by the corpses swinging on the gibbets. The message is clear and a potential crime wave is averted.

Martorell's hero exhibits the same kind of preventive wisdom as an administrator/governor. Observe the measures he takes to ensure an orderly municipal government in Constantinople in Ch. 124:

> — the organization of the Emperor's vassals and servants —indeed of the entire citizenry of the capital— into fighting units of 50 men, each led by a captain; these reserve units are to be activated in time of emergency or attack;
>
> — the establishment of a permanent palace guard to protect the lives of the Imperial family; this elite unit of a hundred soldiers will stand guard in two shifts during the night while the Emperor and his family sleep; another patrol of 300 guards will keep watch outside the palace;
>
> — the institution of a system for illuminating the city's streets during the evening hours by having half the homes place a lighted candle in the window from dusk until midnight, the other half from midnight until dawn; the purpose of this is to diminish the after-dark burglary rate in the town;
>
> — in conjunction with the previous measure, Tirant establishes a double-shift night patrol to monitor activities in the city after nightfall; Tirant commands the first shift, Diafebus and the other lieutenants relieve him at midnight;
>
> — the initiation of a grain-rationing plan for the city that will distribute the food reserves equally among the citizens; Tirant also sets a fixed price at which grain surpluses may be sold; the effect of this is to do away with the widespread hoarding that had taken place prior to Tirant's arrival.

Tirant's crowning achievement as a governor, however, takes place during the North African campaign when he assists Escariano in raising a powerful army to conquer the Barbary region (Ch. 334). Martorell's hero simply establishes a new feudal system among the Africans: he grants titles and privileges to vassals according to the number of horses each man owns; the various categories constitute a military and political hierarchy that will provide the basis for a totally new social structure. Eventually problems arise from the petty jealousies that develop among the new nobility, but Tirant is quick to stifle this budding lawlessness by imposing serious penalties — usually beheading for capital crimes, loss of one's title of nobility for lesser offenses — that serve to keep the fractious nobles in line.

Tirant the Perfect Courtier

When I speak of Tirant as the model *soldado cortesano*, I am referring to more than the simple issue of etiquette and good breeding. Martorell's protagonist indeed exhibits the finest manners and is capable of the most sophisticated comportment (as we shall see in Chs. 100-109 when Tirant stands out in contrast with the ill-bred Felip), but there is an even deeper issue addressed in this novel: the question of social rank vs. personal gentility. Should the one imply the other? Are those born into the highest social classes necessarily the most genteel? And more to the point, might not a person of inferior social standing actually possess all the social graces normally associated with only the upper crust of society? In his book Martorell presents a rather democratic view insofar as his hero, a member of the lower nobility in Brittany, aspires to achieve royal or imperial rank by virtue of his heroic deeds and personal qualities. Tirant's successful quest indicates that Martorell viewed social mobility as a positive feature of a modern society. There is only one major figure in the novel who can be said to represent the ultra-conservative point of view, the Duke of Macedonia. The nefarious Duke is a member of the highest level of the Greek aristocracy and opposes from the start Tirant's participation in the war effort. He is the spokesman for the old, rigid class system that has traditionally resisted the efforts of talented social inferiors to ascend within the Greek hierarchy; with the arrival of Tirant and his men, the Duke merely widens his horizons to include foreigners among those he opposes. Martorell's treatment of this character is totally negative; we are reminded time and again that the treacherous Duke has been a major contributor to the precarious military and political situation that has prompted the Emperor to summon Tirant to Constantinople. His ineptness as a field commander has caused the Greeks to lose several important battles to the Turkish invaders; furthermore, it is rumored that the Duke's perfidy was actually responsible for the death of the Emperor's only son in one of the battles. If we broaden our view to project the Duke of Macedonia as the representative of an entire segment of society, the target of Martorell's social criticism in the novel becomes readily apparent.

We should begin by examining the contrast Martorell makes between his genteel hero and the uncouth French prince, Felip. The situation develops because the King of Sicily, for reasons of political expediency, wishes to establish familial ties with the French royal family. Tirant docks at Palermo on his way to relieve the besieged Christians on Rhodes (Ch. 100); with him is Felip, the youngest son of the French monarch. During the Sicilian sojourn the young Prince and Ricomana, daughter of the island's ruler, discover a mutual sexual attraction. The only impediment to what appears to be an ideal political and marital union is Ricomana's insistence upon selecting for her consort a man who is both intelligent and witty, and in no way unpolished or niggardly. It becomes Tirant's very difficult task to convince the Infanta that Felip is the man of her dreams, when in fact he is precisely the type of mate she seeks to avoid. (Ricomana has confessed to Tirant that she would prefer to marry a man of lower social standing and humbler lineage than a coarse and stingy royal suitor.)

Tirant begins by instructing the ignorant Felip in the matter of table manners. It is the Commander's sage advice that pulls the French prince through the awkward hand-washing ceremony that precedes the banquet at the Sicilian court (Ch. 101). Whenever Felip is about to commit a faux pas during the meal, Tirant literally comes running to the rescue. For example, he notes that the Prince has blundered by cutting into his bread before the main course has been served; Felip has, in fact, cut his entire loaf into twelve slices. The quick-thinking Captain immediately extracts twelve gold ducats from his purse, places one on each of the slices, and orders them to be distributed among a dozen poor persons in the name of the twelve Apostles. He then explains to the bewildered Sicilians that this unusual ceremony is actually the custom at the French court (Chs. 101-02).

Her suspicions aroused as to the true nature of her intended spouse, Ricomana devises a test for Felip regarding his manner of dress in Ch. 109. Tirant, ever mindful of what the crafty Infanta is seeking to uncover, again enables the Prince to stifle his niggardly nature and behave in a fashion more appropriate of a member of the French royal house. When Ricomana suggests an after-dinner ride through the muddy streets of the city (following a hard rain), the childish Felip balks, but Tirant convinces him to ride and not pout about soiling his brand-new outfit. As a result of Tirant's constant coaching, the parsimonious Prince eventually learns to comport himself in a regal fashion and succeeds in winning the heart and hand of Ricomana.

The point of the Felip-Ricomana episode is to show that there is no connection between social rank and the social graces; the French prince has to be instructed in the finer points of etiquette by a soldier who is not of royal blood, but whose personal gentility is at least the equal of that of any royal figure.

Martorell continues to underscore his protagonist's courtly demeanor during the subsequent Constantinople adventure. Upon his arrival at the Byzantine capital Tirant offers a gesture of obeisance to the Emperor by lowering his flag into the water as his ship passes the Imperial reviewing stand. When the two men finally meet, Tirant falls to his knees in homage and attempts to kiss the ruler's feet — which the Emperor graciously refuses to allow (Ch. 116).

The real test of Tirant's knowledge of courtly protocol is to be found in his dealings with the outrageous Duke of Macedonia. Immediately upon his arrival in Constantinople, when the Emperor offers him the solid gold baton that signifies the rank of Imperial Captain, Tirant is humble and gracious enough to decline the post, partly because of his relative inexperience in commanding an army and the fact that he brings with him a force of only 155 men, but also because he recognizes that his acceptance would constitute an affront to the dignity of the Duke of Macedonia who is of the highest social rank and a native of the Empire (Ch. 117). Martorell's hero is ultimately persuaded to accept the Captaincy by the Emperor, but his original fears about the Duke's reaction are soon borne out. The two rivals do not actually meet until the Duke has foolishly led his troops into a Turkish trap and has been forced to retreat to a village near the city of Pelidas (Ch. 133). When Tirant arrives with reinforcements to rescue the encircled Greeks, the new Captain demonstrates the utmost consideration for the sensitive circumstances under which they meet; he attempts to diminish the awkwardness of the scene by dismounting and approaching the embarrassed Duke on foot. The Greek noble, however, remains astride his mount and disdainfully places his hand on Tirant's head, a gesture which is taken by the other officers present as a sign of great discourtesy. Even so, Tirant continues to treat the Duke with honor and respect; he attempts to engage the Greek leader in polite conversation, but each effort is rebuffed with a brusque reply. The same kind of churlishness is displayed by the Duke when the new Captain offers him a choice of campsites and invites the Greek to dine with him that evening. The tension reaches a breaking point on the following day when Tirant sends two of his officers to demand that the Duke surrender to him (as Commander) his rightful share of the booty which the Duke's men have seized from the Turks. The Duke's refusal is so haughtily phrased that the envoys are nearly provoked to violence (Ch. 134). [19] Preparations are made for a battle between the forces

---

[19] It is in the arrogant reply of the Duke in Ch. 134 that Martorell casts him as a representative of the conservative military faction that continually rejects the progressive attitude and modern values exhibited by Tirant in his campaign. The Duke casts aspersions on Tirant's courtly demeanor and resents the fact that the "intruder" has come from the capital where he has reveled in carnal delights, slept on perfumed sheets, danced, played musical instruments, engaged in idle recreational activities with the ladies of the Imperial Court, etc., while the Duke and his men have supposedly been sweating, fighting and dying like true warriors of ancient tradition. The Duke's harangue, reproduced below, epitomizes the archaic attitudes that Martorell was trying to combat in his book; the fact that these sentiments are expressed by so foul and utterly despicable a figure as the Duke is an accurate indication of the author's low opinion of that point of view.

> —¡Oh, com són plenes d'alegria les mies orelles — dix lo Duc —, com sent paraules que no han neguna eficàcia, de gent mal entesa! ¿E com podeu vosaltres pensar jo fes tal cosa ne menys consentir, com ab tan gran treball de suor de sang de nostres persones, nit e dia exercint les armes, conservant aquell gentil orde de cavalleria, obrant tots dies contra los enemics de la fe, no donant-nos a delits carnals, ni dormir entre llançols perfumats ni algaliats, car les nostres persones no olen ni saben a res de tot açò, sinó que olen a ferro acerat; e les nostres mans no són veades de sonar arpa ni esturments, mas de tenir contínuament, nit e dia, l'espasa al costat e altres armes ofensives; los nostres ulls no acostumen de veure dames en cambres ni per les esglésies; los nostres peus no acostumen de dansar ni anar a solaços ni a deports, mas los ulls miren los enemics e los peus

of the Marquis of Sant Jordi and the Duke's troops, but Tirant, fearful that such open dissension will lift the defeated Moors' spirits and ultimately deprive him of a hard-won victory, personally intervenes to restore harmony among the allies.

Another occasion on which Martorell's hero patiently abides the insults and effrontery of an adversary takes place in Ch. 148 when Tirant receives the King of Egypt in his tent. The Christian leader orders a reception and banquet befitting his royal guest, but the Moslem ruler repays him with a tirade in which he declares his hatred of Tirant, accuses him of extreme cruelty, and promises to kill him in a most painful manner. Rather than reply in kind and sink to the same level of dishonorable conduct, Tirant simply excuses himself and leaves.

The next opportunity for Tirant to demonstrate his gentility comes after he has been shipwrecked on the Barbary Coast and is sent as the King of Tlemcen's envoy to King Escariano of Ethiopia, who has just declared war and invaded Tlemcen (Chs. 308-09). Escariano decides to test the patience and breeding of the

> porten tot lo cos a les batalles cruels? E si nosaltres ab just títol, havem sabut guanyar, eixint del setge com a virtuosos cavallers, ¿per què ha tan poc saber en vosaltres demanar ço que a vosaltres no pertany? E digau a aqueix vostre Capità, que faria bé que se'n tornàs en sa pròpia terra, si no jo li faré beure tanta d'aigua que de la meitat n'hauria prou.
>
> (*TB*, 436)

" 'Oh, how delighted my ears are,' said the Duke, 'to hear such useless words from ill-informed persons. How could you think that I would do such a thing or even allow it when we are engaged in such honorable work that must be accomplished through the sweat and blood of our people, fighting day and night to preserve the exquisite order of chivalry, working every day against the enemies of our faith, foregoing carnal delights, not allowing ourselves the privilege of sleeping on perfumed sheets? Our men don't smell or taste of such soft materials, but rather of forged steel; and our hands are not accustomed to playing the harp or any other instruments because they are used instead to clutch swords at their side day and night and handle other offensive weapons; our eyes aren't accustomed to seeing ladies in their chambers or in church; our feet are not used to dancing or engaging in idle recreational activities. Our eyes look rather to the enemy and our feet carry our bodies into fierce combat. And if we, with some justification, have managed to emerge victorious and come out as worthy knights, why are you so foolish as to demand booty that is rightfully ours, not yours? Tell your captain that he would do more good if he would simply return to his own homeland; otherwise, I shall force him to drink so much water that he would have been content with half as much.' "

ambassador with a sumptuous banquet at which Tirant acquits himself admirably by selecting only the finest and most elegantly prepared viands. The final test comes when Tirant is led to a room filled with luxurious items and told that he may select any single object for himself. The Christian passes over the mounds of gold and silver coins, fine robes and jewelry, several fine stallions and saddle trappings, etc.; he chooses instead one of the King's hunting falcons. Escariano is stunned by so wise and so unusual a choice and determines that the ambassador is indeed a man of quality and noble virtue.

Another demonstration of Tirant's diplomatic skills and sense of protocol takes place in Chs. 345-46 when one of the enemy chieftains, the King of Tunis, succumbs to his wounds while being held prisoner in Tirant's camp. The Christian commander informs the Moorish leaders of their comrade's death and requests a cortege to escort the King's corpse back to the opposing camp for burial. In the meantime, Tirant arranges for a most impressive wake; when the Moorish escort arrives they find the deceased's remains laid out on plush mattresses, covered with gold cloth, and guarded by a hundred knights bearing unsheathed swords. As one of the Moorish envoys remarks, Tirant has ennobled himself even further by the honor he has accorded the memory of the valiant King.

The final occasion on which Martorell's hero displays a gentility and decorum worthy of a king takes place after Tirant has returned to Constantinople to blunt the Turkish invasion. Having defeated the Turks at sea and cut them off from escape on land, Tirant receives the ambassadors of the Sultan and the Grand Turk with great pomp. The Turks are welcomed at the bridge and escorted to the Christian commander's huge tent of red brocade by five hundred armed and mounted horsemen (Ch. 425). They are graciously welcomed by Tirant and the other Christian leaders, then shown to their own luxurious quarters where they are wined and dined in an elegant fashion. The sight of four thousand combat-ready horsemen and the rest of Tirant's ostentatious exhibition is sufficient to intimidate the Moslem leaders into suing for peace immediately.

The evolution of Martorell's hero as a *soldado cortesano* gives an additional dimension to the novel's design. The author is not content with merely chronicling Tirant's military success; his diplomatic triumphs must become equally important if Tirant is to be presented as a model for fifteenth-century Christendom. And on the social level, the stark contrast of the genteel but relatively inferior in lineage Tirant with the ill-mannered Prince Felip and the vile Duke of Macedonia serves to underscore Martorell's sober warning that the solution to the Turkish problem may lie somewhere other than among the moribund ruling classes of the Christian kingdoms.

Tirant the Military Apostle

No study of Tirant's character would be complete without taking into account his activities on behalf of the Christian faith. The Moorish-Christian opposition is a constant in Martorell's novel and the hero never fails to demonstrate the clear superiority of Christian dogmas, moral values, social institutions, etc. Tirant is at all times a perfect model for his followers, whether it be by beginning each day with a Mass (e.g., Ch. 133 at Pelidas), requesting a Mass per day to be said for his soul as repayment for lifting the siege at Rhodes (Ch. 108), ransoming 473 Christian slaves at Alexandria (Ch. 108), or having recourse to the Blessed Virgin to plead for mercy on his soul when all appears lost during a storm at sea (Ch. 299).

It is during the adventures of Tirant on the North African Coast (Chs. 299-413) that the hero truly begins to function as a warrior-evangelist. The emphasis here is on converting and baptizing the Moors of the Barbary region, most notably Queen Maragdina of Tlemcen (Ch. 326) and King Escariano of Ethiopia (Ch. 329). Tirant converts literally thousands of Moslems at a time to Christianity while he is in Africa, with as many as 334,000 baptisms being recorded during one three-day period (Ch. 404). We are also informed that Tirant is responsible for the construction of many churches and monasteries in the North African region, plus the importation of a multitude of Christian friars and secular clergy from other parts of Christendom to minister to the new faithful.[20]

---

[20] The most notable example of this is a Mercedarian friar who arrives from Valencia in Ch. 330 to ransom Christian captives in Tunis. Upon learning of Tirant's astounding success at Tlemcen, the friar hastens to join

Martorell's hero serves as a model Christian in many ways other than as a mere proselytizer. For example, when the newly Christianized King Escariano slays the Cabdillo because the latter has foolishly suggested that the new converts abandon the Christian faith and return to their previous Moslem beliefs to appease their hostile neighbors, the Christian leader refuses to be ruled by his emotions. Rather than attempt to take vengeance on the assailant, Tirant holds himself firmly in check. Escariano immediately realizes how intemperately he has acted, confesses his guilt, and humbly begs for forgiveness, which Tirant willingly grants in spite of the deep hurt he feels at the loss of his dear comrade (Chs. 333-34). [21]

Another area in which Martorell's hero sets a perfect example for Christian military leaders is in providing an honorable Christian burial for those who have made the supreme sacrifice under his command. After a fierce battle with the Moors in Ch. 349, Tirant agrees to a truce so that the Christian women may arrange for the proper interment of their fallen warriors — something which the Moors under the King of Tlemcen consider a strange innovation and contrary to their custom of treating the dead with violence and disrespect. [22]

---

the Christian commander and remains with him to assist in the mass baptism of 44,327 Moorish converts. He is later named Papal Legate to the Barbary States at Tirant's request (Ch. 372). In Ch. 402 we are told that his name is Juan Ferrer, a Moorish-speaking Spaniard from Lleida (*Lérida* in Castilian), not Valencia, as originally reported in Ch. 330. In the next chapter the friar delivers a supremely chauvinistic pro-Christian harangue that results in the conversion of another 334,000 Moors.

[21] Ironically, the contrite Escariano eventually becomes Tirant's principal cohort during the African campaign, and again later during the final stages of the Byzantine adventure. As for Christian example, in Ch. 409 Escariano and his bride Maragdina are credited with introducing Christianity — and especially the sacrament of Matrimony — within the previously Moorish and polygamous kingdom of Ethiopia.

[22] A similar, but purely propagandistic, episode is recounted earlier in Ch. 340 when Tirant prays for and receives a miracle that enables him to identify the dead Christian soldiers so that they may be properly buried. In answer to his prayers, the Christian cadavers roll face-up on the ground with their hands clasped while giving off no foul odor; at the same time the Moslem corpses lying beside them turn facedown and emit a horrible stench. Many critics have observed that this episode is strikingly divergent from the normally realistic tone of most of Martorell's novel. The most plausible explanation I can offer for this unusual deviation from the norm

Not to be ignored are Tirant's formidable skills as an orator on behalf of the Christian cause. On more than one occasion — most notably at Tlemcen (Ch. 340) and Caraman (Ch. 387) — Martorell's hero calls upon his considerable rhetorical gifts to stir up the Christian troops in preparation for what he knows will be a savage confrontation. He calls upon his men to fight valiantly for their own honor as well as for their sacred Christian faith, and advocates martyrdom as a preferable alternative to captivity among the Moors. On both occasions Chivalric Honor and the Christian Faith are presented as the twin bases upon which he builds his case.

Notwithstanding all of the above, the greatest single example of Christian conduct that Tirant provides is that of his own death. Martorell takes pains to provide his hero with the perfect Christian demise. When he realizes that he is mortally ill, Tirant summons a Franciscan friar to confess him and help him receive the Eucharist for the final time (Ch. 467). He then offers thanks to God for all the success He has accorded him in his earthly life, and declares that he accepts his death obediently for the remission of his sins, sentiments not unlike those expressed by Jorge Manrique in his *Coplas* regarding the equanimity with which his father accepted his fate (Ch. 468). As his final official act before expiring Tirant dictates his last will and testament and a short note to his beloved Carmesina (Chs. 469-70); he then commends his spirit to Jesus Christ and succumbs (Ch. 471). Lest the reader miss the point, Martorell later duplicates the performance on the female side in the chapters that recount the equally perfect demise of Carmesina (Chs. 476-78).

Summary

If we concentrate on Tirant's evolution as a Christian warrior, we observe that he begins by rising from the lowly rank of squire up to the more prestigious position of a full-fledged knight-errant; he subsequently assumes an even loftier role as a naval commander

---

is that Martorell — or perhaps Galba at this late point — intended this adventure to be symbolic of Tirant's newly acquired missionary qualities in Africa among the hostile Moors, as opposed to the emphasis on Tirant's purely military prowess that we find in most of the novel.

and eventually achieves the exalted title of Captain General, which signals his role as supreme commander of a large military force. Along the way he schools himself in a variety of novel strategies and technological innovations that will eventually enable him to overcome tremendous disadvantages in troop strength and firepower. He becomes adept at defending against attacks at sea, breaking naval blockades, and using the terrain to his advantage when fighting on land. He also learns methods for taking and defending walled fortresses and cities, and how to coordinate joint land and naval operations. His modernity and flexibility are best demonstrated by his easy accommodation to the use of heavy artillery (e.g., *lombardas*): his first task is to learn how to defend against the use of such powerful weaponry, but by the close of his African campaign he has also mastered the use of cannon power as an *offensive* weapon. In the same vein, he makes use of the relatively modern strategy of employing mercenary agents to handle special support duties such as the shipping of grain and foodstuffs to his allies.

One important aspect of Tirant's evolution as a warrior/commander is his increasing reliance upon cleverness *(indústria)* and deceit to defeat a numerically superior enemy. He frequently calls upon his native intelligence and wiliness to extricate himself from seemingly impossible situations. He also discovers how to create a false impression of the size of his forces to dishearten the enemy; he resorts to the use of camouflage, guerrilla warfare, scouts, messengers, and spies to achieve victory, not to mention the element of surprise; he realizes that the ethics of war have changed since the days of the knight-errant and the old chivalric code, and he is quick to adapt to the new reality that confronts him.

In general, the figure of Tirant is a paragon of military virtue: he is living proof of the warrior's need for skill and dexterity in handling a multitude of offensive and defensive armaments; he also demonstrates the importance of flexibility and adaptability in dealing with new technology like long-range artillery; at the same time he is a perfect example of the benefits to be gained from a rigorous program of physical conditioning. As a leader Tirant exhibits impressive rhetorical skills, a keen insight into human psychology, plus superb administrative and judicial talents like patience, fairness, resourcefulness, innate wisdom, and attention to detail.

Not to be overlooked are the diplomatic skills that make Tirant a model for the military courtier of the fifteenth century. His most important virtue in this area is his political savvy, which is then coupled with a set of impeccable courtly manners to produce what Martorell considered a working model for the perfect diplomat. He knows when to hold his tongue, when to speak out; he is circumspect both in his speech and in his correspondence; although he is not of noble birth, his breeding is of the highest calibre; when it becomes important to maintain good appearances, Tirant's fine manners and gentility never fail him.

Finally — and from Martorell's point of view, equally important — there are Tirant's Christian virtues. His moral perfection, extreme generosity, and abundant mercifulness are unsurpassed in chivalric literature. Tirant's military and political/diplomatic successes are attributable as much to his Christian values as they are to his military skills. Martorell is careful to contrast at all times the exemplary behavior of his Christian hero with the inferior virtues and values of his Moslem adversaries; even when an occasional Moorish or Turkish leader may approach Tirant in valor or physical prowess, the Christian will always emerge victorious by reason of his Christian faith and virtues. Clearly, what Martorell had in mind was the prototype for a new kind of Christian commander — with equal emphasis given to each term.

CHAPTER III

TIRANT LO BLANCH: A NEW KIND OF COURTLY LOVER

The second theme of Joanot Martorell's novel encompasses the many romantic interludes involving Tirant and Carmesina and several other pairs of lovers at the Byzantine Court. These sections of the book provide us with a full treatment of the customs and conventions associated with the institution of Courtly Love; a related topic is Martorell's treatment of the much-abused practice of clandestine marriage (i.e., the secret exchange of vows), which was still very much in vogue during the fifteenth century and was not outlawed by the Church until the Council of Trent (1563).

The social and erotic nature of *TB*'s secondary plot has been examined by comparatively few distinguished critics; [1] however, the most thorough analysis of the novel's amorous episodes — and the only one I shall cite — can be found in Chapter Three of Justina Ruiz de Conde's study of love in the romances of chivalry. [2] While fully acknowledging my deep debt to the Ruiz de Conde work for its penetrating examination of the love theme in *TB*, I must express some reservation about one of her conclusions. It is Ruiz de Conde's contention (pp. 147-52) that Martorell's novel is a strong reaction against the outdated conventions of the Southern School of Courtly Love (as opposed to the North European practices); she feels that

---

[1] See Frank Pierce, "The Role of Sex in the *Tirant lo Blanc*," *Estudis Romànics*, 10 (1962), 291-300; William J. Entwistle, "*Tirant lo Blanc* and the Social Order of the End of the 15th Century," *Estudis Romànics*, 2 (1949-50), 149-64.

[2] *El amor y el matrimonio secreto en los libros de caballerías* (Madrid: Aguilar, 1948), pp. 101-70.

the author's intention was to ridicule the idealistic modes of the old Provençal model, while at the same time proposing a more realistic kind of courtship ritual. My own view is that Martorell's purpose here was merely to streamline and modernize the traditional Southern Courtly Love pattern, not to ridicule it. As we have already noted in the previous chapter, Tirant is adept at accommodating himself to all sorts of changing political and social circumstances and whatever new customs and practices they may require. The same sort of flexibility Tirant demonstrates regarding the evolution of the martial arts and military conventions is again evidenced in the romantic interludes.

Aside from this point, I agree completely with the rest of Ruiz de Conde's thesis about *TB*: Martorell wished to propose in his novel the somewhat unorthodox notion that Courtly Love can indeed be compatible with marriage (or more precisely, with the sacrament of Matrimony), and that lasting romantic love can and does exist within the married state. Author Martorell demonstrates, first in the courtship and marriage of Diafebus and Estefania but then principally in the case of Tirant and Carmesina, that the traditional courtship conventions of Courtly Love can be successfully combined with more practical measures (e.g., the exchange of certain written promises and guarantees prior to or at the time when the marriage vows are exchanged — but definitely before consummation takes place (to produce a stable, binding, yet romantically satisfying conjugal arrangement). Martorell does *not* reject Courtly Love as totally unworkable; he merely shows how the romantic and erotic elements of Courtly Love can and should be combined with the practical security of a legal contract — not to mention the sacramental blessings of the unbreakable marital bond. [8]

---

[8] Ruiz de Conde shows (p. 170) that Tirant and Carmesina are considered wed in the eyes of the Church prior to their initial act of sexual intercourse in Ch. 436. The wedding bond was forged earlier during their exchange of marital vows in the palace garden in Chs. 271-72. At that time they were informally following the example set earlier by Diafebus and Estefania, whose exchange of promises was considerably more formal and legalistic in nature: Estefania presented the would-be bridegroom with a signed contract outlining the various terms and conditions of their agreement (Chs. 146-47). During the medieval period in which Martorell wrote,

An ancillary issue that is addressed in Martorell's novel is the controversial practice of clandestine marriage: the secret exchange of vows (for a variety of social or political reasons) which often resulted in unpleasant legal consequences for one of the parties — usually the woman — when such private vows were not subsequently ratified at a public ceremony.[4] Ruiz de Conde's entire first chapter (pp. 3-31) is devoted to a discussion of the history of this custom and its attendant problems. Given the fact that a member of Joanot Martorell's own family had indeed fallen victim to this troublesome convention, we might reasonably expect his novel to offer a scathing condemnation of the practice. Surprisingly, however, Martorell's treatment of the subject is quite temperate; he simply proposes the legal safeguard of a formal contract, plus the sensible precaution of having witnesses present when such vows are exchanged, which is precisely how Diafebus and Estefania handle the matter (Chs. 146-47).

In the following pages I would like to examine the various phases through which the Tirant-Carmesina relationship passes in the course of the novel. Using Ruiz de Conde's important work as a springboard, I plan to compare and contrast the courtship of Martorell's hero and the Princess with similar romantic adventures shared by several other pairs of lovers in the book. In so doing I will demonstrate that Martorell's plan was actually more complex and carefully executed than even Ruiz de Conde's excellent study has indicated. We will see that *TB* presents a complete and balanced treatment of various medieval conventions dealing with romantic love and courtship, Courtly and otherwise; the various pairings are neither casually drawn nor haphazardly introduced

---

espousal followed by copulation was tantamount to a valid and binding (although technically illegal) marriage.

[4] Martorell's younger sister Damiata was seduced and abandoned to a life of spinsterhood by an untrustworthy cousin, one Joan de Monpalau, who refused to honor such a secretly given promise of marriage. The affair served as the pretext for a prolonged and often vituperous exchange of letters between Monpalau and Joanot Martorell and very nearly resulted in a duel. See Riquer's Introduction to *Tirante el Blanco*, 5 vols. (Madrid: Espasa-Calpe, 1974), I, xi-xxi. For the complete text of the several letters exchanged by the feuding cousins, see M. de Riquer and M. Vargas Llosa, *El combate imaginario: las cartas de batalla de Joanot Martorell* (Barcelona: Seix-Barral, 1972).

into the narrative, which indicates that a great deal of artistic control has indeed been exercised by author Martorell and his collaborator, Martí Joan de Galba.

* * *

THE INITIAL STAGE: TIRANT AS COURTLY LOVER (Chs. 117-213)

Just as Tirant's military career begins with a period of apprenticeship at the jousting lists in England, so also does he pass through a brief probationary period as a suitor during his sojourn at the Greek Court. With his first glimpse of the fair Carmesina's alabaster breasts (Ch. 118), the valiant knight is hopelessly smitten — a totally novel experience for him, one for which he has not been prepared to this point. In his pursuit of the Princess, Tirant attempts to follow the conventions established by the Provençal poets; with the exception of the fact that Tirant eschews the use of a musical instrument (Ruiz de Conde, p. 127), his courtship of Carmesina is conducted strictly "by the book."

The Princess ably plays the role of the disdainful *belle dame sans merci* while the fretful knight suffers all the pangs and anxieties of the typical courtly lover. For example, immediately following their first encounter, Tirant's newly kindled ardor deprives him of all desire to eat or to sleep; he immediately sinks into a deep depression marked by all the perfunctory and attendant sobs, sighs and tears (Ch. 118). Soon thereafter Tirant makes the required inventory of his beloved's physical charms, then he sends her a richly adorned prayer book as a token of his esteem. And so it goes.

Throughout the early stages of their relationship Tirant is too timid to express his true feelings toward Carmesina, even in moments when they are alone; his innate shyness obliges him to resort to the hackneyed strategem of employing a mirror to represent a portrait of his beloved, so that when the curious Princess seizes it and glances at her own reflection there, she comes to realize the embarrassing truth that the tongue-tied Tirant cannot bring himself to reveal (Ch. 127).

To compound matters, Carmesina is rather reluctant to offer her suitor any kind of encouragement. For example, at first she actually refuses to allow Tirant to kiss her hand, despite his many ardent entreaties. She eventually accedes to his harmless request, but only after her most trusted handmaidens prevail upon her to do so. She is careful, however, to insist that he kiss only the inner part of her hand (as a sign of affection), rather than the outer portion, which would be a more compromising expression of *señorío* (Ch. 125). Her reaction to Tirant's aforementioned clever confession of love is also reproachful; she harshly upbraids him on that occasion for failing to treat her with the proper honor and reverence (Ch. 128). When the chastened lover apologizes and retreats in tears, Carmesina immediately repents of her harshness and follows him to his quarters, where she ultimately agrees to allow him to kiss her hair, forehead and eyes in the future, provided that he solemnly promise not to make additional amorous advances beyond those limits in subsequent encounters (Ch. 130). This is the general tone of the courtship of Tirant and Carmesina in the preliminary stage: the timid hero attemps to woo the Princess by adhering strictly to the precepts of Courtly Love, while the honor-conscious Carmesina begrudgingly gives ground, but never enough to compromise her delicate reputation. Their relationship advances fitfully as Tirant presses for more and more physical gratification and Carmesina is obliged to grant him additional liberties at every turn, often against her will and better judgment. A brief chronological outline of some of the more important occurrences that take place in the early chapters will suffice to trace the gradual development of the novel's principal romantic intrigue: [5]

> *Ch. 131:* Tirant becomes physically ill when he learns that the Emperor may send Carmesina to live with her sister in Hungary until the invading armies have been repulsed. The threat of separation from the object of his affection is sufficient to cause severe stomach pains in the smitten warrior.
>
> *Ch. 132:* Tirant requests and receives from the Princess one of her undergarments (a shirt) which he swears to wear over his armor in the next battle as a token.

---

[5] See also Ruiz de Conde, pp. 137-47.

Ch. 133: Carmesina refuses Captain Tirant's request to kiss her hand in the presence of the Emperor and Empress.

Ch. 138: Estefania, handmaiden and closest confidante of the Princess, reproaches Carmesina for her disdainful attitude toward the Captain, whom she considers a most worthy suitor.

Ch. 159: On the battlefield following a decisive victory over the Turks, Tirant learns that the Princess is lodged at the nearby castle of Malveí; he immediately sends an emissary to request permission in writing (in the form of a *guiatge* or safe-conduct pass) to join her there. Carmesina sees no need for this kind of formality, but the Captain, following to the letter the conventions of Courtly Love, refuses to appear before her without such a formal invitation. (In this chapter Martorell appears to inject tones generally associated with the *novela sentimental*.)

Ch. 161: Carmesina now begins to feel the effects of Cupid's dart and suffers a loss of appetite. When she gives signs of returning Tirant's affection, he immediately presses for a sexual favor, which she refuses to grant as a threat to her honor (Ch. 162).

Ch. 163: The famous *bodes sordes* episode in which Tirant and Diafebus attempt to seduce Carmesina and Estefania, respectively, during a secret nocturnal rendezvous at the castle of Malveí; Diafebus is successful (more about that later), but the Captain is again rebuffed by the determined Princess.

Ch. 172: A pivotal episode in which Tirant confesses that his passion for Carmesina has weakened his resolve to defeat the Turks; he is torn between his desire to remain with her in the capital and his professional duty to return to the battlefield.[6] In a lengthy (and somewhat wandering) exhortation, Carmesina seizes the opportunity to play the inspirational role required by the Provençal conventions: she exhorts him strongly

---

[6] At this point Tirant is recuperating in Constantinople from wounds received in one of his many battles with the Turkish invaders and their Moslem allies. He has recovered almost completely and realizes that it is his duty to return to the front and resume command of his troops. Nonetheless, the sensual pleasure and delights of the *vida cortesana* — and the abundant charms of the lovely Princess Carmesina in particular — have distracted him momentarily from his duty.

to return to the front so that he may continue to gain honor and glory from the many valiant deeds that he will perform there. For his part, Tirant has already been moved to acts of great magnanimity in the name of his beloved; for example, in Ch. 136, simply because the Turkish Sultan has invoked the memory of the Captain's lady in the course of requesting the release of *one* particularly important captive, Tirant agrees to free an additional *forty* Moorish prisoners-of-war.

Ch. 173: Love takes its toll physically again on the Princess as she swoons from an excess of love that we are told has affected her heart. No longer able to resist fully Tirant's sexual entreaties and her own awakening erotic desires, Carmesina soon thereafter (Ch. 175) entertains the Captain in her chamber and grants him permission to kiss her breasts. Tirant's goal of complete carnal gratification appears to be near at hand, but . . .

Ch. 178: A temporary reversal of fortune occurs as Tirant is dismayed to learn that the Emperor is seriously considering the Sultan's offer of a peace settlement, in return for which the Moslem leader demands the hand of the Greek Princess in marriage. (The offer is ultimately rejected, much to the relief of the Captain.)

Ch. 189: The rituals and conventions of Courtly Love have just about been exhausted at this point; Tirant can no longer restrain his sexual drive and boldly enters Carmesina's boudoir in search of erotic adventure. In one of the most memorable comic scenes of the novel, Tirant behaves like an overanxious adolescent as he chases the Princess about the room, making several clumsy attempts at seduction. The hero's rather unsophisticated sexual advances are generally unsuccessful and he is eventually subdued by Carmesina's attendants; nonetheless, he does manage to break new ground by placing his hand under her skirt, his right toe into her crotch, and a kiss on her upper thigh (*over* her skirt, however). Tirant is so pleased with his progress in this episode that he orders the stocking and shoe that touched the Princess's genital area to be embroidered with pearls, diamonds and rubies.[7]

---

[7] Tirant's adolescent behavior in Ch. 189 is one of the areas in which Ruiz de Conde sees Martorell ridiculing the conventions of Courtly Love (p. 151).

Ch. 208: The passionate Captain once more implores Carmesina to grant him complete sexual gratification; she, wavering noticeably, again declines, this time on the grounds that the knowledge of such lascivious conduct on her part would be most hurtful to her father, whose love and trust she would never wish to betray.

Ch. 212: Tirant now despairs completely of the conventions of Courtly Love and seeks the counsel and complicity of Estefania and the other damsels of the Court in conquering the strong resistance of the Princess. The wily damsel Plaerdemavida enthusiastically accepts the challenge of bringing together the ardent Tirant and the reluctant Princess; under her tutelage the Captain abandons the heretofore only partly effective rituals of Courtly Love and enters the second, more sexually aggressive stage of his courtship (Ch. 214).

At this point some mention ought to be made of a curious contrapuntal element that forms an integral part of the preliminary phase of the Tirant-Carmesina story. I am referring to the parallel romantic involvement that blossoms between Estefania and Diafebus. The latter relationship is a streamlined version of the main romantic intrigue, simultaneously conducted but without the many and diverse complications that beset the principal pair of lovers. The affair takes a serious turn in Chs. 146-48 when Tirant's lieutenant declares his love for Estefania and begs her to allow him to dedicate himself to her service. Her response is to grant him possession of her body *above the waist* (Ch. 146). When Diafebus proceeds to explore his newly won territory, he finds in her bodice a formal legal document (Cat. *albarà;* Cast. *albalá* or *albarán*) drawn up and signed by Estefania, which is designed to serve as a marriage contract.[8] In this document she promises

---

[8] Riquer observes that Estefania's *albarà* is a clever transposition into the romantic sphere of a type of legal document that was commonly employed in fifteenth-century Valencian society among gentlemen of honor who wished to engage in a secret duel; they would draw up a detailed agreement that would specify all the attendant conditions and penalties desired or required (*Tirante el Blanco*, II, 297, n. 2). For the text of Martorell's own collection of feisty *albaranes,* see Riquer and Vargas Llosa, *El combate imaginario....* The only point I would wish to add — and one

before God to take him as her husband, with the full intention of ratifying the union in sacramental Matrimony at a later time ("en contemplació de matrimoni"); in addition to granting him all the normal conjugal privileges, she bestows upon him as well the title of Duke of Macedonia (which had belonged to her late father) and a handsome dowry in jewels, clothing, and gold and silver coins. A most interesting — and highly significant, as we shall see — feature of the contract is the penalty clause she adds near the end: if she should prove false to her promises, she will not take refuge in any law, past or present, that has been traditionally used to shelter damsels, widows and female heirs from punishment; furthermore, she renounces all recourse to the laws of chivalry and specifically requests that no knight attempt to defend her cause in battle; she prefers instead to suffer the normal penalty for such transgressions: to have her hand pierced by a spike. As a further indication of her sincerity, the document is signed and sealed with her blood (Ch. 147). [9] When Tirant and Diafebus depart for

---

which the critics appear to have overlooked heretofore — is that Martorell in this instance offers a concrete and very practical suggestion for obviating many of the abuses that had crept into the practice of clandestine marriage; he advocates the simple transference of an existing legal formula from the field of honor to that of social intercourse (no pun intended).

[9] The complete text of Estefania's *albarà* (plus the English translation) follows:

> De tots jorns nos mostra experiència quant natura ha sàviament ordenat ses coses per los gloriosos passats. Havent atesa llibertat de fer de mi lo que vull, tenguda aquella honestat que sol ésser dada a donzelles, veuran e sabran en aquest albarà com jo, Estefania de Macedònia, filla de l'il·lustre príncep Robert, duc de Macedònia, de grat e de certa ciència, no constreta ni forçada, tenint Déu davant los meus ulls e los sants Evangelis de les mies mans corporalment tocats, promet a vós, Diafebus de Muntalt, ab paraules de present prenc a vós per marit e senyor, e done-us mon cos lliberalment sens frau ni engan negú; e port-vos en contemplació de matrimoni lo sobre dit ducat de Macedònia ab tots los drets a ell pertanyents; més, vos porte cent deu mília ducats venecians, e més tres mília marcs d'argent obrat, joies e robes per la majestat del senyor Emperador ab los de son sacre consell estimades uitanta-tres mília ducats; e més, vos porte la mia persona, que estime més.
> E si contra res d'açò venia ni em pot ésser provat, vull ésser encorreguda per falsa e fementida, e no em puga alegar, ni ajudar de neguna llei que los nostres emperadors passats ni presents, hoc encara los de Roma, renunciant en aquella llei que féu aquell gloriós emperador Július Cèsar, la qual se nomena llei de més valer, la qual és en favor de donzelles, viudes e pubiles.

the battle from the capital in Ch. 148, the lieutenant takes leave of his cherished Estefania in a tearful scene and receives from her a gold chain that will serve as a token of her affection.

The *bodes sordes* scene of Ch. 163, referred to earlier as one of deep frustration for Tirant, is for Diafebus an event of paramount significance in that it represents the consummation of the vows exchanged by him and Estefania in the *albarà;* it is the successful coupling of the secondary pair of lovers that gives this

---

> *E més, renuncie al dret de cavalleria: no sia negun cavaller qui en camp per mi entre ni dona que em gose raonar, ans me puguen clavar la mà ab la cerimònia entre cavallers e dones d'honor acostumada.*
> *E per ço que major fe hi sia dada pose lo meu propi nom sots signat ab sang de la mia persona.*
>
> ESTEFANIA DE MACEDÒNIA.
>
> (TB, 494)

"Experience shows us every day how wisely nature has arranged things through the example of our glorious ancestors. Having achieved the freedom to do whatever I wish while maintaining the modesty that is customary for maidens, I, Estefania of Macedonia, daughter of the illustrious Prince Robert, Duke of Macedonia, as you will come to recognize from this letter, willingly and with full knowledge, without being constrained or forced in any way, having God before my eyes while swearing upon the Holy Gospels, promise you, Diafebus of Muntalt, in these words to take you as my husband and lord and give you my body freely and without any deceit or fraud; and I offer you, in contemplation of marriage, the aforesaid Duchy of Macedonia with all the rights and privileges associated with it; furthermore, I bring to you the sum of one hundred ten thousand Venetian ducats and more than three thousand marks of wrought silver, jewels and clothes from His Majesty the Emperor and those of his Sacred Council, estimated at some eighty-three thousand ducats; and above all that I bring you my very person, which I esteem most of all.

"And if anyone should prove that I have not told the truth in this matter, I want to be denounced by all as a false and treacherous liar and to be denied any appeal or aid from any law that was passed by any emperor, past or present, even going back to the times of the Romans; and therefore I renounce that law which was dictated by the glorious emperor Julius Caesar, which is called the Law of the Greatest Worth, which favors maids, widows and heiresses.

"Aside from all this, I renounce all appeals to the order of chivalry: let there be no knight who will enter the field of battle on my behalf, nor any lady who will dare to argue my case; first let them drive a spike through my hand in the ceremony prescribed for knights and maids of honor.

"And to certify the absolute veracity of this document, I affix here my name signed in my own blood.

Estefania of Macedonia"

episode its title. From this point forward they both act and think as married persons; for example, when Estefania writes to reproach her lover for remaining so long away from her at the front, she expresses a fear that he may have committed *adultery* in the interim (Ch. 187). Their romance culminates in formal bethrothal and wedding ceremonies (plus lavish celebrations following each) on consecutive days (Ch. 220).

The importance of the Diafebus-Estefania relationship cannot be stressed too strongly; theirs is conceived by author Martorell as a model courtship, a simplified and very sensible version of the elaborate, wasteful, seemingly unending mating dance that Tirant and his Princess have been performing throughout the novel to this point. Martorell lays before the reader a concrete example of how clandestine marriages *ought* to be contracted in fifteenth-century society: a brief courtship, a firm legal contract agreed upon by both parties, the exchange of vows (to be followed by consummation), and finally the formalities of an engagement ceremony and a Church wedding at the appropriate time. The proof of this can be seen in the fact that once the comic episode of their wedding night has been narrated (Ch. 220), both Diafebus and Estefania cease to function as important characters in the novel and their subsequent sexual conduct — now as man and wife — is ignored completely. Diafebus and Estefania retire to the sidelines after Ch. 220 and serve thereafter as mere observers of the actions of others.

THE SECOND STAGE: PLAERDEMAVIDA IN COMMAND (Chs. 214-99)

By entrusting his romantic fortunes to the resourceful Plaerdemavida, Tirant relieves himself of the obligation to follow the precepts of Courtly Love (although Carmesina will still expect him to do so for a while longer). Several other changes in tone can also be noticed from this point forward: there is a sharp increase in the number of erotic encounters as Plaerdemavida schemes to give Tirant entry to the Princess's bedroom with greater frequency; another member of Carmesina's retinue, the middle-aged Viuda Reposada, becomes a blocking agent for the young lovers because she secretly lusts after the virile Captain herself and hatches a series of plots designed to sow discord where love should bloom. Tirant is now cast in the role of the fainthearted suitor while the aggressive Plaerdemavida is assigned the part of instigator of all new romantic intrigues; in the meantime, Carmesina continues to struggle with the question of her honor, which causes her at times to become wrathful in the face of Tirant's new aggressiveness. The major developments of this second stage are:

Ch. 215: The jealous Viuda Reposada begins her campaign to undermine the delicate relationship between Tirant and the Princess. As a result of her malicious counsel, Carmesina turns cool to the Captain's charms, fearing that his interest in her is more political than amorous.

Ch. 225: Plaerdemavida, fully cognizant of the Viuda's role in turning the Princess against Tirant, conceives a plan to smuggle the Captain into Carmesina's chamber while she bathes. Tirant balks, fearful of the wrath such a bold act may provoke in the Princess; Plaerdemavida urges him to show more forcefulness, to act as boldly in the bedroom as he does on the battlefield (Chs. 228-29). At the same time and on another front, the wily go-between finally persuades the Emperor to offer his daughter in marriage to the brave Captain as soon as the Turks are defeated (Ch. 230).

Ch. 231: Tirant is successfully concealed in a box or chest in Carmesina's room, from which vantage point he is able to view her entire bathing procedure; after the Princess has fallen asleep, Plaerdemavida leads the Captain by the hand to her bedside. Trembling with nervousness, Tirant is afraid to advance any further; his brazen counselor scolds him for his cowardly conduct and exhorts him to show here the same kind of daring for which he has become so famous on the field of battle (Ch. 232).

Ch. 233: With the indispensable aid of Plaerdemavida, Tirant spends more than an hour touching freely all the forbidden regions of the sleeping Princess's body; before he can advance any further in his plan for seduction, however, Carmesina awakens with a start and loudly orders him to desist. The ever-vigilant Viuda comes to suspect that Tirant may be in the Princess's bedchamber and sounds the alarm; Tirant is forced to beat a hasty retreat through a bedroom window in order to save Carmesina's reputation, but in so doing he falls hard to the ground, breaking his leg in three places.

Ch. 243: Realizing that Carmesina is justifiably outraged at the manner in which he has compromised her delicate reputation, the contrite Tirant sends her a letter of apology. A subsequent exchange of notes between the lovers moves the matter closer to resolution, and we notice the Princess's wrath beginning to abate (Chs. 246-47).

Ch. 251: Carmesina is suddenly obliged to reconsider her attitude toward Tirant's aggressive wooing when his messenger, Hipòlit, upbraids her for clinging to some rather outmoded notions of courtship. Hipòlit's rebuke is occasioned by the Princess' strange reply to Tirant's most recent apology: she announces that she plans to send him three hairs from her head instead of a letter; this is an apparent throwback to the rites of Courtly Love and a gesture whose symbolic meaning she fully expects her lover to comprehend. The young messenger censures her sharply for entertaining such an antiquated notion and reminds her that modern times demand new conventions, that Tirant is no longer playing by the rules set down by the Provençal poets, and that the Captain seeks — quite reasonably — a sexual liaison with her, a desire which is in no way compatible with the quaint kind of courtship she prefers. [10] Plaerdemavida gives immediate support to

---

[10] Hipòlit's remarks (Chs. 251-52) consist of the following two outbursts:
—No em valla Déu —dix Hipòlit— si jo los prenc, si ja no em dieu la significança per què són estats més tres que quatre, que deu o vint. E com, senyora!, ¿pensa vostra altesa que siam en lo temps antic, que usaven les gents de llei de gràcia? Car la donzella, com tenia algun enamorat e l'amava en estrem grau, dava-li un ramellet de flors ben perfumat, o un cabell o dos del seu cap, e aquell se tenia per molt benaventurat. No, senyora, no, que aqueix temps ja és passat. Lo que mon senyor Tirant desija bé ho sé jo: que us pogués tenir en un llit nua o en camisa; posat cas que lo llit no fos perfumat, no s'hi daria res. Mas si la majestat vostra me dóna tres cabells en present a Tirant, no acostume jo tal cosa portar: trameteu-los-hi per altri, o diga'm vostra excel·lència sots quina esperança són eixits del vostre cap.
... ...
—Jatsesia que la majestat vostra diga que violència vos és estada feta, e sots nom de força vullau cobrir la culpa vostra e dar a Tirant pena qui és pijor que mort, és ver que sou estada

the words of Hipòlit by scolding Carmesina for her cruel and disdainful treatment of the brave Captain, an action which may cause the downfall of the Empire

> retreta en la cambra de vostra mare, mas no sou estada violada. Digau, senyora, ¿quina culpa pot ésser dada a mon senyor Tirant, si ell ha temptat de fer un tan singular fet com fer volia? ¿Qui el deu condemnar a pena neguna? Foragitau de la celsitud vostra, bellea, gràcia, seny e gentil saber, dinitat ab perfecció de tota virtut, e no siau tan dura en amar aquell qui us desija tostemps servir e us ama en extrem. Car bé deuria ésser en record la majestat vostra quant vos obliga lo seu molt amar e la glòria que en posseïu; ¿e voleu-li llevar l'esperança, la qual departir no es pot? Estic admirat del que les orelles mies han oït, la deliberació de tan penada vida com l'altesa vostra vol fer passar a mon senyor Tirant, car deuríeu deixar tots los dubtes que en ofensa sua fossen, ni causar-se porien, com, lo pensar que ell fa en absència de vostra majestat, no li és permès la gravitat del dan que li aporta, si ja la vostra grandíssima discreció no contempla los infinits mals e desolacions que a càrrec de vostra celsitud se siguiran, qui ara a vós paren molt pocs, car sereu causa de fer perdre lo millor dels millors, e passar n'heu en aquest món i en l'altre condigna pena. Car les sues nafres, com sent alegria de vostra altesa, aumenten en tot bé, e si sent lo contrari sereu causa de molta dolor així per a vós com per a tots los del llinatge de la casa de Bretanya. E perdent a ell, se perdran passats deu mília combatents, qui faran gran fretura per dar compliment a la conquista. Mirau lo rei de Sicília quanta gent té en servei de vostra altesa; e lo gran Mestre de Rodes, lo vescomte de Branxes, la gent que ha portada. Car si Tirant no fos, negú de tots aquests no hi aturaria. Veureu llavors la Viuda Reposada si farà les batalles per vostre pare ni per vós. La majestat vostra és metge sens medecina, e aquell és bon metge qui dóna sanitat al cos i a l'ànima, però veig que aquell desventurat no pot haver sanitat ni goig de lla on hi ha tan gran malvolença.
>
> (*TB*, 738-40)

" 'May God abandon me if I take [these three hairs],' said Hipòlit, 'unless you tell me their meaning. And why should there be three of them, and not four, ten or twenty? For heaven's sake, My Lady, does Your Highness think we are still back in olden times when these quaint customs were fashionable? When the maiden had a lover and fancied him greatly, she used to give him a bouquet of fragant flowers or one or two hairs from her head, and the poor fellow considered himself very lucky to have them. I'm sorry, My Lady, but those days are gone forever. What my Lord Tirant wants I know very well: he wants to have you in bed, whether naked or clothed only in a nightshirt; the bed doesn't even need perfumed sheets. But if Your Highness should give me three hairs for me to present to Tirant, I must reply that I am not accustomed to carrying such things. Send them with some other messenger, or tell me for what purpose they have been plucked from your head.' "

... ...

" 'Even though Your Majesty says that some violence has been done to your person, and that you want to use this issue of force to hide your own

if a heartbroken Tirant should suddenly withdraw from the fighting (Ch. 253). [11]

Ch. 271: Having clarified most of the past misunderstandings, Tirant and Carmesina exchange secret wedding vows in the palace garden (cf. Estefania and Diafebus in Chs. 146-48, but without the legal formality of an *albarà*). This represents a double triumph for Tirant in that he gains not only the long-sought conjugal rights to Carmesina's body, but also a firm claim to the Imperial Crown because the Princess renounces at the same time all her rights of inheritance

---

guilt and make Tirant feel pain that is worse than death, the truth is that you were held captive in your mother's room but not raped. Tell me, Lady, how can my Lord Tirant be blamed for trying to do something so special as that? Who can pass sentence on him? Why don't you come down from your pedestal of beauty, grace, knowledge and elegant manners, your dignified perfection in all virtues, and try not to be so hard and cold toward a man who wants nothing more than to serve and please you forever and who loves you with all his heart? And Your Majesty should remember how indebted you are for his great love and the glory that has come to you as a result of his love. And you want to take away his hope, without which no man can live? I am astonished by what my ears have heard about the arduous kind of life Your Highness wishes to impose on Lord Tirant. You should put aside all the doubts you have about him, and which could never be true, and you should think about the dreadful life he is leading when he is away from you, a life which he can no longer endure. If from this point forward your great wisdom doesn't take into account the infinite damage and destruction that will occur because of you, very few people will take your part because you will be the reason why the best of all great men will be lost, and you will have to suffer the punishment for it in this world as well as in the next. For when he is happy about you even his wounds seem less painful; but if the opposite should occur you will be the cause of much pain to yourself as well as to the House of Brittany. Losing him would mean more than losing a thousand soldiers, for he is essential if we are to finish the job of conquest that stands before us. Look at the King of Sicily and how many people he has brought to serve Your Highness; and the Great Master of Rhodes, and the Viscount of Branches and all the troops they have contributed. If it weren't for Tirant, none of these would be here now. And then you will see if the Viuda Reposada will fight the battles for you and your father. Your Majesty is a doctor without medicine, while he is a good physician who brings health to the body and the soul; but I can see that it is impossible for that unfortunate man to have either health or happiness when there exists such great ill will towards him.' "

[11] This stern warning is followed by one of the most memorable monologues of the novel (Ch. 254), wherein Plaerdemavida imagines a scene in which Carmesina, following her death, will be asked by the Lord and St. Peter to account for her harsh and foolish treatment of the Captain. This passage (*TB*, 741-42) was cited earlier in my Introduction.

(Ch. 272). Nonetheless, she requests here that they postpone consummation of their marital vows until after the Turkish threat has been obliterated (Ch. 273).

Ch. 277: On Tirant's next nocturnal visit to Carmesina's room he finds her dressed in her wedding gown and wearing the Imperial Crown, which she immediately places on his head to confirm and ratify the promise made to him earlier about ceding her inheritance rights to him. To the accompaniment of Plaerdemavida's strong vocal support, he attempts once again to consummate their relationship (Ch. 280); a tearful Carmesina manages to dissuade him one more time and the bridegroom is content simply to spend the night in her bed without complete sexual gratification (Ch. 281), which angers Plaerdemavida to the point of her refusing to serve as his counselor any longer (Ch. 282).

Ch. 283: The malevolent Viuda puts into action her final and most elaborate plan to drive apart the Captain and Carmesina. Through the use of a great deal of false circumstantial evidence, Tirant is made to believe that the Princess is carrying on sexually with a black gardener (Ch. 286). Ironically, it is now the Captain's opportunity to turn a deaf ear to Carmesina's pleas. The misunderstanding is corrected a short time later, but at the very moment that Tirant hears the truth from Plaerdemavida's lips (Ch. 296), they are both swept away by a fierce storm and shipwrecked somewhere on the North African coast (Ch. 299). And so, because of this incredible stroke of misfortune, Tirant's golden opportunity for a reconciliation with Carmesina is delayed until the fourth stage of their courtship, Ch. 434 to be precise.

Just as the Diafebus-Estefania relationship provided an interesting contrast within the preliminary stage of Tirant and Carmesina's romance, author Martorell places a similar contrasting pair in the second phase of their courtship by describing the adulterous affair carried on by the middle-aged Empress (Carmesina's mother) and Tirant's new second-in-command, the young knight Hipòlit. Their liaison shares several common features with the main romantic intrigue, but their behavior is notable for running in almost every way counter to the actions of Tirant and the Princess. For example, the romance is totally illicit from beginning to end, with definite incestuous overtones (the Empress is obviously attracted to the young man because of his strong physical resemblance to her recently deceased son). Furthermore, the relationship is characterized by unabashed frankness and unrestrained sensual delight. The affair begins with Hipòlit's startling confession in Ch. 249 of his secret passion for the middle-aged Empress (the reader has been given absolutely no hint of any sexual attraction between them to this point). Hipòlit's boldness here is in sharp contrast with the parallel case of Tirant's shyness and plodding attempts at seduction. And if Carmesina is concerned about her good name and the threat of public exposure, her mother's only preoccupation is with whether she will be able to satisfy completely her lover's sexual appetite (Ch. 258). In further contrast with the principal romantic intrigue, the Empress assumes an equally aggressive role here: it is *she* who arranges for a two-week liaison with her lover in her bedchamber. And when her young lover first asks for a sexual *don,* she immediately and unhesitatingly pulls him to the floor of her boudoir where they make love for the first time (Ch. 260). A potential blocking agent to parallel the Viuda Reposada is provided in the person of the Empress's servant girl, Eliseu, who is initially distrustful of the young knight but later warms to his charms; eventually Eliseu becomes a willing accomplice to the Empress's adulterous machinations.

At the close of the torrid two-week liaison between the Empress and Hipòlit (Ch. 264) the reader might well expect the narrator to include additional erotic adventures featuring these two illicit lovers, but he will have to wait until the closing chapters to find them. Martorell makes no further report on this adulterous/incestuous relationship until Ch. 479, but from that point until the end of the novel they play a significant role in the book's ironic denouement. What must be borne in mind is that the Hipòlit-Empress affair is nothing more than an ironic comment on the Tirant-Carmesina relationship; these two pairs of lovers are intended to represent opposite poles in the matter of courtship and sexual relations. [12]

---

[12] Contrast also the illicit Hipòlit-Empress liaison with the perfect courtship of Diafebus and Estefania in the first stage.

THE THIRD STAGE: PHYSICAL SEPARATION OF THE LOVERS (Chs. 299-414)

Coincidental with Tirant's physical removal from the Greek Capital to the Barbary Coast by the hand of fate, we find Carmesina living in self-imposed exile at a convent near Constantinople and awaiting word as to the fate of her lover. As we saw earlier with the hero's development as a military commander, the African adventure here again represents a pivotal step in his evolution toward becoming the perfect suitor and fiancé. His faithfulness is put to the supreme test when he encounters the extremely beautiful Maragdina of Tlemcen, a queen who confesses to a wild passion for the Christian warrior and offers him her hand in marriage — not to mention a share of her royal crown (Ch. 322). Tirant recognizes the proposal as a sincere and exceedingly generous one, but politely declines on the grounds of their religious differences. The Moorish beauty persists by declaring herself prepared to embrace Christianity, if that be necessary to win him (Ch. 324). It is absolutely essential to Martorell's plan that Tirant's fidelity to the Greek Princess be severely tested in this manner before they can be joined definitively in a binding marital union. (It must be remembered that their exchange of conjugal vows has not yet been consummated.) But because he is flattered by the Moorish Queen's generous overture, he returns the favor by 1) personally pouring the waters of baptism that initiate her into the Christian faith (Ch. 326), and 2) arranging for her marriage to Escariano, King of Ethiopia and Tirant's comrade-at-arms, the only other figure in the novel who can be said to approach Tirant's perfection as a warrior or diplomat.

Tirant's relationship with Escariano is worthy of further comment. They meet originally as diplomatic adversaries when the Christian warrior is sent as the King of Tlemcen's ambassador to Escariano to arrange for a truce between their warring kingdoms (Ch. 308). The initial wariness of the two warriors soon gives way to deep admiration, and a firm friendship is forged; they eventually become allies and *hermanos en armas*. If Escariano can be conceived as Tirant's double as a warrior-diplomat, he is precisely the *antithesis* of the Christian hero as a lover; there is nothing of Tirant's timidity or passiveness in the Ethiopian's courtship of Maragdina. While Tirant has been wont to fret back in Constantinople about the inequality of lineage that appears to constitute an impediment to his union with the Imperial Princess, Escariano never doubts for a moment his worthiness to claim Maragdina as his bride. As the outraged Moor informs Tirant in Ch. 309, the hostilities between Tlemcen and Ethiopia have resulted from a broken promise on the part of Maragdina's father, who has recently reneged on an earlier agreement to marry his daughter to the Ethiopian monarch in order to surrender her instead to the son of one of his own generals. Seeking only what he thinks is rightfully his, Escariano has declared war on Tlemcen and laid siege to that kingdom to press his claim. Martorell's plan calls for the black warrior first to succeed in kidnapping his intended bride (and assassinate her father and fiancé in the process), then to be defeated and captured by Tirant, at which point their friendship is allowed to blossom.

If the political advantages of aggressive courtship as demonstrated by Escariano serve as a lesson to the romantically timid Christian hero, Tirant likewise causes a change in the Ethiopian warrior's behavior by showing him the moral benefits of the Christian religion and the sacramental blessings of Holy Matrimony. Martorell's hero personally oversees the doctrinal instruction and conversion to Christianity of both Maragdina (Ch. 326) and Escariano (Ch. 329); the repercussions of Tirant's good example are felt in even more remote corners when the newly Christianized royal couple later introduce their new faith to the Ethiopian people and institute monogamy within their culture (Ch. 409). By the time Escariano and Maragdina rejoin Tirant for a triumphant return to Constantinople (Ch. 456), the Christian hero has been markedly influenced for the better by his earlier experiences with them in Africa, and returns to the scene of his earlier victories as an even more admirable warrior and lover than he was previously.

A second — albeit minor — romantic pairing that is presented in the North African interlude is the courtship and marriage of Plaerdemavida (shipwrecked along with Martorell's hero on the Barbary Coast in Ch. 299) and Tirant's cousin, Lord Agramunt, who joins the Christian commander in Ch. 321. The future sovereigns of Morocco and Bougie overcome a nearly disastrous beginning of their relationship: Plaerdemavida appears before the conquering Tirant disguised as an ambassador in the service of the Queen of Montàgata, and a misinformed Agramunt is led to believe that she has poisoned the Christian leader; he comes within a hair's breadth of cutting her throat but he is quickly prevented from doing so and sharply upbraided by the Captain (Chs. 363-64). The impetuous Agramunt later apologizes to both Tirant and Plaerdemavida for his impetuous behavior (Chs. 367-69) and is eventually joined in marriage to her at the suggestion of the Christian commander, who has taken to acting as a matchmaker (Chs. 382-83); they are then designated by Tirant to become the rulers of Fez (Morocco) and Bougie and they live happily thereafter in those roles.

By the time Tirant's adventure in Barbary draws to a close, he has personally overseen the bethrothal and marriage of two important pairs of lovers who will serve as a frame for his own eventual union with Carmesina. The African adventure — just as in the military episodes — is intended to represent the final stage of preparation for Tirant's ultimate role as the perfect courtly suitor and consort; the lessons learned during his forced absence from the Byzantine Court are as pivotal in his romantic life as they are in his development as a military commander.

STAGE FOUR: REUNION, CONSUMMATION AND DEATH (Chs. 414-78)

With Tirant's triumphant return to Constantinople and his stunning defeat of the Turkish invaders, the groundwork for a happy and successful conclusion of the hero's quest for the hand of Carmesina appears to have been laid. The young lovers are joyfully reunited at the Imperial Court (Ch. 436) and all opposition to their marriage disappears with the suicide death of the scheming Viuda Reposada (Ch. 416). Chapters 430-39 represent the complete and final triumph (on the romantic front) of the counsel and philosophy of Plaerdemavida, who reappears now as the Queen of Fez and immediately sets out to complete the task of Carmesina's seduction by Tirant — this time without opposition or hindrance from any quarter. The long overdue consummation of the Tirant-Carmesina relationship takes place in Chs. 436-37, despite the half-hearted protests offered by the Princess when she belatedly discovers that Plaerdemavida has once again smuggled the Captain into her bed. Ire is soon turned to ardor as the lovers spend the night in a makeshift conjugal bed, renewing their interrupted courtship and sharing their first taste of marital bliss and carnal delight. A second night of love is spent in Plaerdemavida's chamber a few chapters later (Ch. 445), this time without all the delicious — and often hilarious — detail Martorell has provided in describing their first carnal encounter. The author is content here merely to inform us that Tirant has at last achieved his goal of becoming as valiant in the bedroom as he is on the battlefield.

The final and complete fulfillment of Tirant's desires is achieved in Ch. 452 when the old Emperor presides at the formal betrothal of his daughter to the Captain, who is thereupon named the Emperor's heir and successor and given the title of Caesar of the Greek Empire. Before he can begin to enjoy his newly acquired rights and title, however, he is obliged to depart the capital one more time to supervise the surrender of the final Turkish strongholds and oversee the repatriation of the numerous Greek prisoners of war (his friend Diafebus among them). At Adrianople the hero falls gravely ill (Ch. 467) and dies unheroically in Diafebus' arms (Ch. 471) on the return trip to the capital. Upon learning of Tirant's sudden demise, the distraught Carmesina dresses in the gown her father ordered to be designed for her wedding (which still has not taken place, it must be recalled) when she goes to view her lover's embalmed remains. She proceeds to pronounce a long and tearful lament over the body of Tirant and then collapses in a paroxysm of mortal consequences. She lingers at death's door long enough to allow her father the Emperor to precede her into the next life (Ch. 477); eventually she too succumbs, but only after making a perfect Christian confession and profession of faith (Ch. 478).

THE IRONIC EPILOGUE (Chs. 479-87):

The physical and moral perfection of Tirant's life and works is masterfully undercut by author Martorell in the final nine chapters of his book when we learn that it is the adulterous knight Hipòlit who is destined to reap the glory and honors that should rightfully have gone to the Captain. As the principal beneficiary of Tirant's will, young Hipòlit is designated to succeed to the Imperial throne following the death of the Emperor; furthermore, it is suggested that he then contract marriage with Carmesina's heir, who turns out to be the former Empress, in order to consolidate all claims to the throne. Fate has played perfectly into the hands of this incestuous and adulterous couple. The author informs us that the two former sinners rule happily for a period of three years, at the end of which time the old woman passes away. Hipòlit's grief is sincere but short-lived, as he soon thereafter marries an English princess closer to his own age and they proceed to enjoy a most happy and fruitful conjugal relationship, living to a ripe old age — they even manage to die on the same day — and leaving behind an unspecified number of children and grandchildren who (we are told) will carry on the noble and chivalric tradition for generations.

* * *

No discussion of the love theme in *TB* would be complete without a comment on some of the minor male-female relationships that are presented in the early chapters of Martorell's novel (i.e., those episodes that precede the hero's arrival in Constantinople). The function of these premature romantic adventures, we must remember, is to prepare Tirant for his eventual encounter with Carmesina; they serve as a kind of amatory apprenticeship that complements his early training as a warrior at the English jousting lists and the lessons in naval warfare that he receives from Cataquefaràs.

The most interesting aspect of these primitive romantic encounters is the changing role of women in medieval society up to and including the establishment of the conventions of Courtly Love. The conjugal bond between Guillem de Varoic and the Countess, for example (Chs. 1-28), is intended to represent the earliest stage of marital relations within the military class. As Ruiz de Conde notes (p. 128), women are viewed as both victims and enemies of the chivalric order; they are little more than chattels whose sole function is to serve the males by bearing and raising their sons, i.e., the next generation of warriors. In Varoic's society a woman is not perceived as either a love-object or a confidante, but rather as a subversive element whose softer, more "civilized" social values are inimical to the interests of the military caste and must be suppressed. The Countess is expected to sacrifice continually her own happiness to satisfy the more important desires and needs of her husband and the chivalric ideal. We observe this in Ch. 22 when the tearful Countess pleads (in vain) that her only son be spared from military conscription.[13] Her pleas fall on deaf ears — even her son refuses to accept her reasoning — and she is obliged to return home to weep alone. As a symbol of the first generation of chivalric warriors, Guillem de Varoic is portrayed as a superb fighting machine, but a man devoid of tenderness and romantic sentimentality. His world is a dark, cruel and pessimistic one in which compassion and other such "soft" feminine qualities have no place.

At a later point, in the chapters that treat of the founding of the English Order of the Garter (Chs. 85-97), Martorell shows how the woman's role was eventually elevated from a negative to a positive position; here she is held in some sort of esteem, but her rank is still of definite secondary importance and she must be careful never to interfere in matters of chivalry or knightly duty. In Ch. 95, for example, we learn that twenty women of honor will be permitted to serve the Order, but only after vowing never to implore their husbands, sons or brothers to abandon any military campaign on their behalf. With regard to a woman's role as the legitimate object of a knight's affection, this new romantic convention is dealt with in the episode of Tirant and the beautiful Lady Agnès, the hero's first encounter with the customs of Courtly Love and one which very nearly costs him his life (Chs. 60-68). During his apprenticeship — both as a knight and as a courtly lover — at the English Court, Tirant unwittingly becomes an interloper in the secret romance between Lady Agnès and Lord Vilesermes when he innocently requests that he be allowed to

---

[13] She is speaking to a person whom she believes to be the King, but who in reality is her husband, absent these many years on a pilgrimage to the Holy Land. Her plea is rooted in the fact that with her husband removed from the scene, perhaps never to return, she should not be obliged to sacrifice her only son as well.

wear one of her jewels during his next appearance on the jousting lists. The young knight is in no way enamored of her and is merely following a convention of the times. On her part, Agnès is quite astonished to learn that a knight would vow to fight to the death over such a worthless trinket, but she accedes to his demand. Vilesermes, angered by Tirant's effrontery and doubly outraged when the intruder's hands accidentally graze Agnès' breasts in the act of removing the bauble, immediately challenges the young hero to mortal combat. The result is a very strange duel involving long linen shirts, sharp, double-edged swords, papier-mâché shields and helmets made of flowers; at the end we find Vilesermes brutally slain and Tirant hovering near death from his many and severe wounds.

This episode is significant because it is the first adventure in which the love and war themes intersect in the life of Martorell's protagonist. Furthermore, as Ruiz de Conde points out (pp. 128-129), there is an undeniable symbolic quality to the episode insofar as Agnès' bauble may be said to represent the role of the female in chivalric society as reflected in the conventions of Courtly Love: she is now viewed as a kind of jewel, a beautiful but ultimately useless adornment for the gentleman, an object for display, one more conventional element among many. In another sense, the Agnès-Vilesermes affair is also a grim foreshadowing of the unhappy fate that awaits Tirant and Carmesina. Both Vilesermes and Tirant seek to overcome an inequality of social rank in pursuit of a woman of higher birth, and they are destined to be frustrated in their quest by a cruel fate that will cut both of them down before they can achieve their goal.[14] We should note that Agnès' sorrowful lament delivered over the corpse of her beloved suitor (Ch. 67) is doubly powerful as 1) a condemnation of certain

---

[14] The symbolism in Vilesermes' name should not be overlooked here. Despite the explanation of his title given in Ch. 67 (that he was the lord of many towns, cities and castles, among them a city called Ermes and a strong fortress by the name of Viles), it would seem that Martorell's intent can be more clearly perceived in a literal translation of the name Viles-Ermes (in Castilian, *villas yermas,* 'uninhabited towns'). Although he may have inherited title to some 37 castles, cities and towns, his is essentially an empty inheritance insofar as it fails to raise his social standing to a point prestigious enough to allow him to marry the beautiful and high-born Agnès of Berry.

insane dueling customs that can easily lead to tragedy in the name of so trival a matter as a trinket, and 2) a strong negative comment on some of the stifling courtship conventions and restrictions that have traditionally been invoked to keep apart worthy lovers who merely happen to be of different social ranks.

Tirant's final preparation for his inevitable affair with the Greek Princess takes place in Chs. 100-11 when he presides over the courtship of Prince Felip of France and the Infanta Ricomana, daughter of the King of Sicily. Ironically, no two suitors could be more antithetically presented than the elegant Tirant and the ill-mannered Felip, nor could two courtships be more dissimilar than their respective pursuits of Carmesina and Ricomana. The question of social rank is the principal unifying element in these two otherwise disparate cases. The French prince and the Sicilian princess *on the surface* appear to be a perfect match because each is of royal blood; in the matter of breeding and courtly comportment, however, they are on completely different levels: she is the epitome of good taste and noble demeanor while he possesses some of the grossest and most uncouth social vices imaginable. It is Tirant's unenviable task to camouflage Felip's bad manners and general niggardliness until the Sicilian princess will consent to marry him. On a personal level Felip is not nearly worthy of Ricomana's hand; their suitability as a royal couple is restricted to the political level (i.e., equality of social rank).

The stumbling block for Tirant's wooing of Carmesina, on the other hand, is their *in*equality of rank: she is of royal parentage but he is not. Martorell's hero is shown time after time to be deserving of her hand by reason of his personal valor and many great military achievements, not to mention the superb manners he displays on various occasions during his sojourn at the Byzantine Court. There is never any doubt about Tirant's worthiness to share the Imperial Crown with her. It is also clear that Martorell intended the parallel cases of Felip and Tirant to serve as an ironic comment on the question of social rank vs. personal qualities as the basis for a sound marriage; he demonstrates here that there is absolutely no correspondence between the two and that we should never automatically infer the one from the other.

Both suitors eventually succeed in their courtship (although Tirant's triumph is short-lived). Ricomana's father immediately approves of the proposed marriage because he views it as a desirable political link for his small island kingdom with the powerful French crown; the old Greek Emperor likewise comes to realize — although rather belatedly — that many political benefits would accrue from marrying his daughter to a glorious military figure like Tirant.

Martorell injects still another ironic note by having his hero play the role of the procurer/go-between for Felip and Ricomana, which is precisely the function that Plaerdemavida will later have (after Ch. 214) in the courtship of Tirant and Carmesina; the hero at that later point will find himself reluctant or fearful of heeding the same kind of libidinous counsel he dispensed earlier to Felip. Ricomana is eventually won over by a single sexual encounter with her suitor, a liaison orchestrated and presided over by Tirant in much the same manner that Plaerdemavida will subsequently attempt to win sexual fulfillment for the Captain with Carmesina. The only difference lies in Carmesina's firmer resistance and determination to maintain her virginity.

* * *

In summarizing the role of the romantic interludes in *TB* let us keep in mind that Martorell's narrative technique here is essentially the same one used in the military episodes: to present first a kind of pre-history of romantic love within the chivalric tradition; this is to be followed by several stages of the hero's gradual development as a lover, capped by his emergence in the final chapters as the perfect courtesan and noble suitor for the 1400s. Broken down into narrative sections the following plan takes form:

> *Chs. 1-28:* Guillem de Varoic and the Countess: a primitive view of male-female relations within chivalric society; the woman is perceived as both the victim and the enemy of the warrior class.
>
> *Chs. 60-67:* Lady Agnès and Lord Vilesermes: here we note that women have advanced to the point of being considered a desirable trophy or a prize to be won in competition; their status is little more than that of an

appendage or adornment to be displayed by the conquering male. The question of social rank as a possible obstacle to romance/marriage is introduced in the case of Vilesermes, a knight of great courage and renown who in a sense could serve as Tirant's double; his frustration at being prohibited from marrying Agnès and his tragic and senseless death are a foreshadowing of the unhappy fate that awaits Tirant with Carmesina.

Chs. 100-11: Felip and Ricomana: if Vilesermes can be considered almost Tirant's twin, the uncouth and miserly Felip is portrayed as the antithesis of Martorell's hero. His courtship of the Sicilian princess is justified solely on the basis of a pre-existent equality of social rank between the lovers, not by his personal qualities. The unwarranted success of Felip's courtship — with no small assist from Tirant — should be contrasted with the earlier frustrated failure of the noble Vilesermes and the similarly disappointing conclusion of the Tirant-Carmesina affair that will follow.

Chs. 117-213: The courtship of Tirant and Carmesina, conducted strictly according to the conventions of Courtly Love: the rules are followed faithfully by Tirant, but the results prove to be unsatisfying from the standpoint of carnal gratification. For contrast Martorell provides the affair between Diafebus and Estafania, a parallel courtship that succeeds where Tirant and Carmesina's fails; sexual gratification precedes the marriage ceremony in this secondary courtship, but proper legal safeguards are wisely taken to ensure the protection of Estefania's interests. In this manner the Diafebus-Estefania affair is presented as a model for "modern" (i.e., fifteenth-century) courtship and marriage that avoids both the silliness inherent in some of the precepts of Courtly Love and the potentially tragic consequences of the then popular practice of clandestine marriage.

Chs. 214-99: Tirant abandons the conventions of Courtly Love in favor of the uninhibited and often licentious counsel of Plaerdemavida, but he fails to achieve his goal of physical union with Carmesina simply because of his own timidity in the bedroom. The jealous Viuda Reposada serves as a blocking agent for Tirant, but the wily Plaerdemavida, acting as procuress and chief instigator of romantic intrigues, manages to frustrate the evil Viuda repeatedly. The adulterous and incestuous affair between Hipòlit and the Empress is injected here to move in counterpoint to the main love story; theirs is a totally illicit romance that is intended to represent the antithesis of Tirant and Carmesina's morally righteous one. As such, the Hipòlit-Empress affair is the negative counterpart of the Diafebus-Estefania courtship in the previous section.

Chs. 299-414: The physical separation of Tirant and Carmesina during his exile on the Barbary Coast provides a stern test of his faithfulness to her. He is sorely tempted by the charms of the beauteous Queen Maragdina, but he succeeds in resisting her offer of marriage and a share of her throne. Tirant's former timidity is contrasted here with the aggressive courtship methods of King Escariano of Ethiopia whose bold persistence is eventually rewarded with marriage to the very desirable Maragdina. Escariano, who is in many ways an ebony version of Tirant on the battlefield, serves here as the model suitor whom Tirant will emulate upon his return to Constantinople.

Chs. 414-78: Tirant's triumphant return to the Greek capital occasions his reunion and reconciliation with Carmesina; unfortunately, the long awaited consummation of Tirant and Carmesina's secret marriage vows is followed closely by the sudden death of both. They enjoy only two nights of love before they are taken from this world.

Chs. 479-87: In a master stroke of irony, Martorell concludes his novel by having the unworthy Hipòlit achieve Tirant's dream; the young knight marries his maternal paramour and ascends to the Imperial throne to rule with her. They enjoy three years of marital happiness, despite the illicit beginnings of their relationship. After her death Hipòlit marries again and lives blissfully to an advanced age.

Although at first glance the secondary couples appear to have no more than a casual connection with the main romantic intrigue, a close examination reveals that each one of them has a direct relationship to the central pairing. The subordinate couples may serve as an interesting parallel to the principal couple (Agnès and Vilesermes) or as a ridiculous case in the opposite extreme (Felip and Ricomana); they may provide a perfect model for courtship and marriage (Diafebus and Estefania) or they may represent precisely the type of behavior that is antithetical to the ideal social model (Hipòlit and the Empress).

It is indeed tempting to let our final judgment of Martorell's novel be determined by the ironic epilogue he brilliantly provides. On the basis of the last five chapters a careless reader might well conclude that Martorell had a rather jaundiced view of the world and its way; with regard to the relationship between material success and inherent personal virtue, the respective fates of Tirant and Hipòlit appear to confirm the acrid observation made centuries later by actress Mae West about material success in this world: "Goodness ha[s] nothing to do with it." But such a reading would do a disservice to Martorell and his well-conceived plan for the romantic interludes in his book. His message regarding matters of the heart is a most positive one: marriage (i.e., the sacrament of Matrimony) is the only viable solution for the problems of love and sex— even for illicit relationships. Every one of the romantic couples who ratify their relationship in a marital bond is blessed with happiness; this is true even for unlikely pairs such as Ricomana and Felip and the Empress and Hipòlit. One of the major points Martorell makes in his novel is that true love is found only in the married state, a view which totally contradicts the old precepts of Courtly Love, which generally proposed that the most enduring kind of love can be had only *outside of* marriage.

A second theme of these amorous adventures is that of clandestine marriage. Martorell demonstrates in his book that the many abuses that have resulted from this practice of exchanging secret wedding vows without witnesses can be remedied easily by taking a more careful and legalistic approach to the exchange ceremony, as in the *albarà* presented by Estefania to Diafebus (Ch. 147). In light of his sister Damiata's unpleasant experience with this custom and the violent confrontation that nearly took place because of it, Martorell's handling of this very delicate subject in his novel is marked by much more restraint and calm reflection than one might have at first expected.

All in all, the romantic episodes of *Tirant lo Blanch* are much more than mere "filler" or comic diversion from the main theme of the hero's military exploits. They constitute a separate theme of nearly equal importance. Love and marriage are serious topics for

Martorell, despite the sometimes hilarious escapades that punctuate the chapters that take place in the palace bedrooms. Unfortunately, Martorell is so adept at portraying the comic side of sex and romance that he often succeeds in distracting the reader from the serious message that lies beneath all the erotic and comic events he presents. Perhaps a fifteenth-century reader would have perceived the serious social comment inherent in Martorell's novel; for the reader of our own times who is either ignorant of or unconcerned with the problem of clandestine marriage and Courtly Love, only the erotic or farcical elements are of interest — which is one of the principal reasons why this novel has for so long been grievously misunderstood and sadly unappreciated.

Chapter IV

ON QUAINT CHIVALRIC RITUALS:
VOWS AND PERSONAL CHALLENGES

One could conceivably write volumes concerning the many and various ceremonies that are so minutely described in *TB*,[1] but here I shall limit myself to an examination of two particular rituals that are given special treatment by author Martorell: 1) the chivalric practice of proclaiming publicly a personal vow to perform some noteworthy — and often bizarre — deed; 2) the formal letter of challenge (*lletra de batalla* or *deseiximent* in Catalan, *carta de desafío* in Castilian) that served as the preliminary to either a private duel or an armed public encounter on the jousting lists.

The reason for their special handling can be found in the unusual critical attitude that the author brings to their delineation in his novel. In each case the tradition or ritual in question is presented as a curious, lingering, but relatively useless art form that initially may have been quite sensible and of a practical nature, but which has evolved over the centuries to such an ultra-sophisticated and contrived state that the original spirit and meaning has long since been undermined, lost or perverted. The final stage of the ritual is always portrayed in Martorell's novel as something so far removed from the meaningful and valid nature of its original form, so completely degenerate as a social custom, as to be only a ridiculous and grotesque caricature of its former self.

---

[1] In the novel we find baptisms, jousts, parades and processions of diverse kinds, weddings, betrothals, dances, victory celebrations, inductions into the chivalric orders (and expulsions therefrom) — all reported in the fullest detail.

According to Martorell's plan, each of these rituals, having degenerated to the point of self-parody, simply disappears as a social entity within the novel — which is precisely the fate that the progressive-minded author seems to be advocating for all such once-meaningful but ultimately useless customs, rituals and traditions. Let us examine these two social phenomena in close detail, beginning with the chivalric vow.

* * *

A) QUAINT VOWS AND BIZARRE PROMISES

The pattern we observe here is one of gradual trivialization. In the early chapters of the book the solemn chivalric vow is portrayed as a noble custom that has developed naturally as a just and meaningful personal response to some serious threat and/or provocation. In subsequent chapters, however, we find these solemn promises being made for increasingly frivolous reasons, and occasionally with near-disastrous results. Eventually these vows evolve to the point of having little or no real significance; Martorell shows that they become hollow rhetorical forms, nearly devoid of substance, and frequently issued with two distinct — and at times incongruous — levels of meaning, one of which is intended to disguise the *real* cause or provocation for the solemn utterance. At one point the once-hallowed custom of the solemn chivalric oath even degenerates to the depths of burlesque, the substance of a mean-spirited practical joke. The final stage is reached during the North African campaign when with increasing frequency the provocation for these vows is discovered to be frivolous, often imaginary, and largely based on ignorance or misinformation. The practice ultimately passes out of existence after one great and final debasement: an excessively harsh promise, rashly issued by one of Tirant's lieutenants in the heat of anger, that ultimately threatens the lives of thousands of innocent civilians. Having degenerated in this way to the point of producing unwanted, embarrassing and possibly calamitous results, the institution of the chivalric vow is then mercifully put to rest for the final hundred chapters of Martorell's book.

The initial appearance of the solemn chivalric vow occurs in Ch. 20, within the Guillem de Varoic section. Curiously enough, there is no mention or reference to such a vow in the fragment of the Warwick legend that is preserved in Ms. 7811 of the Biblioteca Nacional in Madrid and reproduced by Martín de Riquer.[2] This suggests that the original source contained no reference to such a custom and that Martorell has added the incident in the course of integrating the Varoic fragment with the more comprehensive plan for *TB*. The vow in question is Varoic's response to the treachery of the Moorish leader, Cale ben Cale, who has cruelly assassinated two English ambassadors and all their attendants, then sent their severed heads back to the English camp in a packsaddle (cf. the treachery described in the Castilian legend of the Seven Infantes of Lara). The English count cries out in defiance

> ¡Oh infels crudelíssims e de poca fe, car no podeu donar lo que no teniu! Ara jo faç vot solemne, així nafrat com estic, de jamés entrar dins casa coberta, si no és església per oir missa, fins a tant que jo haja llançat tota aquesta morisma fora de tot lo regne.
>
> (*TB*, 149)[3]

and swears to refrain from enjoying the comforts of civilization — such as sleeping under a roof — until he has driven all the Moorish invaders from the kingdom. A partial consequence of this vow is seen a scant five chapters later during a fierce battle in which Varoic, having just rescued 309 female hostages, refuses to accept the offer of the Moors within the besieged castle to surrender; instead he sets the fortress ablaze and orders his men to kill all those who attempt to flee the inferno or to drive them back into the flames. We are told matter-of-factly that some twenty-two thousand Moors perish in the flames that day, and the entire matter

---

[2] See Martín de Riquer, ed., *Tirant lo Blanc i altres escrits de Joanot Martorell* (Barcelona: Ariel, 1979), pp. 1235-49.

[3] "Oh, you extraordinarily cruel unbelievers of such little faith that you cannot possibly give to others what you do not possess yourselves! I hereby solemnly vow, offended as I am, never again to enter a roofed building, except to hear Mass in a church, until I have expelled all the Moors from the entire kingdom."

is treated as merely a natural and righteous consequence of the Moors' earlier perfidy.

The subject arises again in Ch. 33 with the reference to a vow made by a certain Quinto lo Superior, the Pope's ambassador to Constantinople, upon his arrival when he noted the many forms of profanation and desecration that had taken place in the Holy City under the conquering Turks (e.g., stabling their horses in the city's most beautiful cathedral).[4] Quinto's ire is directed not at the offending Moslem invaders but at the pusillanimous Christian inhabitants (beginning with the timid Greek Emperor) who have meekly shrunk from their sworn duty to defend the Church against those who would defile her. He angrily charges them with being unworthy Christians who have shown no confidence in God's Divine Assistance; he then vows to smite with his mighty sword the first Christian who dares to speak in favor of their passive acceptance of Turkish rule in the city:

> ¡Oh gent de poc ànimo e de poca fe! Bé mostrau ésser mals cristians, que no confiau de l'adjutori divinal. Ara jo faç vot a Déu que lo primer qui parlarà, jo li daré ab aquesta mia tallant espasa un tal colp, que los crits sentiran los qui estan dins l'església.
>
> (*TB*, 176)[5]

As a vow, Quinto's threat may not be particularly noteworthy, but the provocation is indeed interesting. This brief anecdote is offered by Varoic solely to emphasize the duty of every member of the chivalric orders to defend the Catholic/Christian faith against those who would desecrate her temples of worship. (Varoic goes on to add that Quinto, having made his point, soon thereafter meets with a Turkish captain to negotiate for the removal of the horses from the cathedral.)

---

[4] Riquer believes this to be a reference to the behavior of the Turks on 29 May 1453, when Constantinople fell into their hands (*Tirante el Blanco*, I, 107, n. 4). See also Marinesco, "Du nouveau..." (pp. 179 and 184).

[5] "Oh, you people of such small spirit and little faith! How well you show yourselves to be bad Christians by the fact that you do not trust in Divine Assistance. I now swear before God to strike with this sharp sword the first man who dares to speak, and I shall do it so mightily that the screams will be heard even by those inside the church."

The process of trivialization begins in Ch. 113 when the King of France's expedition arrives to battle the Moors at Tripoli.[6] As the Christian troops gather to hear Mass immediately before the first battle, Tirant rises and — without the slightest provocation — places his hand upon the missal and utters a solemn vow to God, to all the saints in Paradise, and to his lord the Duke of Brittany, that he will be the first warrior to land on the shore during the assault and the last to return to his ship:[7]

> —Com per la divinal gràcia de Déu omnipotent jo sia posat en l'orde de cavalleria, franc e llibert de tota captivitat e altre empediment, no constret ni forçat, mas com a cavaller qui desija guanyar honor, faç mon vot a Déu e a tots los sants de paraís, e a mon senyor lo duc de Bretanya, capità general d'aquest estol, portantveus del molt excel·lent e crestianíssim rei de França, de jo ésser hui lo primer qui eixirà en terra e lo darrer qui es recollirà.
>
> (TB, 358)[8]

---

[6] There is some disagreement among scholars with regard to the location of this city. Vidal Jové's edition of *TB* (1969) refers to it as the famous Libyan port, but Riquer's 1974 version footnotes "Tripoli de Suria" (as it appears in the 1490 Catalan original) to be the Syrian — or today, Lebanese — city of the same name (*Tirante el Blanco*, II, 87, n. 2). Given the fact that the French expedition embarks from the island of Corsica, I would be inclined to believe that Martorell had the Libyan city in mind.

[7] The custom of the solemn vow among medieval knights has been discussed by Huizinga, *The Waning of the Middle Ages* (London: E. Arnold, 1924; rpt. 1963), pp. 77-80. Riquer refers to a medieval tradition of making such vows in the presence of a roasted pheasant or peacock in the courts of England, France and Germany. He makes special mention of an occasion in Lille (1454) when Geoffroy de Thoisy — one of the suspected historical models for Tirant, we should recall — uttered a vow very similar to Tirant's promise here in Ch. 113 (*Tirante el Blanco*, II, 87-90 in footnotes). See also Marinesco, "Du nouveau..." (p. 160).

[8] "Because by the divine grace of Almighty God I am a member of the military order, free and unencumbered by imprisonment or any other such impediment, neither constrained nor forced in any way, but rather acting as a knight who seeks to gain honor and glory for himself, I hereby vow to God and to all the saints in Paradise, and to my lord the Duke of Brittany, admiral of this fleet and spokesman for the most excellent and Christian King of France, to be the very first man to set foot on the beach and the very last to leave it."

In quick succession a litany of similar utterances flows from the mouths of Diafebus and several other knights who have been inspired by Tirant's bold example:

> Aprés jurà Diafebus, e féu vot d'ell escriure lo seu nom en les portes de la ciutat ja nomenada de Trípol de Suria.
> Aprés féu vot altre cavaller, e votà que si lo Rei eixia en terra, d'acostar-se tant a la muralla de la ciutat, que posaria un dard dins la dita ciutat.
> Llevà's altre cavaller, e féu vot dient, que si lo Rei eixia en terra, d'ell entrar dins la ciutat.
> Aprés jurà altre cavaller, e féu vot d'entrar dins la ciutat e pendre donzella mora del costat de la mare, e posar-la dins la nau e dar-la a Felipa, filla del rei de França.
> Féu vot altre cavaller de posar una bandera en la més alta torre de la dita ciutat.
> Molts cavallers anaven dins la nau del Rei, qui passaven nombre de quatre-cents cinquanta cavallers d'esperons daurats, e lla on són molts d'un ofici tostemps s'hi engendra enveja e mala voluntat, car lo pecat d'enveja té moltes branques, per aquells cruels envejosos qui tenen dol e despit del bo e virtuós cavaller.
>
> (*TB*, 358-59)[9]

The inevitable complication of jealousy among peers is presented in the very next chapter in the person of Ricard lo Venturós

---

[9] "Then Diafebus swore an oath and took a vow to write his name on the gates of the aforementioned city, Tripoli of Suria.

"Then another knight vowed that if the king should also land on the shore, he would approach so close to the city that he would be able to fire an arrow into it.

"Another knight stood up and took a vow, saying that if the king would set foot on the land, he would actually enter the city.

"Following this still another knight swore and took a vow to enter the city and capture a Moorish maiden from her mother's side, then carry her back to the ship and present her to Felipa, the King of France's daughter.

"Another knight vowed to place a flag on the highest tower of the city.

"More than 450 golden-spurred warriors were gathered there on the king's flagship; and where so many people of the same profession are assembled there is always generated a certain amount of envy and ill will, for the sin of Envy offers many opportunities to those who are jealous and cruel by nature and who feel resentment and rancor toward a good and virtuous knight."

(Richard the Lucky), an extremely courageous warrior, a soldier deserving of the greatest honor, but also a man who is somewhat envious of Tirant's reputation. He approaches the hero as the battle winds down and proposes that he (Ricard) be permitted to share in the glory that is sure to come to Tirant for his performance on the beach. More specifically, he requests that Tirant allow him to be the final soldier to return to the galley, an act which would technically prevent Tirant from fulfilling his vow but would also constitute a chivalric gesture of the first order, one that would permit Ricard to reap what he considers a fair share of the glory. But rather than suffer the shame of having to alter or suspend his publicly uttered promise, Tirant counters with a proposal that they both return to the shore (they are standing chest deep in the surf as this conversation takes place) to die there heroically. Ricard's initial reaction is to accept what he considers a challenge made in jest, but when he notes that Tirant is quite serious about his foolhardy plan and has actually moved back toward the beach, Ricard reconsiders and proposes a more sensible alternative: if Tirant will consent to being the first to place his foot on a rung of the ship's ladder, Ricard will then agree to precede Tirant up the ladder. As a torrent of Moorish spears, lances, darts and stones rains down upon their exposed position, Tirant agrees to compromise his vow and allow Ricard to share a small share of his glory. Both heroes manage to return unscathed but the reader is left with the distinct impression that Tirant's vow has perhaps been somewhat precipitous and has very nearly resulted in the senseless death or injury of two very noble warriors. From this point on, Tirant will have to balance the anticipated benefits of each new chivalric vow against whatever inherent detrimental effects it will also have.

Ricard's jealousy continues to debase this chivalric custom in Ch. 114 when he challenges Tirant to a duel to the death, which he declares is the only remaining chivalric course of action that will enable him to gain recognition from his peers as Tirant's full equal in the use of arms. In one sense, Ricard's complaint is valid: a rightful share of the honor and glory has been denied him because of Tirant's penchant for bizarre promises about his performance in each subsequent battle; and as a result of an ill-timed and ridiculous utterance, Tirant later saw himself obliged to deny Ricard's rather reasonable request to be the final soldier to leave the combat zone. Unfortunately, the offended party opts to present his grievance in a rather childish manner. Taking his cue from Tirant's previous utterances, Ricard begins by declaring that he will thereafter go barefoot until the King of France and the other nobles publicly acclaim him as the knight who has fought most valiantly at Tripoli. He then demands that Tirant do battle with him "a tota ultrança" to settle the issue, and throws down his gloves in challenge. Tirant's response is at once measured and provocative: he delivers a crashing blow to Ricard's head — a capital offense when committed in the presence of the French monarch, as is the case here — and censures his temperamental colleague for wanting to duel over so trivial a matter (cf. Lady Agnès' comment earlier at the conclusion of Tirant's battle with the hot-headed Vilesermes to settle a dispute over the lady's brooch). He goes on to point out that such a duel can have only negative consequences because at least one good Christian warrior must perish in the process. Having justified his rather extreme reaction to Ricard's challenge, Tirant makes a hasty retreat to the safety of his own ship so that the matter cannot be pursued further. Apparently, he has learned a valuable lesson from the Vilesermes affair.

With Tirant's appearance at the Byzantine court in Constantinople comes a new level of sophistication regarding chivalric promises: the two-tiered (or double-entendre) vow. This phenomenon begins when Martorell's hero feels he must invent a false pretext to explain his deep melancholy, a moodiness attributable solely to a severe case of love-sickness and to his dismay at having to march off to war and separate himself from his new-found romantic interest, the Princess Carmesina. When the Emperor inquires about the reason for Tirant's gloominess, the Captain concocts a phony story about a secret vow that he says he has taken to avenge personally the death of the Emperor's son (Ch. 126). As part of this façade he also creates an imaginary provocation: a mournful sigh that he is supposed to have heard issue from the lips of the grieving Empress. Tirant declares that at that moment, feeling great compassion for the dolorous mother, he uttered a solemn promise to avenge the boy's death, but decided not to reveal it publicly for fear that others would censure him for jeopardizing his honor and reputation in the pursuit of vengeance. Even the text of his vow is a sham: the Prince died in battle against the Turks, and Tirant deliberately makes it appear that his ire is directed against them:

> E jamés la mia ànima no haurà repòs fins a tant que la mia mà dreta sangonosa e cruel haja fet morir aquells qui malament escamparen la sang d'aquell gloriós e estrenu cavaller, lo Príncep fill vostre.
>
> (*TB*, 402) [10]

In point of fact, however, the Captain has recently been informed by Carmesina that one of the Greek commanders, the villainous Duke of Macedonia, is believed to have been the one responsible for the Prince's murder. It is rumored that the Duke secretly cut the strings of the Prince's helmet during the skirmish with the Turks, thereby rendering the young man extremely vulnerable when the armor fell — as inevitably it would — from his head. In the light of this revelation, the vow Tirant appears to utter in Ch. 126 is totally inoperable; it is intended to be nothing more than a smokescreen to cover the real cause of his depression (lovesickness), and is deliberately directed against a party other than the known malefactor. We see in this incident a symbolic account of how the convention of the chivalric vow gradually came to be employed in some less-than-honorable ways. Two levels of meaning can now be perceived: 1) the *real* one and 2) the "official" or surface issue. Tirant's vow on this occasion consists almost entirely of form, with little or no substance.

A similar double-tiered vow appears in Ch. 189, when Tirant is embarrased during a joust with someone called the Grand Noble (*lo Gran Noble*). His angry utterance is provoked by the fact that Tirant's horse falters during the final charge and stumbles to its knees, thereby obliging the Captain to place his right hand on the ground to avoid a fall and defeat. Although Tirant is declared the

---

[10] "And my soul shall never rest until my cruel and bloody right hand has slain those who so vilely spilled the blood of that brave and glorious knight, the Prince, your son."

victor, the judges decide to impose on him a slight penalty for future jousts: the Captain will thereafter be required to battle without colorful trappings or ornamentation, and without a spur on his right foot or a glove on his right hand. Taking great umbrage at the judges' decision and feeling shamed by the shortcomings of his mount, Tirant immediately announces his withdrawal from the competition and renounces all future participation in such jousting tournaments — save if some opportunity should arise to joust with a king or the son of a king. All in all, the incident hardly seems sufficient to provoke such a strong vow and the entire matter takes on a rather trivial air. Tirant's petulance about a silly technicality is difficult to explain on the surface. There is, of course, a *second* level of meaning at which Tirant's decision can easily be understood. The Captain has presented himself at the beginning of the tournament with the stocking and shoe of one foot heavily studded with pearls, rubies and diamonds. The reason for such a peculiar ornamentation — a mystery to all the others present at the lists — is that on an earlier occasion the ardent Tirant had succeeded in placing the large toe of one foot into Carmesina's crotch; in honor of this momentous (to him) achievement he has decided to bejewel the fortuitous appendage. The decision of the judges to require Tirant to appear *without ornamentation* for the remainder of the tournament is clearly unacceptable to him because it will prevent him from celebrating a cherished moment of sexual triumph. Here for the second time we observe the utterance of a vow with two distinct levels of interpretation; again the reader must separate the hidden, *real* motivation and meaning of Tirant's vow from the "official" ones that he offers on the surface.

Tirant's bizarrely decorated stocking and shoe continue to play an important role in the next step in the progressive debasement of the chivalric vow that takes place in Chs. 203-06. On this occasion some of the Captain's friends conspire to elicit from Tirant a confession of the real reason for his strange footwear; they persuade the Moorish slave who is charged with carrying the Captain from a skiff to dry land to pretend to stumble in the surf and soak Tirant's bejeweled foot; they hope that in his anger the Captain will reveal his secret intention. The plan almost succeeds but Tirant becomes suspicious and hatches a scheme that will turn the tables on his would-be tormentors. He feigns anger and gently obliges the Moor to assume a prone position on the beach; the Captain then proceeds to place his studded foot squarely on the unfortunate Moor's head and utters a totally ridiculous vow:

> —Jo faç vot a Déu e a la donzella de qui só, de no dormir en llit ni vestir camisa fins a tant jo haja mort o apresonat rei o fill de rei.
>
> (*TB,* 643) [11]

Moving his foot then to the Moor's right hand, Tirant adds his intention to turn the offense against him into a criminal act:

> —Tu que est moro m'has envergonyit, mas no só ofès. Davant la majestat de la senyora Emperadriu has comès cas civil, mas jo faré que serà criminal, encara que de la fortuna sia ofès.
>
> (*TB,* 644) [12]

The Captain's intention here clearly is to goad his playful friends into similar ludicrous postures and statements of their own; he succeeds magnificently as first the Viscount of Branches, then Diafebus, and finally Hipòlit seek to surpass Tirant in making outlandish vows. Observe the following pronouncements, each one stranger and accompanied by a longer preamble than the previous one:

> —Puix tu has abandonada la virtut de gentilea, e com a catiu lo crim que has comès és civil, no en mereixes punició, puix complit has lo que t'havien manat; per què jo faç mon vot solemne a Déu e a tots los sants de no tornar jamés en la mia pròpia terra fins sia estat en batalla campal on hi haja de quaranta mília moros en sus, e que

---

[11] "I hereby vow to God and the maiden whom I serve not to sleep in a bed nor wear a shirt until I have killed a king or the son of a king, or have taken him as my prisoner."

[12] "You, a Moor, have shamed me, but I am not offended. In front of Her Majesty the Empress you have committed a civil offense, but I will turn it into a criminal one, even though I may have been offended only by accident."

sia vencedor capitanejant jo los crestians, o trobar-me sots la bandera de Tirant.

(*TB*, 644) [13]

—Ab paraules suaus assajaré si de tan deslimitat desig me pogués retraure, però puix veig ja lo foc encès de mon lleal voler, lo qual porte a Tirant, resestint més aumenta, puixa ab novella esperança restaurar ma vida. E per satisfer al gran voler que tinc en les armes, faç vot a Déu e a aquella gentil dama de qui só catiu de portar senyal en la barba, ni menjar carn, ni assegut, fins a tant la bandera del Gran Soldà, dins batalla campal, haja presa, ço és, la bandera vermella on és pintada l'hòstia e lo càlzer, e ab açò sia mon vot delliure.

(*TB*, 644-45) [14]

—No dubte de soferir lo mal perillós per tan esdevenidor delit, lo qual, no vençut ne jamés sobrat, moltes voltes he sofertes les grans forces dels turcs per aument de ma honor, per lo gran desig que tinc de servir a mon senyor Tirant, del qual só criat; e per exercitar la mia persona e per mills obtenir la gràcia de la mia bella dama qui tant val, sens mijà de la qual a mi seria molt difícil pogués desijar major bé que la sua amor, per què he proposat de fer tal vot com oireu: de no menjar pa ni sal, e lo que menjaré serà tostemps agenollat, e de no dormir en llit, fins a tant que jo haja mort ab les mies pròpies

---

[13] "Since you have abandoned the virtue of gentility and because as a prisoner your crime is a civil one, you do not deserve to be punished for it, for you have merely complied with the commands given to you by others. And so for that reason I solemnly vow before God and all the saints never to return to my homeland until I have been in pitched battle with forty thousand or more Moors and have emerged triumphant either in the role of Christian commander in my own right or by fighting under Tirant's banner."

[14] "With soft words I will try, if I can, to avoid expressing such a limitless desire, but already I can see the fire of my loyal affection for Tirant, and the more I resist it, the more it grows; would that this fire could restore my life with new hope. And in order to satisfy my great affection for bearing arms, I take a vow to God and that gracious lady whom I serve as a prisoner to let my beard grow as a sign, to abstain from meat, and never to sit down until I have captured the Great Sultan's flag in pitched battle, that is to say, the red banner on which are painted the host and the chalice, thereby freeing me from this vow."

> mans trenta moros sens ajuda de negú, e en tal cas mon vot sia complit.
>
> (TB, 645) [15]

The Viscount makes his vow with a foot planted on the poor Moor's body; Diafebus and Hipòlit pronounce theirs with a foot pressed against the luckless slave's head and neck, respectively. The effect of this grotesque mistreatment of the Moor is at the same time comic (for Tirant and the reader) and menacing (for the Sultan's ambassadors who witness this strange scene and conclude that the Captain and his lieutenants are quite mad). Tirant caps his performance by removing the jewels from his shoe and stocking and presenting them to the bewildered slave, who is also given the Captain's outfit — except for the stocking and the shoe — and granted his freedom. Although the episode ends happily for almost all those involved, the reader cannot escape the conclusion that the chivalric vow, once so solemn an utterance, is now being reduced to the level of practical jokes.

The downward spiral continues during Tirant's adventures in North Africa, where he unwittingly vows to perform acts of violence against a monarch whom he believes to be an intruder, only to learn subsequently that the antagonist's cause is a just one that he (Tirant) would ordinarily wish to support. The Christian commander's rashness here is somewhat excusable in light of the circumstances surrounding his vow and his ingenuousness regarding the political situation among the Moorish rulers along the Barbary Coast; nonetheless, Tirant is guilty on this occasion of allowing his emotions to sway his judgment and of making an ill-advised commitment on that basis.

---

[15] "I am prepared to suffer any hazardous evil for the sake of such a future reward for my spirit, which neither timid nor bold, so often has suffered at the hands of the Turkish forces so that I may add to my honor, and also because I wish to serve my lord Tirant, who is my master. And so to train myself and to obtain more easily the blessing of my beautiful lady who is most worthy and without whose mediation it would be difficult for me to desire any greater good than her love, I have proposed to take the following vow: to eat neither bread nor salt, to take all my meals in a kneeling position, and to refrain from sleeping in a bed until I have slain thirty Moors with my own hands without anyone else's aid; and if I should do all this, my vow will then be fulfilled."

Shipwrecked on the North African coast (Ch. 299), Tirant eventually becomes the prisoner of the Supreme Commander *(Cabdillo sobre los cabdillos)* of the King of Tlemcen's forces. As a reward for the Christian's successful efforts to rescue the king from the clutches of his enemy, Escariano of Ethiopia, the grateful monarch grants Tirant his freedom. Under these circumstances, and given the totally negative picture that has been painted for him about the figure of Escariano, Tirant feels moved to swear allegiance to Tlemcen and promises as a faithful Christian ("a fe de crestià") not to leave the king's service until he has a) killed Escariano, b) captured him, or c) forced him to withdraw his invading force from Tlemcen's soil (Ch. 307). A short time thereafter (Ch. 309) Tirant comes face-to-face with the dreaded Ethiopian and finds, much to his amazement, a great deal to admire about the man. From Escariano's account of the events that have led to the war between Ethiopia and Tlemcen it becomes obvious to Tirant that he may have been working under a misconception when he made his vow to King Tlemcen, and he begins to question the wisdom of that action. As fate would have it, subsequent events permit the disillusioned Christian warrior to fulfill his vow by capturing Escariano at the castle of Mount Tuber (Ch. 318); in combination with the death of the King of Tlemcen earlier (Ch. 310), this event ultimately paves the way for the establishment of a firm friendship between Tirant and the Ethiopian warrior-king. In a relatively brief period of time Escariano becomes the Christian commander's brother-in-arms and his most dependable and trustworthy ally; the irony of this situation does not escape Tirant's notice.

A similarly ironic consequence can be observed in a parallel episode during the siege of Mount Tuber (Ch. 312). Tirant seeks at this point to enlist the aid of a Christian slave (named simply the Albanese) in order to defeat the forces of Escariano who are trapped within the fortress. The Captain once more allows his emotions to cloud his judgment and the result is another impetuous and ill-advised promise that he will eventually regret. The tears and lamentations of the Albanese about being beaten with sticks by his Moorish masters and having to suffer other kinds of cruel abuse arouse in Tirant strong feelings of compassion for his fellow

Christian. Consequently, he once more swears, this time as a knight ("a fe de cavaller"), to refrain from taking solid food until he has secured the Albanese's freedom. Tirant eventually makes good his promise, but not without serious misgivings, for the Albanese proves to be an excessively cruel, sly, and generally ignoble comrade. Even so, Tirant carries out his promise as soon as the city is captured. He grants the Albanese his freedom, rewards him handsomely for his efforts, but then summarily dismisses him from his service and sends him back to Albania.

Tirant's tendency toward impulsiveness in making vows is in evidence one more time during the defense of the city of Tlemcen against a federation of Moorish forces who are attempting to re-conquer it from its newly Christianized rulers, Queen Maragdina and her husband Escariano. In Ch. 340 a truce is declared between the Moors and the Christian defenders, and Tirant naively trusts the enemy to honor the agreement while he sends a small squad to escort back to Tlemcen his friend and ally the Marquis of Luçana, recently arrived in Tunis. As one might expect, the treacherous King of Africa sends a force of ten thousand soldiers to ambush the Christians as they approach the city. When the naive Christian leader learns of the treachery that has been perpetrated by his Moslem adversary, he curses himself for being so ingenuous, for not following a more reasonable and prudent course of action, for allowing his enemy to deceive him, and principally for accepting a temporary truce instead of pushing for a total victory. Noting that the Moors have also technically violated the truce by receiving reinforcements — both infantry and cavalry — during the cease-fire, Tirant issues still another solemn promise that may bring unexpected and unwanted consequences. He swears that for as long as he remains in Africa he will refuse to grant any temporary cease-fire to the enemy, and if such a truce should be granted by one of his colleagues without his knowledge, he will immediately and unilaterally withdraw from the campaign (Ch. 341).

The potentially disastrous consequences of the Captain's vow are readily apparent to Escariano, who immediately begs Tirant to reconsider. For the first and only time in the novel, the Christian commander agrees to retract a precipitously uttered ultimatum. Tirant's new-found moderation and self-control are displayed again shortly thereafter in Ch. 349, when the Moors petition once more for a temporary halt in the fighting. Tirant, true to his word, refuses to accede to their request, but when four of his Christian allies consent to the truce, he graciously accepts their decision and issues no threat to abandon the cause. On still another occasion, he generously makes a ten-for-one restitution to the Moors for a technical violation committed by his troops, despite the fact that he personally never swore to abide by the agreement in question.

After this point Tirant is wise enough to abandon the custom of making such solemn utterances; there is, however, one final example of a careless and injudiciously pronunced chivalric vow. It comes from the mouth of Tirant's cousin, Lord Agramunt, who makes a foolish promise at the gates of the city Montàgata (Ch. 349). Once again the provocation comes from the treachery of the Moors who first offer to surrender the city to Agramunt, then renege on the agreement. Agramunt is subsequently wounded by a small arrow that pierces his cheek, which provokes him to offer a solemn vow to God and all the Apostles that he will not leave until the city has been captured and all the inhabitants — men and women, old people and small children — have passed under his sword. Agramunt is now obliged to learn the same lesson that Tirant did earlier about impetuous outbursts. By Ch. 372 Agramunt's anger has abated and he no longer thirsts for vengeance and the wholesale slaughter of the populace. But how can he avoid such an unpleasant consequence without breaking his solemn vow? Plaerdemavida saves the day by presenting an ingenious plan that will obviate both bloodshed and embarrassment: they will have the Montagatans pass in single file under Agramunt's sword as it is held aloft jointly by him and Tirant — in short, a *literal* application of the statement that fulfills the letter, if not the spirit of the vow. Although the resolution of Agramunt's dilemma may seem uncomfortably flip and light-hearted, its significance within the novel can easily be discovered by comparing it with the sensible alternative selected earlier by Tirant in Ch. 343. The absurd extreme to which Agramunt must go in order to satisfy, technically, his intemperate vow is intended by Martorell to appear ridiculous in comparison with Tirant's simpler and far more reasonable retraction.

Let us now summarize the lessons Tirant absorbs in the course of his sojourn on the North African coast:

1. Moors cannot be trusted under any circumstances;
2. a wise warrior must avoid over-reacting to adversity or provocation;
3. vows should not be made in anger or under the influence of any emotional stress;
4. rashly formulated vows may often prove to be counter-productive, or at least difficult and/or embarrassing to fulfill; you may be required to do some harm to a friend or an innocent party;
5. impetuous vows may eventually have to be retracted, which is embarrassing, but not nearly as awkward as some of the ridiculous lengths to which you may be obliged to go in order to avoid such a retraction.

Martorell wants the reader to compare the exemplary action of Tirant in Ch. 341 with the ridiculous one of Agramunt in Chs. 349-72; the key element in these parallel episodes is Tirant's newly acquired patience and prudence. The intemperate vow Tirant utters in Ch. 341 is wisely recanted only moments later (Ch. 343). The Christian leader learns to choose the patient course of action: he allows the beaten Moorish troops to withdraw in peace, and although he personally refuses to grant them another truce, he agrees to abide by a subsequent cease-fire agreed to by his allies. When he learns of Agramunt's hasty threat to annihilate the population of Montàgata (Ch. 349), Tirant begs God to grant him the patience to deal with his impulsive subordinate and censures Agramunt for his shameful treatment of a certain outspoken Moorish woman — who turns out to be Plaerdemavida (Ch. 364). A short time later Martorell's hero is able to find it in his heart to forgive his quick-tempered cousin and compassionately welcomes him back into his good graces (Ch. 367). Tirant even agrees to play a role in the strange plan devised by Plaerdemavida to enable Agramunt to fulfill his reckless vow (Ch. 372).

Let us pause now to consider precisely how far away from its original purpose the chivalric vow has envolved since its introduction in the opening chapters of the book. The vows of Varoic (Ch. 20) and Quinto lo Superior (Ch. 33) are made only in response to strong provocation and are designed to provide an immediate and significant response to that provocation. But with the encounter of Tirant and Ricard (Chs. 113-14) we observe the onset of trivialization that progressively undermines the value of the chivalric vow. In Chs. 126 and 189 we note a new and different kind of debasement of the solemn oath with the addition of an unspoken or secret purpose behind each elaborate promise. We are now faced with two distinct levels of meaning — the "real" vs. the "official" one — not to mention a measure of hypocrisy. At Chs. 203-06 the genre has degenerated into almost total frivolousness and self-parody; the chivalric vow, which ought to be reserved for serious matters and solemn occasions, has become instead a tool for practical jokes among members of the military establishment.

During Tirant's sojourn among the Moors on the Barbary Coast he experiences the ultimate disillusionment that comes with the knowledge that the vows he has uttered there have often been based on faulty information, ignorance and self-deception. His early encounters with Escariano (Ch. 307) and the Albanese (Ch. 312) occasion him to make vows that bring unplanned, unwanted or embarrassing consequences. The final step in Tirant's liberation from the stranglehold of this outmoded custom occurs in Ch. 341 when he is confronted with his own rashness in reacting — or rather, over-reacting — to what has really been only a minor provocation. He soon realizes his error and the potentially disastrous consequences of his promise to withdraw from the conflict; with that he retracts his threat. After this point Tirant's behavior is characterized by a new degree of patience and forbearance in dealing with his adversaries and comrades; the hero's righteousness in this final stage is highlighted by the contrast Martorell offers between Tirant's model comportment and that of the impulsive Agramunt who utters an imprudent vow in Ch. 349 and later finds himself resorting to absurdly extreme measures to fulfill it (Ch. 372).

Having completed at this point his history of the birth, the development, and finally the inevitable degeneration and perversion of the chivalric vow, Martorell allows it to pass silently out of his story during the final hundred-or-so chapters. But in retrospect we can see that his unique historical and evolutionary treatment of one of the more elegant and solemn chivalric traditions is one of the most interesting and significant — if heretofore unappreciated — elements of Martorell's novel.

* * *

B) Formal Challenges, Written and Oral

Given the author's historically documented penchant for issuing scathing formal challenges for the purpose of settling personal, family and business disputes on the field of battle, one might reasonably expect to find substantial excerpts — perhaps even entire paragraphs — from his personal files within *TB*. [16] Precisely the opposite is true: rare are the phrases from Martorell's own correspondence that find their way into his novel. The few cases in which sections of an actual *lletra de batalla* actually do appear in *TB* are not from the author's own letters, but rather from documents exchanged by certain contemporaries of his. Riquer's 1974 Castilian edition of *TB* footnotes these careful borrowings as they occur, as I shall also do in the course of my discussion below. The plagiarized portions uncovered to date are traceable to MS. 7811 of the Biblioteca Nacional in Madrid, which appears to be a sixteenth-century copy of a volume of fifteenth-century documents, including the Guillem de Varoic fragment that was used as the foundation for Chs. 1-28 of *TB,* plus a series of actual letters of challenge exchanged by various noblemen of the 1400s, several of them written by or to Joanot Martorell. Whether Martorell actually possessed or had easy access to the original volume is a matter of speculation; however, because so much of the material therein touches upon the same themes as those treated in *TB,* it is probable that at least a portion of the collected documents passed through Martorell's hands at some point. As

---

[16] Martorell's participation in such activities is well documented — with the complete text of his letters provided — by Martín de Riquer and Mario Vargas Llosa in *El combate imaginario: Las cartas de batalla de Joanot Martorell* (Barcelona: Seix-Barral, 1972).

we did with the subject of the chivalric vow, let us now examine in chronological order the oral and written challenges to duel that appear in the course of Martorell's novel; at the same time we will observe the unique historical and evolutionary approach author Martorell adopts toward still another of chivalry's most cherished traditions.

The phenomenon of the personal challenge makes its initial appearance in Ch. 13, during the Varoic interlude, when the King of England receives the following epistle from Abraim (Abraham), the Moorish King of Grand Canary, whose forces have just invaded the island:

> *A tu, rei cristià, qui senyorejaves l'illa d'Anglaterra, dic jo, Abraïm, rei e senyor de la Gran Canària, que si tu vols que aquesta guerra fine entre tu e mi e cesse la mortaldat entre lo teu poble e lo meu, si bé jo en esta illa d'Anglaterra sia més poderós que tu no est, així de viles com de castells com de gent e esforç de cavalleria, car si lo gran Déu t'ha donada victòria sobre la mia gent, jo e los meus l'havem haguda de tu e de tots los teus moltes vegades dins la tua pròpria terra, emperò si tu volràs que no hi haja més escampament de sang, entrem en camp clos rei per rei, sots tals pactes e convinences: que si jo venç a tu, tendràs tota Anglaterra sota la mia potestat e senyoria, e em faràs de traüt dos-cents mília nobles cascun any, e en la festa del gran Sant Joan vestiràs unes robes mies, les quals jo et trametré, e aquell dia t'hages a trobar en l'una d'aquestes quatre ciutats, ço és, en la ciutat de Londres, o de Conturberi, o de Salasberi, o en esta ciutat de Varoic per ço com ací só estat desconfit. E ací vull que es faça la primera festa, e açò serà en memòria e recordació de la victòria que jo hauré haguda de tu; e si fortuna administra que tu sies vencedor, jo me'n tornaré en la mia pròpria terra e tu restaràs ab pau en la tua, e ab gran repòs e tranquilitat tu e tots los teus, e més te restituiré totes les viles e castells que ab la mia pròpria mà victoriosa he guanyat e conquest.*
>
> *Aquestes paraules no són per vanaglòria ne per menysprear la corona real, mas per ço com Déu és gran e darà a cascú la part que per sos mèrits serà mereixedor.*
>
> (*TB*, 136) [17]

---

[17] "I, Abraham, Lord and King of Grand Canary, wish to inform you, Christian king who used to rule over the island of England, that if you

As we can easily note, the preamble is very short and contains no insult of any kind. The Moorish king simply asserts the superiority of his forces over those of the English defenders — despite a recent English victory, it should be added — and proposes a plan that will put a quick end to the bloodshed: single combat between the respective sovereigns, winner take all. His challenge is both brief and general, offering very little in the way of specifics. There is no mention of any need for one of the participants to forfeit his life; simple victory will suffice. Furthermore, the letter is completely silent with regard to the conditions of the proposed combat; the challenger is more concerned with the eventual outcome of the battle than with the nuts-and-bolts details of how they will do battle. If the Moor is victorious, all of England will fall under his power and an annual tribute of 200,000 coins per year will be paid; furthermore, the English king must agree to dress in the robes of his Moorish sovereign each St. John's Day in one of four designated cities: London, Canterbury, Salisbury or Warwick. On the other hand, if the English monarch should triumph, the Moor will immediately return to his homeland and

---

desire to put an end to this war between you and me, and if you wish to stop the slaughter between your people and mine, even though I am more powerful on this island of England than you are with regard to castles and towns under my rule, not to mention in infantry and cavalry, and since Almighty God has seen fit to make you victorious this time over my troops, similarly, my forces and I have defeated you and your armies many times in the past right here in your country; but if you wish to stop this bloodshed, let us enter a closed field together, king against king, facing each other in battle under the following pact and agreement: that if I defeat you, the whole of England will come under my authority as part of my realm and you will surrender to me in tribute the sum of 200,000 coins each year, and on the feast of St. John you will don my clothing, which I will personally send to you, and on that feast I shall be able to find you in one of these four cities, namely London, Canterbury, Salisbury, or in this city, Warwick, where I have been defeated. And I declare that the first celebration shall be held here in memory of my victory over you; but if fate should dictate that you be the victor, I will return to my homeland and you will be left in peace in yours, and you and your people will enjoy peace and tranquillity; and furthermore, I shall return to you all the cities and castles that have been captured from you by my triumphant hand.

"These words are not written out of vainglory nor with any intention of slighting your royal crown, but rather because God, since He is great, will give each of us exactly what he deserves according to his own merit."

leave the island in peace; all captured cities will be restored to English rule as well.

The closing paragraph is remarkable for its humility insofar as the Moorish challenger disclaims any vainglory in bringing forth his proposal, as well as any offense to the royal crown of England that may be inferred; his final words express his faith in a just God who will ordain the winner according to the merits of the respective combatants. The need to beware of treachery or trickery is at no time expressed; the dominant tone of the letter is one of complete trust in the will of the Supreme Being. And as a final confirmation of the informal nature of the document, there is no signature or seal to authenticate it; it is intended to be no more than a practical and spontaneous agreement between two honorable men — a memorandum of sorts — for the purpose of putting an end to the senseless bloodshed of the war that they are waging.

Because this document is the prototype for the several other letters and oral challenges that will ultimately appear in the course of Martorell's book, and because it will be useful to note the gradual evolution of the genre away from its original simple format, the outstanding characteristics of this initial *lletra de batalla* bear repeating:

1. extreme cordiality: the lack of any insulting tone;
2. a humanitarian — but also practical — goal: to avoid needless bloodshed;
3. vagueness with regard to the conditions of battle; deliberate sketchiness and lack of specifics concerning armor, weapons, etc.;
4. the absence of any reference to the death of either combatant; victory is not contingent upon slaying one's adversary; in fact, it is assumed from the terms of the agreement (see below) that the loser will survive the experience so that he may pay homage to the victor on future occasions;
5. considerable concern for the consequences of the event; the document spells out clearly and in great detail (vs. § 3 and 4 above) the penalties and forms of obeisance the vanquished warrior will pay to the victor in future years;
6. humility in the final paragraph; no intention to deprecate the worthiness of either the adversary or his kingdom;

7. complete trust in the Divine Will to bring this matter to a swift and just conclusion;

8. not the slightest hint of concern about treachery or deceitfulness on the part of the enemy; the honorability of one's adversary is *assumed;*

9. lack of a formal, legalistic close: no signature, no seal, no date or time or place mentioned; no measures taken (or assumed to be needed) to assure the authenticity of the document.

As I shall show in the next few pages, the frankness and simplicity of this opening challenge and its inherent assumption of chivalric honorability in the opponent gradually give way to a subversive and highly legalistic approach. We will observe that subsequent letters of challenge become evermore vituperous and personally insulting in tone; the intent of these personal confrontations in time grows less and less humanitarian — not to mention decreasingly sensible and practical — as the tone waxes more and more egotistical. Interest in the result of the combat (i.e., the penalties to be imposed) is soon replaced by an intense — virtually monomaniacal — concern for the terms and conditions of the battle itself; the intended result will in all cases be the same: certain death for the conquered warrior. In future challenges all humility will be cast aside, as will any expression of faith in Divine Providence; in its place we'll find an increased reliance upon trickery and other deceitful means of gaining a strategic, tactical or technical advantage on the field of battle. Eventually it will be treachery, not honorability, that will be assumed in one's adversary; and as a consequence, the letter of challenge as a literary sub-genre will soon evolve into an elaborate, obscure and legalistic document that will require a variety of checks to assure its authenticity (e.g., notarization by means of signatures, seals, or even division of the document into two halves along a designated line, with the halves to be matched upon receipt).

The first step along these lines is taken in Ch. 62 when the Lord of Vilesermes challenges Tirant to a duel over the matter of Lady Agnès' brooch and the fact that Tirant's hands have touched the lady's bodice in the act of removing the bauble.[18] What the

---

[18] Some background information should be provided here. During the jousting tournament at the English court, at one point Tirant requested the

document lacks in length it more than atones for in hyperbole and vituperation:

> —*A tu, Tirant lo Blanc, qui est estat principi de la destrucció de la sang militar:*
> *Si lo teu ànimo esforçat gosarà mirar lo perill de les armes que entre cavallers són acostumades, armat o desarmat, a peu o a cavall, vestit o despullat, en la manera a tu més segura, concorda't ab mi ab condició que l'espasa tua e la mia ajustar se puguen a mort determenada. — Escrit de mà mia e segellat ab lo segell secret de mes armes:* LO SENYOR DE LES VILESERMES.
>
> (*TB*, 218) [19]

In the preamble Vilesermes avoids mentioning the real cause of his resentment (Agnès' trinket and Tirant's hands upon her breast) while conjuring up instead the notion that Tirant has some-

---

right to wear Agnès' colors into combat as her champion — a perfectly legitimate and proper request according to the chivalric tradition. Tirant also asked to be allowed to wear into battle a small piece of her jewelry. For her part, Agnès was quite astonished to learn of such a strange custom and declared her incredulity at such silliness in no uncertain terms:

—Ah, Santa Maria val! —dix la bella Agnès—. ¿E per una cosa tan mínima e de tan poca valor voleu entrar en camp clos a tota ultrança, no tement los perills de la mort e lo dan que seguir poria?

("In the name of Holy Mary," said the beautiful Agnès, "and for such a trifling and worthless object you would enter into a closed field to duel to the death, fearing neither the danger of death nor the injury that you might suffer?")

Nonetheless, she invites him to remove the desired bauble from the bodice of her dress. Vilesermes, a long-time and secret admirer of Agnès who witnesses Tirant's action here, later accuses Martorell's hero of excessive boldness in touching her breasts and demands that the brooch be given to him instead. When Tirant refuses, the angry suitor attempts to seize the trinket by force, to which Tirant responds by drawing his dagger. In the ensuing scuffle, we are told, a dozen nobles are slain. Three days later Vilesermes delivers his *lletra de batalla* to Tirant.

[19] "To you, Tirant lo Blanch, who have initiated the destruction of the warrior caste and the bloodlines thereof:

"If your brave spirit dares to face the peril of armed combat, as is customary among knights, then enter into an agreement with me to fight with or without armor, on foot or on horseback, dressed or completely naked, in whatever form you feel is safer for you, with the condition that your sword and mine shall clash until one of us lies dead.

"This is written by my own hand stamped with the secret seal of my coat of arms:

The Lord of Vilesermes"

how initiated the downfall and destruction of the military orders — a charge that is clearly misleading, needlessly insulting, and completely *wrong*. The very personal attack upon his rival's character continues within the actual proposal as Vilesermes questions Tirant's courage and willingness to meet him in hand-to-hand combat. When he finally gets down to specifics, Vilesermes concentrates on the details of *how* the duel shall be conducted rather than on what will be the consequences of one or the other's victory. He offers Tirant three choices as to the mode of combat: with or without armor, on foot or on horseback, dressed vs. naked. These options, offered as they are by the challenger to the defender, represent a significant alteration in the dueling procedure. Other novelties introduced in Vilesermes' letter are his insistence that swords — or a weapon of a similar fashion — be used and his demand that it be a duel to the death ("a mort determenada"). Finally, we should note the absence of any conciliatory closing statement such as the one the Moorish king offered to the English monarch in the previous example; in its place we find Vilesermes' signature and a seal bearing his coat of arms, which are supposed to certify that his challenge is genuine and duly offered within the rules of the chivalric code.

Undaunted but nonetheless confused and uncertain about the formalities that must be observed in such matters, Tirant seeks out the king's chief arbiter *(rei d'armes)*, an old man named Jerusalem, for advice as to how he should proceed. The old judge assures the young knight that he is blameless in the affair and will not be punished or chastized in any manner for his actions; only the initiator of the challenge, in this case Vilesermes, faces that risk. Furthermore, Jerusalem agrees to assist Tirant in selecting a neutral party to serve as judge.

The next issue — and Martorell carefully takes the reader through the formal procedure step by step — is the matter of choosing weapons. As the defending party, Tirant would ordinarily have the right to select the arms of his preference, but he renounces that privilege. He submits instead to Jerusalem a blank letter, signed and sealed in imitation of Vilesermes' earlier example, to be delivered to the challenger; the old judge is instructed to arrange the terms of battle to suit Vilesermes' wishes and to his advantage (Ch. 64).

The challenger opts for a duel on foot, with each combatant wearing only a long, short-sleeve linen nightshirt and carrying nothing more than a paper shield for defense; they will also wear a garland of flowers as a head covering, and fight with double-edged Genoese swords equipped with eighteen-inch blades. [20] The choice of such formidable weaponry, especially when combined with little or no protective covering, seems practically suicidal — which it *will be* for Vilesermes. The battle ends with the brave challenger lying lifeless on the damp earth, beside a critically wounded and profusely bleeding Tirant only a few yards away. It is left to the unlucky Agnès to provide the final comment on this most unfortunate and tragic incident (Ch. 67). Her first remark is addressed to Tirant:

>   —¡Ai trista de mi, Tirant! ¡I tan mal fermall fon aquell que jo us doní! Mal dia, mala hora e mal signe fon aquell quan jo el fiu fer e pijor com lo us doní. E si sabés que tal cas se n'hagués a seguir, no el vos volguera haver donat per cosa en lo món, emperò la ventura cascú la's procura, e jo, trista de mi, reste adolorida de la gran desaventura de vosaltres, car jo puc ésser dit causa de tot aquest mal.
>
>   (*TB*, 231) [21]

Then, placing the head of Vilesermes in her lap, she directs the following tender words to his departed spirit:

>   —Veu's ací amor e dolor. Aquest senyor de les Vilesermes que ací jau tenia de son patrimoni trenta-set castells, e en aquells ciutats e viles forts e circuïdes de moltes torres

---

[20] These details are given in a note by Riquer (*Tirante el Blanco*, I, 184-85). He points out that this peculiar kind of duel, which some critics originally thought to be presented in a strictly humorous vein, is actually historically accurate and verifiable by documentary evidence.

[21] "Oh, woe is me, Tirant. What an evil trinket I gave you. It was a bad day, a bad hour, and a bad sign when I had it made, and an even worse one when I gave it to you. If I had known that this would happen as a result, I wouldn't have presented it to you for anything in the world. But everyone carries his own fate with him and, poor unlucky me, I am left disconsolate by your great misfortune, for I may well be called the cause of this evil."

> e de bell mur; e tenia una ciutat entre les altres, que es nomena Ermes, e un fortíssim castell qui es nomena Viles, e per ço era intitulat lo senyor de les Vilesermes: home de gran riquesa, e molt valentíssim cavaller, que valia tant com negun altre cavaller pogués valer; e confiant del seu esforçat ànimo, podeu veure lo pobre de cavaller en què és vengut: que set anys ha volguts perdre per amar-me, e a la fi aquest és lo premi que n'ha hagut. E ha fetes de singulars cavalleries per amor mia desijant haver-me en sa senyoria per lícit matrimoni, ço que jamés haguera aconseguit per jo ésser de major auctoritat de llinatge e de béns de fortuna. Jamés volguí adherir en cosa que fos en plaer e contentació sua: e ara lo pobre de cavaller és mort per zels, per sa gran desaventura.
>
> (*TB*, 231) [22]

Although at first glance this might seem to be the most opportune moment to banish the matter of dueling from his novel, Martorell is compelled by his artistic goal to provide additional cases that will demonstrate the development of more modern and more sophisticated letters of challenge and forms of hand-to-hand combat. We have only to wait for Tirant's wounds to heal — with a small pause to allow for a tooth-to-tooth encounter with a fierce mastiff in Ch. 68 — to find him again faced with a totally new series of challenges.

Immediately following the battle with the ferocious canine, Martorell presents the curious case of four noblemen from central Europe — the Kings of Friesland and Poland and the Dukes of

---

[22] "Here we have both love and sorrow. This Lord Vilesermes who lies here was the lord of thirty-seven castles and within them fortified cities and towns surrounded by many towers and beautiful walls. And among these he had a city called Ermes and a very strong castle named Viles, and for this reason he was referred to as the Lord of Viles-Ermes. He was a man of great wealth and a most valiant knight who was worthier than any other knight could ever be. Observe now what his reliance upon his bold spirit has gained this poor unfortunate warrior: he has gladly sacrificed seven years of his life wooing me, and this is the reward he has earned. He has performed remarkable chivalric deeds to show his love for me, wanting in return only to be able to take me as his lawfully wedded wife, but this was something that he never would have achieved because of my superior bloodlines and family wealth. I would never acquiesce to his desires or consent to anything that would have given him pleasure or satisfaction. And now the poor knight is dead from his own jealousy, which is his very great misfortune."

Burgundy and Bavaria, to be precise — who appear suddenly and unannounced at the English court and offer a series of unusual challenges to the knights gathered there. The mysterious and suspenseful nature of their arrival is heightened further by their refusal to utter a sound and the unique manner in which the four different challenges are delivered: the documents are borne in the mouths of four trained lions. Each challenge demands a different mode of combat, but Tirant is equal to the task and defeats each challenger at his own special and preferred style of battle.

The first two letters are preliminary in nature, outlining the noble lineage of the four challengers and how they decided to present themselves for battle in England; they are of little or no interest here. The *third* parchment, however (Ch. 71a), specifies not only the terms and conditions under which the first three battles shall be fought, but even the manner in which each challenge should be answered:

> *Qualsevulla cavaller o cavallers que armes a tota ultrança ab nosaltres fer volrà, vinga al nostre alleujament e trobarà allà per divisa una gàbia de nau posada sobre un arbre qui no té fruit ni fulla ni flor, que ha nom Seques amors. Entorn de la gàbia trobaran quatre escuts tots pintats d'oriflama, e cascun escut té son nom: lo u se nomena Valor, l'altre Amor, l'altre Honor e lo quart se nomena Menys valer.*
>
> (TB, 244) [23]

There is a further amplification in a subsequent cedula (Ch. 71b):

> *Qualsevulla cavaller o cavallers qui vendran per tocar aquests escuts, hagen a portar un escut ab les armes pintades d'aquell cavaller qui volrà fer les armes; e aquell escut no puga portar sinó dona o donzella o rei d'armes, heraut*

---

[23] "Any knight or knights wishing to enter into mortal combat with us should present himself at our quarters; there he will find our emblem: a circular platform taken from a ship's mast and mounted on a tree that bears neither fruit, leaves, nor flowers, and is called Dry Love. Around the platform they will find four shields painted in flaming red and golden yellow, each one bearing a dfferent name. One is called Courage or Valor, another Love, another Honor, and the fourth one Scorn or Contempt."

> *o porsavant; e ab aquell escut hagen a tocar en l'escut de la gàbia segons les armes que volrà fer, e lleixar aquell escut al costat de l'altre.*
>
> (TB, 246) [24]

With regard to the terms of the duel, three distinct and increasingly dangerous modes of combat are proposed, each with different specifications as to the weapons to be used, the size and weight of instruments and armor, etc. He who touches the shield marked *Amor* must accept the relatively simple conditions set down in the following paragraph:

> *E lo cavaller qui tocarà l'escut qui es nomena Amor s'ha a combatre a cavall ab tela, ab arnès d'una dobladura, e hagen a córrer tant e tan llongament fins que l'u o l'altre sia mort o vençut, en esta manera: que si perd peça d'arnès, qualsevulla que sia, o tireta alguna se rompés, no la puguen tornar adobar, ans així tinga d'anar e complir les armes. Los arnesos sien sens falsa maestria, sinó tals com són acostumades de portar en guerra guerrejada.*
>
> (TB, 244) [25]

The battle will be fought on horseback wearing reinforced armor; the combatants will charge from either side of a divider until one of them falls. All weapons and protective armor must be standard issue, with no special or deceptive features; no replacement will be allowed for any broken or lost piece of equipment.

---

[24] "Any knight or knights who will come to touch these shields must in turn carry a shield decorated with his own heraldic arms. And that shield can be carried only by a lady, a maiden, an official arbiter of jousts, or a crier. And with that shield they must touch the shield on the platform of the one against whom they wish to do battle, and then they must leave their shield beside the other one."

[25] "And the knight who will touch the shield marked Love must fight on horseback on a field divided by a partition, wearing a double coat of armor; the combatants must continue to charge at each other until one of them dies or is clearly defeated. And the battle shall take place according to the following rules: if any piece of a man's armor should be lost or broken, he cannot repair or replace it, but must instead continue to fight in that condition; the equipment must be of the same type normally used in war, without any additional special features of a false or devious nature."

The conditions for the challenge to the shield marked *Honor* are not only more elaborate, but also slightly different on several points:

> *Qui tocarà l'escut que es nomena Honor, ha de fer les armes sens tela, l'arnès sens guarda neguna ni tarja ni escut, ne vairescut, i la llança o llances sien de desset palms, sens roda ni altra maestria e ferros esmolats; e si perd llança o la romp, ne puga haver tantes com li plaurà fins a tant que mort o vençut sia.*
>
> (TB, 244-45) [26]

Although it is not stated in so many words, this duel will also be fought on horseback, but without a divider or reinforced armor. Furthermore, neither a shield nor a smaller buckler will be allowed. Very long lances (seventeen palms) will be used, their edges finely honed, but with no additional metal attached. In the event that a warrior should lose or break his lance, a replacement *will* be permitted.

The third shield *(Valor)* contains a challenge even more sophisticated and dangerous than the previous two:

> *Qui tocarà l'escut de Valor haja a fer les armes a cavall ab sella acerada e testera, ab estreps deslligats, ab plates de vint lliures enjús, una llança sola de llargària de tretze palms ab lo ferre e ab tot, la punt de diamà, la gruixa cascú tal com li plàcia; espasa de quatre palms de llargària, una copagorja cascú a sa voluntat, una atxa d'una mà poca, al cap una celada ab bavera, per ço que la batalla pus prestament prenga la fi que desijam. E si l'atxa dessús dita sortia de la mà, la puga cobrar tantes voltes com porà, mas que altri no la hi puixa donar, sinó que ell mateix haja a cobrar-la, si pot.*
>
> (TB, 245) [27]

---

[26] "The one who will touch the shield called Honor must fight [on horseback] without a divider or barrier, with a single unreinforced coat of armor, without either a large shield or a buckler; and the lances used shall measure seventeen palms in length and be without a round shield or any other metal or sharpened ornament; and if he loses or breaks his lance, he may replace it as often as necessary until he dies or is defeated."

[27] "The one who touches the Courage shield must fight on horseback with a steel-reinforced saddle and a head ornament for his steed, with loose stirrups, carrying twenty pounds of chest and back armor, a single

The horses will carry steel saddles and a *testera,* a crown piece for its harness; the stirrups will be loose, which is more dangerous than having them tied down (Riquer note, *Tirante el Blanco,* I, 219). Additional specifications include twenty-pound plates of armor for the chest and back of each warrior; a single, regulation-size (thirteen palms) lance per man, of any desired thickness, but with a tournament point (diamond-shaped with three or four sharp tips) rather than a single-pointed head that is normally used only in wartime because of the latter's tremendous potential for penetrating an opponent's shield and/or armor; a regular (four-palms in length) sword; one dagger of whatever design each may choose; a small mace that can be wielded with one hand; and a helmet that covers both the head and the face. A final stipulation is that should a combatant lose his axe, he may retrieve it — but no one may assist him or fetch it for him.

The final duel, which is so different and so dangerous that it is proposed on a fourth parchment and described in a separate chapter (71b), is the one which is given the most complete treatment by author Martorell. Predictably enough, the final challenge is the wordiest and most complicated of the four:

> *Lo cavaller qui tocarà l'escut de Menys valer ha de fer les armes a peu ab quatre bastons, ço és a saber, llança, daga, espasa e atxa de dues mans. La llança, qui la volrà portar emplomada ho puga ben fer, e si millor li parrà espasa de git, que sia sa voluntat de portar-la, e s'hagen a combatre tant e tan llongament fins que l'u dels dos reste mort o vençut l'altre. E si resta sa e sens lesió de sa persona, que s'haja a posar en poder d'aquella dama que el vencedor volrà e que ella puga fer d'ell a sa voluntat.*

---

lance measuring thirteen palms in length (including all metal accessories), and with a diamond-shaped tip that is normally used in jousting tournaments; the lance may be of any thickness desired. The swords used shall be four palms in length; the one dagger allowed may be of whatever design the individual chooses; each man may wield a small one-hand axe and wear a helmet with a beaver to protect his jaw; all of the above conditions are designed to allow the battle to reach its desired conclusion as quickly as possible. And if the aforementioned axe should be dropped during combat, the warrior may retrieve it as many times as he can, but no other person may hand it to him; he himself must retrieve it on his own, if he can."

> *La mort serà egual entre nosaltres, perdonant de bon cor
> e de bona voluntat a tots aquells qui ens ofendran, e
> demanam perdó als qui ofendrem.*
>
> (*TB*, 245) [28]

The challenger against the shield marked Scorn *(Menys valer)* must be prepared to fight on foot with four different weapons: the lance, the sword, the dagger and the two-handed battle-axe. Since this final battle represents a considerable escalation in the seriousness of the challenge, the armaments chosen are of a heavier and more deadly nature. A heavy-duty (i.e., weighted with lead or some other thick metal) lance is permitted, as is the use of a lightweight, javelin-like sword that can be easily hurled.[29] And in a final stipulation that approaches more closely the gallant spirit of the Moorish King of Grand Canary's challenge (Ch. 13) than the hostile tone of Vilesermes' (Ch. 62), it is declared that the battle will endure until one of the combatants is killed or declares himself vanquished; in the latter case, assuming that he is without serious injury, the defeated knight must then place himself at the disposal of the victor's lady. Death is accepted here as a possible and perfectly natural consequence, but hardly an inevitable or desirable outcome. The final sentence of the challenge makes it clear that no malice or rancor will be harbored, and that the Christian spirit of forgiveness should predominate. (The same sentiment of implied pardon is present in the first three challenges as well, although it is not specifically mentioned in their respective letters.)

---

[28] "The knight who touches the shield marked Scorn must fight on foot with four different weapons: the lance, the dagger, the sword, and the two-handed battle-axe. If he wishes to carry a leaded lance, he may; and if he prefers a light, throwable sword, he may choose one; and they shall fight as long and as hard as is necessary until one of them shall die or be defeated. And if the defeated warrior remains in good health and without bodily injury, he must place himself at the disposal of the victor's designated lady, and she may dispose of him according to her whim. Death will be the same for all of us, and we sincerely and willingly forgive all those who may offend us, while begging the forgiveness of those whom we may offend."

[29] In a footnote (*Tirante el Blanco*, I, 220, n. 8), Riquer points out that the original Catalan phrase *espasa de git*, which should have been translated as *arrojadiza* ('throwable') in Castilian, mistakenly became *espada de ginete* ('horseman's sword') in the 1511 Spanish translation.

Considered as a single entity, these four challenges represent the next logical stage in the evolution of the chivalric challenge. As opposed to the first two examples which had serious political or personal consequences — the first duel would determine the fate of all England, the second was fought to settle a personal quarrel and designed to end in the death of at least one of the adversaries — this third case is a purely sporting matter. There is absolutely no personal animosity involved, nor is any political ramification implied. Neither death nor disgrace must necessarily await the defeated party in any of the four battles. In fact, the fourth parchment takes considerable pains to address the matter of the proper penalty to be imposed on the vanquished knight who should survive the encounter.

What we observe here is the development of an elaborate procedure or ritual for what is merely a recreational activity, a peacetime exercise that has been derived from a long established battlefield tradition and may therefore have serious — even lethal — consequences. On the one hand we have a sporting event that superficially seems quite frivolous; on the other there is the recognition that this particular competition may prove to be fatal to one or more parties. For this reason, certain formal precautions and stipulations are required to maximize the chances of felicitous outcome.

As one might expect, Tirant accepts all four challenges and emerges victorious in each of the various forms of combat because of his general expertise in all the martial arts; other contributing factors include his cleverness and superb physical conditioning, which allow him to overcome whatever advantage the other warriors may have with regard to size or physical strength. Martorell's hero is even able to surmount a piece of trickery that the fourth opponent employs to provide himself with an unfair advantage in footspeed: cardboard (i.e., lightweight) leg armor covered with tin plating to resemble normal steel coverings, but without any of the usual cumbersomeness. This is the first instance of cheating we find in the novel, but the reliance upon trickery and skullduggery will begin to appear with greater frequency in subsequent battles, as I shall show.

The next challenge faced by Tirant is interesting from the standpoint of the preliminaries and attendant legal complications, but of little consequence regarding the actual combat conditions. In many ways this fourth incident in the chain, offered by a Scottish knight with the very Latin name of Vilafermosa, provides a refreshing change of pace from the familiar pattern we have observed in the three previous duels. First of all, his challenge is issued orally, not in any formal document; secondly, the entire episode is related in two separate phases, the second following the first by some ten chapters; in the third place, the terms and conditions of the battle are *not* rigidly prescribed by either party, but rather are the subject of continual negotiation; personal insults are kept to a minimum and are never allowed to provoke an escalation of ill will; and finally, there is the strangely truncated conclusion in which the action on the field of battle yields to a fine legal point as the focus of the reader's attention.

The episode begins in Ch. 74 with the arrival of Vilafermosa in London while Tirant is recuperating from the wounds he received in his battles with the four royal challengers. He addresses Tirant at the English court in the presence of the royal newlyweds and issues his challenges in the following statement:

> —Cavaller virtuós, la vostra ínclita fama resplandeix per tot lo món de molta bondat e gentilea. E jo, oint aquella, só vengut de la mia terra deixant lo servir de mon rei e senyor, aquell qui senyoreja l'Escòcia; e la causa de la mia venguda és per quant jo, departint un dia, per mos pecats, ab una senyora que té la mia ànima cativa, no em volgué admetre ma demanda ni pendre'm a mercè, sinó que ab crueltat me dix que jamés me parlaria fins a tant jo hagués combatut e vençut en camp clos a tota ultrança aquell cavaller qui tanta glòria en aquest món havia sabuda guanyar. E per ço com vós, Tirant, sou aquell a qui ma senyora me remet, vos requir per l'orde que haveu rebut de cavalleria que em vullau admetre la mia demanda a tota ultrança a cavall e ab bacinet sens careta; les altres armes vós devisau en la manera que ben vist vos sia, que puix jo he devisat l'una part, que vós deviseu l'altra, e açò us hauré a molta gràcia.
>
> (*TB*, 257) [30]

---

[30] "Virtuous knight, your illustrious fame shines brightly throughout the world with much kindness and gentility. And I, having heard so much

As we can see, he begins by explaining the circumstances that bring him to make his challenge: the refusal of his lady to accept him as a suitor until he has defeated in mortal combat the world's most celebrated knight. He then begs Tirant to accept his invitation as an obligation of his chivalric rank. Assuming that Tirant will agree to his proposal, Vilafermosa proceeds to state the only two conditions he wishes to impose for their battle: that it be fought on horseback and that the principals wear simple helmets without a beaver to protect the face. Although it should be understood from his earlier remarks that theirs should be a duel to the death, he reiterates that stipulation toward the end of his remarks. He closes by offering to Tirant the choice of whichever additional weapons he may desire for the combat.

To this point the Vilafermosa affair is hardly remarkable; however, the matter grows in intensity and interest as the two warriors begin to negotiate the terms of their anticipated confrontation. Tirant starts by dismissing the challenge as frivolous and totally unnecessary; he points out that no serious cause exists to justify a duel to the death, that this is simply something concocted to satisfy a lady's personal whim. Next he reminds Vilafermosa that the wounds from his four previous encounters have not yet healed and that the Scot would be wise to seek some other worthy opponent from among the many brave knights gathered at the English court.

Vilafermosa attempts to provoke Tirant by insinuating that the reluctant warrior is motivated by fear in refusing his request; consequently, he offers to allow Tirant to carry one extra weapon into

---

about you, have come from my homeland, taking leave of my king and lord who rules over Scotland; and the reason for my journey is that one day while I was humbly speaking with the lady who has captured my soul, she dismissed my entreaties and refused to hold me in good favor. She replied cruelly that she would not speak to me until I had fought and defeated on a closed field of battle, in a duel to the death, that knight who had won for himself the most honor and glory in this world. And since you, Tirant, are the one to whom my lady sends me, I demand by the title of knighthood that you have received that you accept my challenge to mortal combat on horseback, each man wearing a headpiece without a beaver or face guard; and you may select whatever additional arms you desire. I have already chosen one part, so you have the right to choose the remainder, for which I will be very grateful."

battle, provided that it isn't a sword (which would represent too great a disparity in arms). [31] Martorell's hero simply refuses to be provoked to anger by the Scot's insulting offer; he accepts the challenge merely to avoid the charge of cowardice but declines the invitation to carry an extra weapon or select additional armaments.

At this point Vilafermosa introduces a new element to the proceedings by obliging Tirant to swear before the king and queen and the entire court that he will accept no other challenge nor enter into combat with any other knight until he has fulfilled his commitment to the Scottish challenger. Tirant willingly gives his word on the matter, but neither he nor the reader can anticipate the ethical ramifications his assent will have a short time thereafter. Having received Tirant's assurance that the desired duel will take place during the next four months, Vilafermosa returns to Scotland to make arrangements with his queen to prepare a field of battle for the anticipated event. The episode concludes in Ch. 84 with Tirant's arrival at the Scottish court and an extremely brief encounter between the two adversaries on the lists. The entire conclusion is presented in the space of two short paragraphs totalling eight lines of print. In this brief space we learn that the queen (who incidentally serves as the official judge for the contest) notices that Vilafermosa has fraudulently altered his helmet in contravention of the terms he himself imposed upon the battle; she immediately calls a halt to the proceedings and refuses to let the duel reach its normal and expected conclusion.

This truncated ending may seem inadequate and unsettling to the casual reader, but Martorell did indeed have a reason for cutting short this promising episode. The brevity with which the matter is resolved in Scotland and the paucity of detail regarding the actual battle between the two warriors is quite *un*characteristic of Martorell's narrative technique. Furthermore, in comparison with

---

[31] Riquer points out (*Tirante el Blanco*, I, 237, n. 8) that this gesture is actually a sly insult insofar as the offer of an additional weapon was traditionally made by a veteran knight to an inferior adversary who was either of an advanced age or a virtual novice in the matter of dueling. Riquer also mentions a historical case in which author Martorell himself made such an offer to one of his antagonists (*Tirante el Blanco*, I, xx-xxi).

the earlier challenges of Vilesermes and the Four Nobles, the Scot's demand appears pointless and trifling — another departure from the very purposeful and didactic style of the author. The most logical explanation for this sudden shift in Martorell's presentation is that on this particular occasion he wanted to emphasize something other than the battle itself or the peculiar modes of combat to be employed therein. Along those lines, two moral issues immediately suggest themselves: 1) the frivolous nature of the challenge (as noted by Tirant himself in his initial reply) as well as the curious case it presents of a damsel who, in counterpoint to the earlier actions and model behavior of the very sensible Lady Agnès, actually provokes an incident and encourages two brave knights to engage in mortal combat merely to satisfy her whim; 2) the question of whether a knight's solemn promise to engage in individual combat with another member of the chivalric order may be abrogated for any reason.

Regarding this second question, it is important to bear in mind that between Vilafermosa's challenge and Tirant's acceptance (Ch. 74) and the unsatisfying conclusion (Ch. 84) Martorell intercalates the fascinating episode of Tirant's encounter with the gigantic brothers Kirieleison and Tomàs de Muntalbà (Chs. 77-84). The Muntalbà challenge constitutes a technical violation of Tirant's promise to Vilafermosa because the hero meets and defeats Tomàs in single combat (Chs. 81-82). The real issue here is Tirant's moral and ethical dilemma in having to choose between keeping a solemn pledge given in good faith to another knight and breaking it in order to respond to the vile and false accusation of treachery leveled at him by the mammoth brothers. Tirant's friend and confidant Diafebus, who narrates the entire episode to Guillem de Varoic, is apparently speaking for the author when he summarizes the extremely difficult choice faced by Tirant in this situation:

> Vejam, senyors, vosaltres cavallers entesos en honor i en les armes: Tirant, en presència del Rei e molts nobles senyors e cavallers, féu jurament solemne de no entrar en batalla ni empendre fer armes negunes fins a tant que aquesta batalla fos venguda a fi. E Tirant de tot açò fon content e així ho jurà e ho promés. Aprés vengué Kirieleison de Muntalbà e requerí'l de batalla incriminant-lo de cas de tració. ¿A qual d'aquests dos devia primer acórrer:

al jurament que fet havia, present los bons cavallers, o al cas de tració que li posaren Kirieleison e son germà? Moltes raons s'hi poden fer d'una part i d'altra: la determinació deixe als bons cavallers d'honor.

(*TB*, 280-81) [32]

It should be noted that at no time does Martorell allow any of his characters to suggest a definite solution to Tirant's dilemma or any workable compromise that would have satisfied all parties concerned. Apparently, the author went to his grave still wrestling with this thorny problem, but not without addressing it — albeit feebly — in his *magnum opus*.

Let us consider now the aforementioned challenges of Kirieleison and Tomàs de Muntalbà. The circumstances surrounding this episode are perhaps the most complicated of any challenge found in *TB*; the incident covers more than ten full chapters from start to finish (Chs. 74-84) and is related with a deliberate abundance of detail. The reason for this close attention may reside in the fact that the Muntalbà affair very closely resembles Martorell's personal experience with a certain Catalan nobleman named Gonçalbo d'Íxer (*Gonzalo de Híjar* in Castilian), who also bore the title of Comendador de Muntalbà (or Montalbán). The similarity in name between the real and fictional characters here is not unintentional, to be sure. Disagreement over the terms of a real estate transaction between Don Gonzalo and the Martorell family eventually led to an exchange of nasty epistles between the Comendador and Joanot in the year 1450. [33] The fact that their

---

[32] "Let us see now, my lords, those of you who know so much about questions of honor and arms: Tirant, in the presence of the king and many noble lords and knights, solemnly swore not to enter into any armed conflict nor engage in any duel until that matter was concluded. And Tirant was satisfied with this agreement and therefore swore to it and gave his word. Afterwards Kirieleison de Muntalbà came forth and challenged him to a duel, charging him with treachery. To which of these two obligations should he have given primary attention? To the oath he had taken in the presence of those worthy knights, or to the charge of perfidy that Kirieleison and his brother leveled at him? Many good reasons can be given to support either choice, but the final decision must be left to all good and honorable knights."

[33] For a detailed account of this real-life chivalric drama, see Riquer and Vargas Llosa, *El combate imaginario*, pp. 126-43, wherein is given the full text of each letter exchanged.

correspondence, subsequently preserved in MS. 7811 of the Biblioteca Nacional in Madrid, so closely mirrors the fictional *lletres de batalla* of *TB* is a testimonial to the historical accuracy of the portrait Martorell paints of chivalric customs in his novel. The similarities of tone and phrasing between the real and imaginary letters are most noteworthy.

Although Kirieleison's initial salvo occurs in Ch. 77, the episode actually begins a few chapters earlier when the giant first learns of the death of his sovereign, the King of Friesland, at the hands of Tirant. (The King was one of the Four Nobles defeated by Martorell's hero at the English court.) Grievously offended by the news, Don Kirieleison decides to journey to England and personally avenge his sovereign's death by taking the life of the offender (Ch. 74). The process of formal denunciation begins in Ch. 75 when a lovely damsel suddenly appears at the English court to charge Tirant with being "un fals e reprobat cavaller" who has vilely slain two dukes and two kings "ab gran tració e maldat e ab armes dissimulades e de gran engan" (*TB*, 260). The accusation of having tampered with his weapons to give him an unfair advantage over his four adversaries is repeated in the next chapter to Tirant's face and he is then presented with Don Kirieleison's formal *lletra de batalla*:

> *A vós, Tirant lo Blanc, més cruel que lleó famejant, falsificador i escampador de la sang real d'aquells benaventurats cavallers mon senyor lo rei de Frisa e lo rei d'Apollònia, ab armes falses e dissimulades, entre cavallers d'honor no acostumades portar: e per quant vós sou desegual cavaller e, per més propi parlar, traïdor, falsificat en armes i en tot lo que d'honor és, e jo, havent notícia de la vostra gran maldat, per bé que só cert que en seré blasmat per molts bons cavallers que a tan vil e desordenada persona e traïdora jo haja admesa per companyia d'entrar dins lliça en camp clos a tota ultrança com si fos de persona en llibertat posada, a tota ma requesta vos combatré a ús e costum de França. E us dó poder de divisar les armes, e vostra resposta esperaré per espai de vint-e-cinc dies aprés que us serà presentada, de la qual estaré a relació de Flor de Cavalleria, rei d'armes....*
>
> (*TB*, 263-64) [34]

---

[34] "To you, Tirant lo Blanch, crueler than a hungry lion, he who tampers with weapons, and he who has spilled the royal blood of those blessed

As we can see, the preamble is rather long-winded and very insulting to Tirant personally; with regard to its function, it merely repeats the charges leveled earlier by the damsel. The next section, the actual proposal for a duel, is the most important part of the document and contains a reference to the French dueling customs that are the principal focus of this episode ("a ús e costum de França"). As for the actual terms of battle, the letter provides little in the way of specifics, but these will eventually become apparent in the course of the battle. At this point Tirant is simply offered the choice of weapons and a twenty-five day period in which to respond to the challenge.

The second part of Kirieleison's letter deals with the action that the challenger will take in the event that Tirant should refuse to accept the challenge:

> ... E si per temor de mi acceptar no la gosareu, siau cert jo us reversaré les armes e us penjaré cap avall segons de traïdor se pertany e per totes les corts dels grans senyors jo iré mostrant la gran tració que feta haveu en les persones d'aquests dos reis e serà notificat a tots aquells qui saberho volran. Escrita e sotscrita de la mia mà, segellada de mes armes pròpies e partida per A. B. C. Dada en la ciutat de Frisa a dos de juliol.
>
> Kirieleison de Muntalbà.
>
> (*TB*, 264) [35]

---

knights, my lord the King of Friesland and the King of Poland, through the use of deceitfully constructed weapons and armor that were tampered with in advance of combat, a trick that honorable knights are not in the habit of practicing; and since you are a dishonest knight, and to be more specific, a treacherous counterfeiter of arms and all other things commonly associated with honor, I, having become fully aware of your great wickedness and realizing that some good knights will condemn me for permitting so low, perfidious and villainous a person as you to enter into mortal combat with me in a closed field as my opponent almost as if you were a free man, hereby declare that I will challenge you to duel with me according to the rules and customs of France. I offer you the choice of arms and I shall await your reply for a period of twenty-five days following the receipt of this letter; please forward your response by means of Flor de Cavalleria, king at arms...."

[35] "... And in the event that you should be fearful of me and therefore not dare to accept my challenge, you may be certain that I will oblige you to paint your coat of arms backwards and I will hang you upside down, as befits a traitor such as yourself, and I will make public the great acts

It isn't clear how Don Kirieleison will manage to carry out his threats — perhaps his enormous physical stature has something to do with it — but he declares that he will oblige Tirant to paint his heraldic coat of arms in reverse, that he will then hang Tirant upside down (as is customary in such cases), and finally that he will denounce Tirant's alleged treachery against the two vanquished kings by publicizing it in various and sundry European royal courts. [86] Curiously enough, there is no mention of what action he will take if Tirant agrees to meet him in battle; apparently, Tirant's death would be sufficient to satisfy his thirst for vengeance.

The closing statement of Don Kirieleison's letter, while harking back to the style adopted earlier by Vilesermes (Ch. 62) in offering a signature and seal bearing his coat of arms, provides still another sophisticated guarantee of the document's authenticity: the practice of dividing the document into halves along a line marked by the capital letters A, B, and C. The recipient is expected to match the halves along this line to assure himself of the genuineness of the challenge. [87] A final novelty consists of the addition of the date and city from which the challenge is issued.

I would like to offer a few comments and observations concerning Kirieleison de Muntalbà's challenge. First of all, there is an obvious return to the highly insulting tone we noted earlier with

---

of treachery you have committed against these two kings by divulging them in the courts of all the great lords so that all who wish to hear me will be informed about them. Written and sent by my own hand, stamped with my own heraldic seal, and divided along a line marked by the capital letters A-B-C. Submitted in the city of Frisa on the second day of July.

Kirieleison de Muntalbà"

[86] Here again art imitates life. Martorell himself made this kind of threat in a letter dated 25 July 1437 to Joan de Monpalau, who had reneged on his promise of marriage to Damiata Martorell, the author's younger sister. Apparently, chivalric custom provided for this particular ceremony — or one very much like it — for occasions such as these when the challenged party refused to accept the challenge and was therefore declared vanquished by forfeit. See Riquer, *Tirante el Blanco*, I, 247, n. 1; Riquer and Vargas Llosa, *El combate imaginario,* pp. 87-89; 92.

[87] This is in reference to the practice of tearing the parchment along a line marked A-B-C, a custom that was evidently quite popular in the fifteenth century. See the note provided in the Castilian edition of *TB* by Vidal Jové (Madrid: Alianza, 1969), I, 554, note to Ch. 77; see also Riquer's 1974 *Tirante el Blanco*, I, 347, n. 6.

Lord Vilesermes, but now in a longer and more elaborate format. Secondly, there is heavy emphasis given to the French (i.e., Burgundian) dueling customs that will govern the eventual combat. Kirieleison insists, as will his brother Tomàs later, that the "ús e costum de França" be observed to the letter when they meet. In light of the vivid detail with which Tirant's battle with the giant Tomàs de Muntalbà is described (Don Kirieleison, it must be remembered, dies of grief before he can fulfill the contract and is replaced by his equally gigantic and outraged sibling), the entire episode has the distinct appearance of being no more than a convenient excuse for author Martorell to display his expertise regarding the dueling customs of the Burgundian court. [38] Finally, we should note several elements that resemble quite closely some of the features of Martorell's own *lletres de batalla:* the aforementioned partition along the letters A, B, and C, a stated period (in this case 25 days) during which the challenged party must respond, and the formal close that includes the challenger's signature and seal, followed by the date and place of issue. This is precisely the pattern that is followed in Martorell's extended correspondence with Joan de Monpalau concerning the alleged refusal of Monpalau to honor his promise to marry Damiata Martorell, sister of the author. [39]

Given the above, it should not surprise the reader to learn that Tirant's reply to Don Kirieleison (Ch. 79) bears a striking resemblance in tone and structure to Monpalau's first letter of response to Martorell. [40] A comparison of the two texts is beyond the scope of the present study, but a few words about the general content of Tirant's answer are in order, if only because they represent an escalation of the hostilities and an advancing step in the evolution

---

[38] Riquer makes more than one reference to the 1306 edict of the Burgundian king Philip IV respecting one-on-one combat, as well as to Martorell's demonstrable knowledge of the terms set down in that edict (*Tirante el Blanco*, I, 171, n. 21; 246, n. 17). Riquer also refers to Siegfried Bosch, "La batalla a ús e costum de França en el *Tirant lo Blanc*," *Estudis Romànics*, 3 (1951-52), 100-01.

[39] Riquer and Vargas Llosa, *El combate imaginario*, pp. 39 ff.

[40] Riquer notes the similarity in a footnote to Ch. 79 (*Tirante el Blanco*, I, 251, b. 16); the text of Monpalau's reply can be found in Riquer and Vargas Llosa, *El combate imaginario*, pp. 45-47.

of the *lletra de batalla* as a chivalric literary convention. Martorell's hero responds as follows:

> Kirieleison de Muntalbà: vostra lletra he rebuda per Flor de Cavalleria, rei d'armes, partida per A. B. C., escrita e sotscrita de vostra mà, ab segell empremtada de vostres armes, la qual conté paraules vils e deshonestes: e par-me que no estan bé tals raons en boca de cavaller, volent mostrar a la gent ab paraules colorades venjar la mort dels dos reis. E si vós tinguésseu tal desig com mostrau haver, no em devíeu escriure, sinó vós venir ací (puix sabíeu que jo era en la cort del senyor rei d'Anglaterra, emperò cavallers hi ha que més amen cercar que trobar), dient que jo ab armes falses e dissimulades hauria morts los dos reis e ab tració ensems mesclada. Dic que mentiu e mentireu tantes vegades com ho direu. Jo els he morts com a cavaller, dins camp clos, ab aquelles pròpies armes per ells devisades així ofensives com defensives; e, si per la victòria per nostre Senyor a mi dada, e les mies mans han sabut guanyar lo preu e la honor davant la majestat del sereníssim rei d'Anglaterra e dels jutges del camp, com a cavaller obrant envers ells, no coneixent ni sabent qui eren, la mort així bé era presta per a mi com per a ells. E si los magnífics jutges del camp seran requests per vós o per altri, trobareu ab tota veritat venir armat contra mi ab armes injustes, no de cavallers, qui ab empresa feta vénen, portant en les cames de paper engrutat, argent pellat e altres coses les quals no cur dir. E lo cas per vós a mi posat malament, defensant mon dret, honor i fama só content, ab l'ajuda de nostre senyor Déu e de la sacratíssima Mare sua, senyora nostra, e del benaventurat cavaller mon senyor Sant Jordi, vostra requesta a tota ultrança, a ús e a costum del realme de França, acceptar. E per lo càrrec per vós a mi dat, jatsia a mi pertanga, devise fer la batalla, no a cavall perquè no diguésseu que ab milloria de cavall vos hagués mort o vençut, mas a peu, ab atxa de set palms sens croixet ne falsa maestria, tal com és acostumat de portar en lliça; espasa de quatre palms e mig del pom fins a la punta; punyals de dos palms e mig. Pregant-vos no m'escrivísseu més, car no rebria pus lletra vostra; sinó que vingau personalment e no ab procurador, e assegur-vos que no tindreu treball d'anar per les corts dels grans senyors ni de reversar armes, e de moltes altres deshonestats que són eixides d'aqueixa falsa boca. Sotscrita

de la mia mà, ab lo segell de les mies armes empremtada, partida per A. B. C., en la ciutat de Londres feta a tretze de juliol.

TIRANT LO BLANC.

(*TB*, 266-67) [41]

---

[41] "Kirieleison de Muntalbà: I have received your letter from Flor de Cavalleria, king at arms, divided along the letters A-B-C, written and signed by your own hand, with the seal of your coat of arms impressed in wax, and which contains several vile and dishonorable accusations; it seems to me that such words are inappropriate in the mouth of a knight who wishes to show people with harsh language that he desires to avenge the death of two kings. And so if you really did have the desire that you profess to have, you shouldn't have bothered writing to me but instead have come directly here (since you knew that I was residing at the court of the King of England — but then we all know that there are knights who prefer to look for trouble rather than find it) and you should have repeated to my face the charge that I have slain two kings with false and illegally altered weapons, that is, in a generally treacherous manner. I say that you are lying and that you will lie as often as you repeat that charge. I have taken their lives in a manner befitting a knight, in a closed field of battle with offensive and defensive arms that they themselves chose; and if the Lord saw fit to give me the victory, and if my hands have been skilled enough to capture the prize and honor before His Serene Highness the King of England and his field judges, then I have comported myself as a knight ought to in their presence, neither knowing them personally nor even their names, for death was as much a threat to me as it was to them. And if the good field judges should be questioned by you or by some other person, you will truly discover that the monarchs in question came against me with unfairly doctored weapons, not like the arms borne by true knights; they deliberately and knowingly wore on their legs pieces of cardboard pasted up with a silver coating to resemble regular steel armor, plus other tricks that I prefer not to mention at this time. I am pleased to accept your ill-made challenge in order to defend my rights, my honor, and my reputation with the help of Our Lord God and his Most Blessed Mother, Our Lady, and of the most fortunate knight, my lord St. George; I accept your request for a duel to the death according to the rules and customs that prevail in the kingdom of France. And you offer me a choice that is rightfully mine in the first place; therefore, I elect not to fight on horseback in order to prevent you from claiming afterwards that you lost or died because your steed was inferior; I choose to fight on foot with an axe measuring seven palms in length, without a cross-piece or any extra or tricky features, precisely the kind that is usually employed on the jousting lists; the sword shall measure four-and-a-half palms from tip to tip; the daggers shall be two-and-a-half palms in length. I urge you not to write to me in the future, for I shall refuse to receive all letters from you; please confront me in person, not through an intermediary. I assure you that you will have no reason to trot about the royal courts, nor to have my coat of arms painted in reverse, nor to carry out any of the other dishonorable acts your lying mouth has threatened

Tirant begins by giving the lie to Kirieleison's charge of treachery; he attempts to set the record straight by attesting to the honorable conditions that attended the death of the King of Friesland. He closes the first part of his letter by revealing a distasteful matter that he has previously allowed to pass unmentioned: the unfair and illegal use of cardboard leg armor fabricated to look like steel by the Frisian monarch. Having disposed of the required preliminaries, Tirant begins the second half of his response by accepting the challenge and the challenger's stipulation that the French rules govern their encounter. Furthermore, since the choice of weapons is his as the challenged party, Tirant opts for a duel on foot so that Kirieleison (or his followers) will be unable to offer a feeble excuse for the giant's forthcoming defeat by pointing to the shortcomings of his mount. Additional specifications include a battle-axe measuring seven palms in length and without any special adornments or extra features of a deceptive nature, swords of four-and-a-half palms, and daggers that are two-and-a-half palms in length. He closes by warning Don Kirieleison that he will refuse to receive any correspondence from him in the future, and he advises the giant to communicate with him personally, not through intermediaries, from that point forward. After firing a final salvo about his adversary's mendacity, Tirant finishes off the reply with his signature and seal, authenticates the document in the manner prescribed earlier by Kirieleison in dividing the letter along the line marked A-B-C, then affixes the date (July 13) and place of issue (London).

Martorell injects an ironic element into this episode by providing for the unusual and premature death of Kirieleison de Muntalbà before he can meet Tirant on the lists. The giant suddenly expires of extreme grief in Ch. 80 while visiting the tomb of his slain monarch, a circumstance which appears to impose a most dissatisfying conclusion to what has been a promising episode full of tension that has been allowed to build carefully and in plentiful detail. But the author is not about to let such a meticulously

---

to perform. Signed by my own hand and sealed with the sign of my heraldic arms, divided along lines A-B-C, in London on the thirteenth day of July.

                Tirant lo Blanch"

prepared scenario evaporate unfulfilled into thin air. The original challenge is taken up by the deceased warrior's equally enormous brother Tomàs, as is required by French dueling custom.[42] At this point it becomes clear that Martorell has purposefully interposed the death of Kirieleison simply to create a legal complication that will require a formal substitute challenge. He continues to demonstrate his profound knowledge of the finer points of the French dueling customs by having Tirant demand — as is required under the circumstances — that each of the disputants deposit with the field judges some article of clothing, a *gatge* (Cast. = *gaje*), that will serve as a bond or pledge of his intention to appear at the appointed time and place. Tomàs offers his cap *(bonet)* and Tirant counters with a gold chain; the adversaries — in strict accordance again with the rules of the French court — proceed to embrace and exchange the traditional kiss that symbolizes the implicit pardon of the victor by the vanquished in the event that death should claim one of the combatants (Ch. 81).

The battle itself is described in minute detail in Chs. 81 and 82; not even the preliminary ceremonies escape the narrator's attention. We are informed, for example, that although Martorell's hero is willing to forgive the torrent of insults he has had hurled at him, Tomàs de Muntalbà curtly rebuffs every one of Tirant's attempts at reconciliation; when the ladies of the English court make a similar effort to seek a peaceful resolution of the problem, the giant rejects their entreaty "ab molta supèrbia." Tomàs' thirst for vengeance is indelibly impressed upon the reader when he stubbornly restates, in the presence of the sacred Host during the final few moments before the battle, his opposition to any compromise or reconciliation.

Martorell's obsession with the French dueling customs is clearly reflected in his blow-by-blow account of the battle; no effort is spared to provide the reader with a clear picture of exactly what the Burgundian rules permit or require in hand-to-hand combat. For example, we are informed that the French rules stipulate that if a warrior's foot, arm or hand should fall outside the marked

---

[42] Riquer notes that Tirant would have been unable to accept such a second challenge unless the accusation had been repeated clearly and categorically (*Tirante el Blanco*, I, 259, n. 2).

boundary of the combat zone, the judge, if requested to do so, must order the offending appendage to be severed on the spot.

Despite suffering from a distinct physical disadvantage when pitted against such a huge opponent, Tirant makes use of his superior intelligence to gain the upper hand. At one point, for example, Martorell's hero appears to be hopelessly and helplessly pinned by the giant, but in his blind fury Tomàs makes a foolish miscalculation: he attempts to raise Tirant's face guard in order to pound the smaller man into submission with his mailed fists; when he discovers that his bulky gauntlets prevent his blows from penetrating the tiny opening in Tirant's headgear, the angry giant throws down his axe and discards his mailed gloves in order to attack with his bare hands. This provides Tirant with the perfect opportunity to inflict telling damage with his own axe on Tomàs' exposed flesh. The giant recoils in pain and Tirant suddenly finds himself presented with a clear advantage in weaponry. The smaller man drives the reeling giant across the lists until he pins him against a fence. At this point the hero makes a totally unexpected gesture of generosity: he offers to allow Tomàs to recover his gauntlets and axe in return for an immediate public retraction of his charge of treachery against Tirant. Tomàs agrees to Tirant's stipulations and the battle resumes on even terms. We note here that Martorell's hero is willing to sacrifice an invaluable physical advantage in order to gain a far more important — to him, at least — legal concession.

The duel continues a while longer but, as frequently is the case in these early chapters, the hero's superior conditioning eventually provides him with the margin of victory. Before long the plodding giant is woozy with fatigue and lurching about on rubbery legs; Tirant eventually fells him with a series of blows to the head with his axe. Faced with the prospect of an immediate and ignominious demise (Tirant's dagger is pointed at his eye), Tomàs wisely and willingly accepts the victor's invitation to renounce all the charges he has made against Tirant. The winner spares his life, as promised, but Tomàs must still undergo a most humiliating experience. In Ch. 84 Martorell describes — again sparing no particulars — the ceremony by which the disgraced giant is divested of his chivalric rank and all its privileges. He is obliged to ride *backwards* to the gate of the lists where he dismounts and is stripped piece-by-piece of his armor (each item of which is hurled over the fence). The judges then pronounce sentence over him, denouncing him in the bargain as a liar and perjurer. He is thereupon required to walk — again, backwards — through the streets to the cathedral where the final ceremony will take place: the pouring of a caldron of very hot water over his head and eyes. Following this, his wounds are cured by the royal physicians and he is allowed to take part in the banquet and ball that are celebrated that night. The final word on Tomàs de Muntalbà is the simple announcement that he later retired to a monastery and became a Franciscan friar.

Because the episode of Tirant and the giant Muntalbà brothers is so long and so complicated, the primary reason for Martorell's including it in his novel is easily overlooked. Certain observations I made earlier about this unique and peculiar adventure bear repeating. First of all, the episode is presented in three distinct stages: 1) the formal challenge issued by Kirieleison de Muntalbà; 2) the equally important formal reply by Tirant; and 3) the oral re-statement of the charges by Tomàs following his brother's death, followed by the inevitable bloody conclusion of the action on the lists. Secondly, the entire incident has been conceived as a tour de force to demonstrate author Martorell's phenomenal knowledge of French dueling customs as established by Philip IV of Burgundy in the early fourteenth century. Martorell is especially interested in showing how a secondary challenge should be issued in the unhappy event that the original challenger may be unable to fulfill the terms of the dueling agreement.

One additional note: with this episode Martorell carries his historical treatment of duels and personal challenges up to the time of his writing. His own *lletres de batalla,* as we find them in MS. 7811 of the Biblioteca Nacional in Madrid, are essentially identical in form to those found in Chs. 77 and 79 of *TB*. The relatively few cases of personal challenge that follow Ch. 84 in Martorell's novel deal principally with aberrations in and perversions of this curious custom.

The first of these aberrant episodes is Tirant's unpleasant encounter with Ricard lo Venturós (Ch. 114), discussed earlier here. It will be recalled that the entire matter is a trivial one that springs from feelings of resentment and jealousy on the part of

Ricard for the many honors that have been heaped upon Martorell's hero during the King of France's expedition to the North African coast. During Tirant's absence the ungracious Ricard denounces him as a coward and timid warrior; he declares, furthermore, that the honors that the young Captain has received for his past acts of bravery rightfully belong to him (Ricard). He unabashedly asserts that he is a more valiant knight than Tirant and plans to demonstrate his military superiority in a duel to the death with his nemesis. The charge and challenge are repeated directly to Tirant a short while later and Ricard hurls down a gauntlet in defiance to emphasize the point.

Rather than accept such an absurd challenge, Tirant replies by delivering an open-handed blow to his tormentor's face and making a quick exit from the King of France's ship to the safety of his own galley moored a few yards away. Before beating such a hasty retreat, however, Tirant pauses long enough to deliver the following words of rebuke for Ricard's frivolous pique and willingness to endanger the lives of two valiant knights over a mere trifle:

> —Senyor, castigue la majestat vostra aqueix desvergonyit cavaller qui és principiador de tot mal. Jamés s'és vist en fet d'armes, ni menys espasa fellona davant los seus ulls, e ara me volia combatre a tota ultrança sobre no res, e si ell venç a mi, haurà vençudes totes les cavalleries que ab mon treball jo m'he sabudes percaçar en glòria e llaor mia, e si jo só vencedor, hauré vençut un home que jamés s'és vist en armes.
>
> (TB, 363) [43]

Because the matter is so trivial in nature, it is never allowed to reach the formal stage; the clash is brief and entirely oral. There are no terms spelled out regarding the manner of combat, nor is

---

[43] "My Lord, Your Majesty should punish this disgraceful knight who has been the instigator of all this unpleasantness. He has never found himself involved in any sort of duel, nor even faced a sword raised in anger against him; and now I learn that he wanted to fight me to the death for no good reason. And if he should somehow defeat me, he will thereby have laid waste to all the chivalrous deeds that I have performed by my past efforts for the sake of glory and praise; and if I should emerge victorious, I will only have defeated someone who has never before been observed taking part in any affair of honor such as this."

any statement offered as to the anticipated consequences of their encounter. Tirant's quick reaction aborts the duel at the earliest possible stage. The only plausible motive for Martorell's including such a potentially volatile but ultimately inconsequential episode in his novel would have been to provide a comment — and a negative one at that — on certain silly and trifling abuses that had infested the hallowed traditions, customs and rituals of the chivalric orders. [44]

If the clash with Ricard lo Venturós can be viewed as an example of an incipient and minor perversion of the chivalric ideal, Tirant's intercourse with the King of Egypt in Chs. 150-52 represents the absolute nadir of his chivalric experience, an almost total perversion of the honor code by which knights were expected and obliged to comport themselves. Not surprisingly, this adventure marks the final occasion on which Martorell's protagonist allows himself to contemplate a duel or any other form of single combat. Because of the Egyptian monarch's unabashed perfidy here, Tirant will henceforth confine his warlike activities to the larger arena of the battlefield. The incident with the King of Egypt, which incidentally closes out this section on the subject of formal challenges and duels, is fraught with frivolous provocations, excessive verbiage and treacherous scheming. But in order to appreciate precisely how distasteful the episode is for Tirant, one must consider the events that lead up to his encounter with the perfidious Moor.

Having been soundly trounced on two occasions by Tirant's Greek forces in battles near Constantinople, the Moorish/Turkish leadership hatches a plan to assassinate the Christian leader, preferably in the course of a duel with their own champion, the King of Egypt (Ch. 148). The latter is received in the Greek camp and granted an interview with Tirant, the most gracious of hosts who prepares a sumptuous banquet in honor of his Moslem guest. Unfortunately, the Egyptian does not return the courtesy, preferring instead to use the occasion to berate his host for alleged cruelties

---

[44] The figure of Ricard lo Venturós plays a similar role, as we noted earlier, in Martorell's criticism of the vow-taking ritual. Martorell obviously created this short-lived but memorable character with the intention of having him represent the antithesis of Tirant's level-headed and unemotional approach to chivalric customs.

committed during the most recent hostilities between their respective forces. The King of Egypt flatly announces his intention to seek Tirant's death for these offenses; he attempts to continue his diatribe, but Tirant, unwilling to abide such distasteful vituperation, abruptly terminates the audience by walking out of the tent.

With the return of the Egyptian monarch to the Moslem camp, the second phase of their nefarious plan takes form. It is agreed that the King of Egypt will send a formal letter of challenge to Tirant with a demand for a duel to the death in terms that no truly brave cavalier could possibly refuse. What will *not* be disclosed in the letter, however, is the Moors' intention to station a bowman at a high vantage point whose task will be to slay the Christian warrior if he should begin to gain the upper hand in the battle (Ch. 149). It is this final twist that marks this episode as the ultimate perversion of the chivalric ideal. Of ancillary interest are the many nonsensical asides and irrelevancies that the King of Egypt introduces to the sub-genre of the *lletra de batalla*. His challenge rambles aimlessly at times and careens from one frivolous item to another before finally settling on the primary issue: their duel and the reason for it. Ch. 150 reads as follows:

> *Abenamar, per la permissió e voluntat de Déu rei d'Egipte, e vencedor de tres reis en batalla campal, e cascú per si, ço és a saber: lo poderós rei de Fes, lo virtuós rei de Botgia e lo pròsper rei de Tremicè; a tu, Tirant lo Blanc, Capità dels grecs.*
> *Deixant tota llonguea de paraules perquè pus clara experiència sia ver testimoni entre tu e mi, a la qual la fortuna serà favorable, puixa haver manera de gloriejar-se en lo dan o deshonor de l'altre. Sobre les tues armes he vist portar hàbit de donzella: mostres, segons lo senyal, ésser enamorat d'ella. E perquè jo puga complir un vot que fiu davant ma senyora, remet lo dit vot a la casa de nostre sant Profeta Mafoma, lla on lo seu gloriós cos jau, ço és en Meca, de requerir de batalla a tota ultrança rei o fill d'aquell o lo major capità dels crestians: e per ço requir a tu, per fer servei a la donzella de qui só, e sia quiti de mon vot, si hi gosaràs venir, de matar-te o de lleixar-te dins la lliça vençut o fementit, e provaré ma veritat públicament ab les mies mans, e tu virtuosament vulles defendre ta honor, com la donzella de qui só sia en major grau de bellea e de virtuts de llinatge acompanyada, que la tua.*

E lo teu cap com a vençut trametré en present a la sua senyoria: e si lo teu ànimo porà comportar beure aquest càlzer de la batalla, seré molt content de la tua persona a la mia s'haja purgar. Emperò atorgant tu bona fe per aquest cas, no tenint ànimo de gosar-te combatre ab mi, hauré a venir en altre cap, e no gos dir aquell espantable mot tan vergonyós per aquells qui amen sa honor. E tot cavaller se'n deu defendre e no restar en openió de gents, de senyores e donzelles menyscabat de ta honor e fama, forçat és que ho diga, ço és a saber: ab gran maldat e, pus propi parlar, tració, has esvaït dos vegades lo nostre camp ab tanta infàmia en ta honor casi inreparable. E per ço del meu bon dret surt una bona esperança obtesa e desijada, e açò dic a fi que acte criminal ne surta si veure'l gosareu, car Déu omnipotent no permetrà que tan lleig crim com és aquest reste en lo món impunit, jo a ma requesta, sostenint la veritat te combatré, lo meu cos contra lo teu, a peu o a cavall segons per ton avantatge ho volràs divisar, davant jutge competent, combatent-nos per tantes jornades fins l'u de tu o de mi reste mort, per ço que lo teu cap puga fer present d'ell a la senyora de qui só. E si a la present me volràs respondre donant o fent donar ta resposta a Egipte, trompeta meu, jo l'hauré per rebuda, lo qual basta per a concordar-nos e portar nostra batalla a la fi que jo desige.

Dada en lo nostre camp de la platja oriental lo primer de la lluna, e pos ací mon signe.

REI D'EGIPTE.

(*TB*, 502-03) [45]

---

[45] "Abenamar, King of Egypt with the permission and by the will of God, victorious in pitched battle over three kings, namely the powerful King of Fez, the virtuous King of Bougie, and the prosperous King of Tlemcen, to you, Tirant lo Blanch, captain of the Greek forces.

"Forsaking all prolixity so that pure experience may provide true testimony between us regarding the question as to whom Fortune may favor, so that the victor may have the means to bring glory upon himself from the injury or dishonor of the other. I have noticed that you wear the garment of a maiden over your armor; by this sign you indicate that you are in love with her. And so that I may fulfill a promise that I once made to my own lady in the house of our Holy Prophet Mohammed, where his glorious body lies in state, that is, in Mecca, to request a duel to the death with a king, or the son of a king, or with the highest-ranking captain of the Greek forces; therefore, I approach you so that I may serve my lady and fulfill my vow by killing you or leaving you on the field of battle as a defeated warrior or as one whose falseness has been proved; and I shall demonstrate the truth of what I say publicly with my

We note that the preamble begins with a self-aggrandizing statement in which the King lists his most recent military conquests in an effort to inflate his stature; Tirant is referred to simply as the captain of the Greek forces. The second paragraph starts with a promise to renounce prolixity in the matter at hand, an affirmation that is immediately disregarded. Rather than arrive at the main point of his letter, the Egyptian detours onto the subject of a lady's garment that he has observed Tirant wearing into battle over his armor; he concludes from this that the Greek Captain is enamored of a lady. He seized this pretext to mention a similar romantic involvement of his own and use it as the basis for challenging Tirant to hand-to-hand combat.

The King of Egypt has apparently abandoned the notion of dueling the Greek Captain simply to seek revenge for past injuries; the tack he now takes is that of fulfilling some ridiculous vow he

---

own hands. And you ought to want to defend your honor in an exemplary fashion, since my lady outranks yours in both physical beauty and noble lineage. And I shall send your severed head to her as a token after I have defeated you. If your courage is sufficient to allow you to drink from the chalice of battle, I will be very pleased to have your person be purified along with mine. But assuming good faith on your part in this matter, if you should decide not to do battle with me, I shall have to take other action; and I do not like to utter that horrible word which is so shameful for those who cherish their honor. And every knight should defend himself so as not to be held in contempt by public opinion or have his honor and reputation scorned by ladies and maidens. It is therefore necessary that I say the following: that with great wickedness, and more specifically with great treachery, you have twice thrown our camp into confusion by infamous methods that serve only to damage irreparably your good name. Therefore, out of my own good nature comes an opportunity to clear your name that you should desire greatly and seize; and I say this so that if any criminal act should evolve from this, should you accept, Almighty God will not permit such a horrible crime to go unpunished in this world. I, in challenging you, will be championing the truth when I meet you in battle, my body against yours, on foot or on horseback — whichever you decide is to your advantage — before a competent judge, both of us fighting for as many days as may be required to leave one of us dead, so that I can then offer your head as a gift to the lady whom I serve. And if you should wish to respond to this letter, you or one of your lackeys may give the reply to Egypt, my bugler and messenger, and I will consider it received, which will be sufficient to seal our agreement to carry our battle to the conclusion that I desire.

"Given in our camp on the East bank of the river, on the first day of the moon; and I hereby affix my seal.

The King of Egypt"

once made to his lady at Mecca to defeat *mano-a-mano* a king, the son of a king, or the greatest of the Christian commanders, leaving the victim dead and defeated, marked as a false knight. Not content to leave his remarks at that, the Egyptian goes on to declare that his lady boasts of more beauty and nobler bloodlines than Tirant's maid; and he concludes by stating his intention to send the Christian's head to his beloved as a trophy.

The next step is an attempt to goad Tirant into accepting the challenge by casting aspersions on his courage. There is a veiled threat to publicize as cowardice any refusal or excuse that Tirant may make. Only after exhausting the themes of the vow to his beloved and the reputed faint heartedness of Tirant does the King of Egypt arrive at the crux of the matter: his desire to avenge the two stinging defeats Tirant's forces have recently inflicted upon the Turks and their allies. The actual challenge is made about two-thirds of the way through the letter, at which point the reader has just about despaired of finding any legitimate reason for the epistle. In the remaining third of the document are found all the necessary and pertinent details concerning the terms under which they will do battle, but even these are sparse and uninteresting. For Martorell neither the conditions nor the expected results of the combat are important factors in this final *lletra de batalla*; the carefully planned treachery of the infidel warrior is the only significant attraction. As a matter of form, Tirant is granted the right to elect to fight on foot or on horseback, but little attention is given to the question of which weapons are to be used, a matter of supreme importance in the earlier letters from Vilesermes, Kirieleison de Muntalbà, et al. The Egyptian challenger's only concern is that they battle, for days on end if necessary, until one of them should fall dead. As for the consequences, which so often in the previous cases were of primary interest to one or both of the combatants, here there are none of importance. The only result promised or alluded to is the Egyptian's intention to send Tirant's head in a sack to his lady as proof that he has fulfilled his vow. Not a single military or political advantage stands to be gained by the victor; no hope is expressed about their being able to avoid future bloodshed by letting this duel settle all issues. In short, what the

King of Egypt accomplishes in his letter of challenge is nothing more than a frivolous exercise in chivalric gamesmanship.

The document closes rapidly with an invitation for Tirant's reply; the date and place of issue are followed by the mark or sign of the Egyptian king, but no outward proof of the letter's authenticity (e.g., division along a line marked A-B-C) is offered.

If any further proof be required of Martorell's obvious and growing disenchantment with the convention of the *lletra de batalla,* one need only consider the tone of Tirant's reply in Ch. 152. Here the hero attempts to match the long-winded King of Egypt's rambling narrative point for point, and the result is the final letter in the series and the most absurd of all such documents to be found in the novel, a true *reductio ad absurdum.* Here is the text of Tirant's prolix response:

> No lleva en res la propietat de verdader, si atènyer poreu bona coneixença; ab tals paraules pensa portar enganosa creença se'n mostre lo ver. Per tal jo, Tirant lo Blanc, vencedor e destroïdor de la gent pagana d'aquell famós e gran soldà de Babilònia, hoc encara del senyor de la Turquia, a tu, rei d'Egipte, signific:
>
> Com per la tua trompeta he rebuda una lletra tua en què dius haver-me vist portar sobre les armes hàbit de donzella, e perquè poguesses complir un vot que tens fet, requis a mi de batalla a tota ultrança, com de la donzella de qui est enamorat sia més virtuosa e més bella que la que jo ame.
>
> Dic primerament: del vot que has fet, has encativada ta honor e fama. E més propi fóra que haguesses votat d'estar deu anys en la casa de Meca, fent esmena de tots pecats, los quals són abominables a Déu e al món. A tot lo món és cert e manifest que la donzella de què jo em nomene servidor, en lo món no ha par, així en bellea, en dignitat e excel·lència virtuosa, més que tota altra; de llinatge, gràcia e saber excel·leix a totes quantes n'ha en lo món. Sabut és com tu ames la filla del Gran Turc e jo la de l'Emperador. La tua, mora; la mia, crestiana; la tua té cisma, e la mia, crisma. Pertot seria aquesta jutjada per millor e de major dignitat: que la tua no seria digna de descalçar-li la sabata del seu peu a la sua gran excel·lència. E dius que lo meu cap com a vençut trametràs en present a la donzella de qui est. Responc-te que a present no hi consent, car fretura em faria per a vençre a tu e als teus.

Posat cas fos així com dius, tal present no deu haver lloc ni deu ésser do de gran preu, per ço com seria d'home vençut. Però jo prometí a la majestat de la senyora Princesa, jo venint en vista de vosaltres, vençre quatre batalles e la cinquena apresonar un rei, e portar-lo davant sa majestat, e ab lo braç armat li faré present de la mia espasa, per ço com serà d'home vencedor. E no és dona ni donzella que sia de valor te dega tenir en estima de res, per ço que fas present de cosa morta e de vençut, e jo no la faç sinó de vencedor. Venint a l'efecte del que vull dir, dius jo haver desconfit dues voltes lo vostre camp ab maldat e tració; dic l'emperador romà féu una llei dient, qualsevulla qui nomenàs a l'altre traïdor, respongués que mentia, e açò et dò per resposta. Però la tua boca bandejada és de veritat, e perquè sia vista en tot la culpa del teu mal parlar, en ço que jo he fet és estat fet justament e bona: conegut per cavallers entesos, aquells qui d'armes saben; hoc encara les dones d'honor ho diran, si en seran demanades, que jo no he feta tració neguna, ans he seguit aquell gentil estil e costum que orde de cavalleria demana en semblants fets de guerra. E si jo per aptea e per ésser més destre que vosaltres, ¿quina infàmia me pot ésser aplicada en ma honor i fama? Si jo hagués feta alguna obligació de paraula o per escrit, en tal cas hauria lloc la tua demanda.

Per què jo, Tirant lo Blanc, en nom de Nostre Senyor e de la sua sacratíssima Mare, e de madama Carmesina, defenent mon dret, ma honor e fama, accepte vostra requesta a tota ultrança. Per la facultat que per dret d'armes a mi com a request és dada, encara per tu a mi atorgada, divís fer la batalla a cavall, ab armes defensives cascú a sa voluntat, tals com són acostumades de portar en guerra, sens falsa maestria. Les armes ofensives, una llança de llargària de catorze palms, la gruixa cascú a sa voluntat, lo ferro de llargària de quatre dits perquè no es puga rompre, e espasa de cinc palms del pom fins a la punta, atxa d'una mà, daga de tres palms e mig; los cavalls encobertats de ço que cascú mills li parrà, de cobertes de cuiro o de lloria, testera d'acer sens espasa ne altra maestria, sella de guerra ab estreps deslligats. Concordes de nosta batalla, venint al jutge dieu competent, ¿qui serà dit jutge competent? ¿Ton rei a qui est tengut de feeltat? E si em seria jo al meu, e tu moro e jo cristià, ¿qui serà aquest jutge competent? Si vols dir: Anem per lo món a cercar jutge; açò poràs tu bé fer, car jo no ho poria fer que hagués a lleixar lo govern de tants ducs, comtes e marquesos, los quals són sots la mia capitania, e jo só cavaller que no em contente d'armes on és dubtosa l'execució. Si vols dir lo Soldà la ens assegurarà, dic-te que, qui no ha fe, no pot donar fe. ¿Qui segura a mi si jo venç tu dins en la lliça, e de la tua persona jo fes a mes voluntats, que jo pogués tornar dins les mies tendes? Si dius vendràs ací dins lo nostre camp, no ho faces, ço que jo no volria per a mi no ho vull per a tu. Havent tu de mi lo que desiges, ¿qui et pot assegurar de mos parents e amics tu tornasses dins lo teu camp? Però jo et daré remei e avís en què poràs complir ton desig. A tots és notori, estant vosaltres ab tot lo vostre poder tenint assejat l'il·lustre duc de Macedònia, jo aní a cercar a vosaltres e us desconfí, e obtenguí la glòria e honor de tants reis coronats. Aprés vosaltres vengués a cercar a mi e vencí-us; fiu fugir a tots aquells que ab supèrbia e vanaglòria se nomenen vencedors de tres reis en batalla campal e cascú per si. Doncs raó vol e demana, jo torne a cercar a vosaltres, puix a mi toca la tanda. Promet a Déu e a la senyora de què só e a la honor de cavalleria, que a vint dies d'agost, quatre dies ans o quatre dies aprés, seré en la platja oriental, davant lo vostre camp ab tot lo major poder que poré per dar batalla, si la volreu. E llavors poràs complir ton desig e no poràs dir que ab tració e maldat ho haja fet. Com lo teu cartell sia tacat de vils paraules, no cur respondre perquè de viltat ab tu no vull contendre; te lleixe en la tua glòria e perquè sia vist d'ara avant de dones e de donzelles e per los cavallers d'honor mon descàrrec, te tramet la present per Egipte, trompeta teu, partida per A. B. C., escrita de la mia mà e segellada ab segell de mes armes en lo camp nomenat Transimeno a cinc d'agost.

TIRANT LO BLANC.

(*TB*, 506-09) [46]

---

[46] "The matter of truthfulness is beside the point if you can achieve clear understanding, for you are trying to persuade us toward a false belief with such words, but you succeed only in making the truth shine more brightly. Therefore I, Tirant lo Blanch, victor over and destroyer of the pagan forces of that great and celebrated Sultan of Babylon and even over the Lord of Turkey, hereby inform you, the King of Egypt, of the following:

"Since I have received the letter from your bugler in which you state that you have seen me wearing a woman's garment over my armor, and in order that you may fulfill a vow you have taken, you challenge me to a duel to the death for the purpose of maintaining that the maid whom you serve is more virtuous and more beautiful than mine.

ON QUAINT CHIVALRIC RITUALS 175

The rebuttal begins with an overblown acknowledgement of the receipt of the Egyptian's challenge and the general terms thereof. Soon thereafter, however, Tirant launches himself into a lengthy

---

"Let me first say the following: your honor and reputation are being held captive by the vow you have taken. It would have been better if you had vowed to remain at the house in Mecca for ten years to atone for your sins, which are abominable in God's eyes and in the eyes of the world. Everyone knows with certainty that the maid I serve has no equal in this world as far as beauty, dignity and virtue are concerned; she surpasses every woman in the world in lineage, grace and wisdom. It is common knowledge that you love the daughter of the Great Turk and I am captured by the charms of the Greek Emperor's daughter. Yours is Moorish, mine is Christian; yours is steeped in schism, while mine is anointed with chrism. All in all, mine ought to be considered the better of the two and with the greater dignity; yours would not be worthy even to remove the shoe of Her Excellency. And you say that my head, once I am defeated, will be sent by you to your maid as a token of your love. I reply that I cannot allow you to use it for such a purpose, since I will need my head to defeat you and your people. And granted that matters may be as you say, such a gift must not be given, nor would it be of much value since it would be the head of a conquered man. However, I promised Her Majesty the Princess when I left for the battlefront that I would win four battles for her and that in a fifth one I would capture a king and bring him back to her as my prisoner; and I will offer my sword to her as a gift with my mail-covered arm, for it would be the sword of the victor. And there is no maid nor lady of dignity who ought to hold you in any esteem at all when you offer a dead object as a token, something that used to belong to a loser, while I offer a prize that belongs to a victor. And more to the point, you charge that I have twice laid waste to your camp in vile manner; I reply that the Roman Emperor established a law that provides that whosoever shall call another man a treacherous malefactor shall be called a liar in return, and that is my answer to you. But your mouth is empty of any truth whatsoever and to demonstrate to all the perfidious nature of your foul utterances I must declare that all my deeds were accomplished in a fair and righteous manner: it is known by knights who are well-versed in these matters, who are experts in matters of arms; even ladies of honor will say, if asked, that I have followed the civilized style and custom which the order of knighthood requires in this sort of military campaign. And if I have won victories by virtue of my superior abilities and because I was more skillful than you and the others, what sort of infamy can you impute to my honor and reputation? If I had betrayed a commitment made in some oral or written agreement, your demand against me would have some validity indeed.

"Therefore, I, Tirant lo Blanch, in the name of Our Lord and His Most Blessed Mother, and Lady Carmesina, hereby defend my rights, my honor, and my reputation; and I accept your challenge to a duel to the death. According to custom, I, as the challenged party, have the right to select the weapons to be used, and you have offered me the choice in your challenge; I therefore elect to do battle on horseback, with defensive

aside in which he enumerates some of the qualities of his fair Carmesina and compares her with the Egyptian king's lady. As part of the comparison Tirant allows himself the luxury of playing

---

weapons and armaments of each man's choice, so long as they are of the kind normally worn in battle and not fitted with any special or deceptive features. As for offensive weapons, I opt for a long lance of fourteen palm-lengths, of any desired thickness, with four finger-lengths of iron so that it cannot be broken; the sword shall measure five palms from the handle to the tip; a one-handed axe shall be used and a dagger of three-and-a-half palms; the horses shall be outfitted with whatever the rider desires, using either leather coverings or a steel cuirass, a plain headpiece without a spike or any feature of that sort, and a regulation battle saddle with loose stirrups. And as a final matter to be resolved regarding our duel, we must choose an impartial referee. Who will serve as such a judge? Your sovereign, to whom you owe fealty? Mine? With you a Moor and I a Christian, who will be this impartial arbiter? Perhaps you would reply: let us go forth and search the world for one. If so, I say: you may be able to do that easily, but I would not because I would have to abandon my command here over all the dukes, counts and marquises who serve under me; and I am a knight who is not content with projects of doubtful execution. If you nominate the Sultan to ensure our mutual safety, I must respond that he who is without faith cannot inspire faith in another. Who can guarantee that if I should defeat you on the lists and have you at my mercy, I will be allowed to return safely to my tent? And if you say you are willing to come here to my camp, I advise against it, since what I do not wish to happen to me I would not wish for you, either. If you should achieve the desired victory over me, who will be able to assure you that my relatives and friends will permit you to return to your camp? But I will offer you the remedy and advice to enable you to achieve your goal. Everyone is aware that with your entire army you had surrounded the illustrious Duke of Macedonia and that I went out to meet you in battle and defeated you, winning much honor and glory from so many crowned kings. Later you sought me out and I defeated you. I put to flight all those vainly and arrogantly self-proclaimed victors over three kings in battle, and I defeated each one separately. It is reasonable, therefore, that I come to you this time. I pledge to God, to the lady whom I serve, and to the honor of chivalry, that on the twentieth day of August, give or take four days, I will be on the East bank of the river, facing your camp with as many men as I can muster to join battle with you, if you so desire. And then you will be able to achieve your goal and you will not be able to say that I have done anything of an evil or treacherous nature. And since your epistle is stained with vile words, I do not wish to reply in kind, for I do not want to compete with you in vileness. I leave you in your glory, and so that my acquittal may be recognized from this time forward by ladies and maidens and honorable knights, I send you this letter by way of your bugler, Egypt; I divide it along points A, B, and C; it is written by my own hand and stamped with the seal of my heraldic arms at the field called Transimeno, on the fifth day of August.

Tirant lo Blanch"

with the words "schism" and "chrism," not to mention taking a gratuitous slap at the Moorish beauty, who he avers is unworthy even to unlace Carmesina's boot or sandal.

The wandering discourse continues with a small joke about not allowing the Egyptian to send Tirant's severed head to his Moorish sweetheart since the Christian will need it to defeat the Egyptian warrior and all the other Moslem invaders. This frivolity is carried over into the next section of the letter where Tirant wishes to make a distinction between the King of Egypt's concept of a worthy trophy (the head of a vanquished warrior) and his own (the victor's sword, which he intends to forward to Carmesina). He also refers parenthetically to a vow that he has made to Carmesina — or so he claims — to win four battles in her name and to capture a king in a fifth and bring him to her as a slave. The truthfulness of this last statement is indeed dubious and not to be found anywhere in Martorell's text; it appears to be nothing more than an empty rhetorical exercise at this point.

With regard to the Egyptian's charge that Tirant has used foul means *(maldat e tració)* to gain the upper hand in the previous victories over the Turks and their Moorish allies, the Christian leader offers a stern *mentís,* as per the custom established by one of the Roman emperors. He reaffirms his contention that he has always adhered to the chivalric code in his campaigns. [47]

The next step calls for Tirant to accept the challenge, which he does while specifying several conditions that must be met regarding offensive and defensive armaments: they will duel on horseback with regular battle armor; no special or sophisticated equipment will be permitted; the size, weight, length and thickness of all

---

[47] The "maldat e tració" refers to a clever ruse Tirant used earlier (Ch. 141) to lure the torpid Turks into a trap; on that occasion he tricked them into dividing their forces into two equal squads, then stationing them on opposite banks of the river. Once this was done, the Christian commander set fire to the only bridge connecting the two Turkish armies. Permanently prevented from reuniting their troops, the foolish Turks were then vulnerable to Tirant's attack on whichever side of the river he chose to do battle. This kind of astuteness is what the King of Egypt refers to as treachery. Tirant, on the other hand, maintains that such trickery is by no means alien to the chivalric code, but merely an intelligent elaboration within the approved groundrules.

offensive weapons are carefully specified, even down to the trappings that may be worn by their respective steeds.

The most important issue — how to select a mutually agreeable and impartial judge — is left until the very end. Tirant's approach to the problem of possible treachery is wordy, to say the least, but handled with thoroughness. He attempts to view the issue from both sides in order to seek a fair solution, but ultimately he is forced to admit that no guarantees can be offered against the threat of perfidy by either side. He has anticipated perfectly the King of Egypt's nefarious plan and consequently is able to propose a countermeasure that will foil the plot completely: he suggests that their armies meet to clash at the river on a specified date and that the two chieftains seek each other out during the battle for a personal confrontation.

Tirant closes with a reminder that he refuses to reply in kind to the Egyptian's vile utterances; he signs and dates the document, seals it with his heraldic arms, divides it along points A-B-C as is his custom, and delivers it to the Egyptian's messenger/bugler.[48] With this, author Martorell closes the book on the *lletra de batalla* as a significant element in his novel, but not without having traced the history of this sub-literary genre within the military tradition. In retrospect we can detect a definite pattern in the waxing and waning of the formal letter of challenge, which warrants a summary at this time.

From the inception of the custom in Ch. 13 to its demise in Ch. 152, we note that the letters grow increasingly more tedious, elaborate and long-winded in form — not to mention more devious. At the same time the amount of meaningful content in each letter appears to diminish. One need only compare the first and last of

---

[48] Riquer observes certain similarities between a number of specifications made by Tirant in this letter and those of author Martorell in some of his own *lletres de batalla*. For example, the demand that the combatants be restricted to the use of regulation battle armor, "sens falsa maestria," is the same one Martorell made in his challenge to Perot Mercader in a letter dated 13 February 1439; the specification as to the length and thickness of the lances to be used is almost identical to Martorell's proposal in a similar letter to Joan de Monpalau, 16 May 1437. These correspondences are noted in *Tirante el Blanco*, II, 319, notes 2 and 4. Additional references are made to the full text of these two letters in Riquer and Vargas Llosa, *El combate imaginario*, pp. 115 and 46, respectively.

these epistles to confirm this. The King of Grand Canary's letter to the King of England in Ch. 13 is short and to the point; furthermore, it has a most serious purpose: to avoid needless bloodshed between two rival factions by resolving the question of England's sovereignty through a simple hand-to-hand encounter between the titular heads of the respective armies. Personal issues are not allowed to intrude into the matter; the content of the letter is entirely political.

The final exchange of letters, on the other hand, is extremely personal and steeped in insulting language. The genre has by this late point evolved into an overblown exercise in bombast and vituperation. Aside from the fact that the last documents are pregnant with circumlocution, the issue seems completely pointless and designed to achieve absolutely no military or political solution. The King of Egypt issues his challenge to Tirant for the most frivolous of declared reasons: to satisfy a vow that he claims to have made some time ago to his lady. The *real* reason for the proposed duel is to lure Tirant into an ambush that will almost certainly result in his death by one means or another. In effect, the true purpose of the letter is hidden or suppressed and a totally false façade is erected to justify the challenge. The final letter, then, is a complete inversion — a *per*version, in fact — of the spirit of the original one. In the course of many generations (and more than a hundred chapters within *TB*), the elements of treachery and deceit have intruded to vitiate what initially was a most honorable exercise and tradition. Tirant is ultimately able to escape the danger to which this final letter would expose him by anticipating the Egyptian king's perfidy and making a counterproposal that effectively disarms the plot against him. Inadvertantly, however, he also orchestrates the demise of the hallowed chivalric ritual of the personal challenge by exposing the weaknesses inherent in it. At the close of this episode it should be evident to the reader, as it certainly is to Tirant, that through the centuries military leaders have become much more sophisticated — which is another way of saying "cunning and deceitful" — and that the fine old traditions of the military orders, customs that were originally based on a strong sense of personal honor and mutual trust among knights, have gradually become obsolete and are now in need of replacement by new, more sophisticated and realistic conventions. We should be noted that in the remaining 335 chapters of Martorell's novel there are no further challenges of this sort, in either oral or written form. The author apparently felt that by Ch. 152 he had made a complete statement about this once-meaningful part of the chivalric tradition that had been allowed to degenerate because of laziness, neglect, and man's innate penchant for perfidy.

* * *

To summarize, then, the major points of this chapter, I have shown that for the custom of vow-taking as much as for the *lletra de batalla* the story is essentially the same: traditions such as these are born of some basic necessity; they evolve slowly through generations as they are gradually altered to meet changing needs and new social conditions; ultimately they die a natural death when their evolution becomes contaminated by moral corruption and the inevitable perversion of their original goals.

In *TB* Martorell presents us with a masterful treatment of the history of two wonderful chivalric rituals that he would doubtlessly have preferred to preserve, but whose usefulness he realized had long before been exhausted. Ever the realist, Martorell recognized that blind adherence to ossified remnants of the glorious past and outmoded traditions was not a feasible option for the "modern" world in which fifteenth-century Christendom faced the formidable threat of the Ottoman Turks and their Moslem allies. He therefore created a new kind of Christian hero who would embody the kind of progressive outlook that was needed to combat the new Turkish aggression. Viewed in another way, Tirant is the perfect antithesis of the idealistic-retrogressive point of view that Cervantes intended to satirize in his *Don Quixote*. It is no wonder, then, that the great Castilian author had so many kind words for the Catalan novel during the famous examination of books in Don Quijote's library (I, Ch. 6). The ironic part is that Cervantes was apparently unaware of the identity of Tirant's clever creator, since the 1511 Castilian translation of *TB* omitted the names of both Martorell and Galba. Fortunately, nothing — not even a translator/editor's failure to give due credit to *TB*'s author(s) — can diminish the timeliness of the book's message.

CHAPTER V

MORE THAN A NOVEL OF CHIVALRY:
MARTORELL'S PLAN FOR *TIRANT LO BLANCH*

The fall of the Byzantine capital to the Turks in 1453 clearly seems to have been the inspiration for Joanot Martorell's unique novel of chivalry. His basic purpose in composing *TB* is unmistakably didactic: he means to show by concrete example the kind of Christian military commander-diplomat-governor that would be needed to stop the march of the Moslem hordes in the Balkan-Eastern Mediterranean region and restore the Greek Empire with its capital at Constantinople. His method is to alloy fact with fiction. He employs a clever fusion of diverse biographical data about several historical heroes of the Christian world, plus a great deal of poetic embellishment, to produce a virtually flawless model of the ideal Christian hero for the fifteenth century. In the course of his novel Martorell also condenses and telescopes several centuries' worth of development in the martial arts, military strategy and technological advancement within the lifetime of his protagonist. The result: a poetic history of the military order that unfolds before us as we read about the exploits of the main character.

For the sake of variety Martorell adds a second theme: the antiquated and oft-abused traditions of Courtly Love and clandestine marriage, not to mention the changes that must be made in them to make them workable in "modern" (i.e., fifteenth-century) society. His narrative plan is similar to that used with the major premise: to show the hero's gradual development — or perhaps "evolution" is a more appropriate term — as a lover. In the early chapters Tirant is portrayed as an ingenuous young man, almost totally naive in matters of the heart; he then begins to serve a period of apprenticeship during which he passes through a series of stages that gradually increase his knowledge and understanding of courtship and the conventions of Courtly Love. The maturation process is capped by the hero's return to Constantinople as a man totally acclimated to the highly sophisticated social mores of fifteenth-century society. Tirant's early timidity has at this point been replaced by a cool self-assurance and a romantic aggressiveness that ultimately gains for him the long-sought sexual union with the princess Carmesina, heir to the Greek Imperial crown.

Tangential to the courtship theme is the matter of clandestine marriage, an old, firmly established tradition that had by Martorell's time degenerated into a much-abused practice that frequently brought forth many unhappy consequences (and would eventually be outlawed by the Council of Trent a century later). Through the example of several pairs of lovers who revolve like satellites around Tirant and Carmesina, most notably Diafebus and Estefania in the Balkans and Escariano and Maragdina in Africa, Martorell demonstrates that this courtship tradition could be made useful and safe again by the simple addition of a few formal legal precautions.

Martorell's book subtly manages to propose meaningful (and necessary) social reform on two distinct planes: the military and the amatory. In the rhetorical passages that unfortunately creep into this very medieval text, the treatment is rather heavy-handed (especially in prolix letters and long-winded tirades) and quite unpalatable to the modern taste in fiction. However, if we set aside the tedious and preachy monologues and epistles and concentrate instead on the occasions when Martorell is content to let his characters speak and act naturally, we are rewarded with a most entertaining yet instructive narration — even by twentieth-century standards. The characters are fresh, multi-dimensional, psychologically complex, and often self-contradictory (an interesting anticipation of Cervantes' characters). Read without the boring and altisonant rhetorical excerpts, *TB* is the most modern of medieval novels, much more than just another chivalric romance.

* * *

Let us examine now the various components of Martorell's narrative plan: the many phases and stages through which the text — along with its hero — manages to pass. Viewed from above, the novel seems to consist of a haphazard arrangement of parts, but as we shall see, Martorell (with the later collaboration of his friend, Martí Joan de Galba) succeeds in keeping the action on its designed course. He achieves an effective blend of the major and minor themes, despite a multitude of intervening episodes and misadventures. What I present below is an outline of the carefully constructed narrative blocks that constitute Martorell's rather deceptive and seemingly amorphous novel.

I. THE GUILLEM DE VAROIC EPISODE (Chs. 1-28)

This opening — and literally primitive — section does not deal with the hero at all, but is instead a re-working of the legend of the famous Norman count Guy of Warwick. These early chapters appear to be based on the oral tradition or perhaps upon some prosified version of the old Anglo-Norman epic that Martorell may have come across during his residence in England (1438-39). A rough draft of the Varoic episode appears in MS. 7811 of the Biblioteca Nacional in Madrid along with many other documents authored by Martorell; it is obvious the author later expanded and reinforced these chapters in preparing the final draft of *TB*.

This section is significant because it is intended to represent the most primitive stage of development for both the military and romantic themes. As might be expected, the emphasis here is on the harsh living and fighting conditions that characterized those early times, not only for the military establishment but for society as a whole as well. The role of women and the proper place of romantic conventions in this early chivalric society are touched upon lightly — and only in the relatively few instances when Varoic is forced to deal with his meddlesome wife. But on those occasions he makes it abundantly clear that women and their sentimental attachments have *no* important place in a spartan society such as theirs.

II. Tirant in England (Chs. 29-97)

In these chapters we find the transition from primitive to late medieval chivalric customs in both love and war. Here Tirant enters the narrative as a young squire who is instructed in the history, function, rules, and rites of the military order by old Varoic; the novice eventually moves on to England to attend the year-long wedding feast of the country's young monarch and to participate there in the attendant jousts and other military exhibitions. It is in England that he is knighted and becomes a member of the Order of the Garter (Chs. 85-97). In essence, the adventures at the English Court are meant to provide us with a carefully arranged catalogue of medieval dueling rituals and many peculiar forms of hand-to-hand combat that were popular in twelfth- and thirteenth-century Europe. For example, he defeats in single combat such notable adversaries as the Knight of Muntalt (Ch. 59), the star-crossed lover Lord Vilesermes (Chs. 60-67), the Scot Vilafermosa (Chs. 74 and 84), four anonymous nobles from Central Europe — later identified as the Kings of Poland and Friesland and the Dukes of Burgundy and Bavaria — (Chs. 67-73), and finally the towering giants Kirieleison and Tomàs de Muntalbà (Chs. 77-82), who demand satisfaction of Tirant according to the Burgundian custom established by Philip IV of France in a 1306 edict.[1] Kirieleison's challenge to a duel "a ús e costum de França" (Ch. 77) and the hero's acceptance of those terms in his subsequent victory over Tomàs de Muntalbà (Chs. 81-82) carry the catalogue through the fourteenth century and into the fifteenth, Martorell's own time.

On the romantic plane, it is the Lady Agnès-Vilesermes affair that is of central interest at the English court. Agnès of Berry represents the idealized "untouchable" lady of the Courtly Love tradition; her brooch is the prize for which two brave knights duel fiercely, a confrontation which results in the tragic death of the valiant Vilesermes. The ironic tone of Agnès' final remarks serves as a kind of epitaph for the early courtly tradition in this novel;

---

[1] See Riquer, *Tirante el Blanco*, I, 171, n. 21.

from that point the victorious Tirant moves on to new and more "modern" romantic adventures in which the female is considered something more than a mere prize to be won, or an ornament to be displayed for the satisfaction of some warrior's ego.

III. Tirant in Sicily and the Siege of Rhodes (Chs. 98-114)

In these chapters Tirant's education is initially concentrated in the area of defensive naval strategies designed to protect his ships from heavy artillery fire; but then the curriculum is expanded to include offensive maneuvers as we witness Tirant's successful penetration of the Genoese blockade around the port of Rhodes, an adventure apparently inspired by the real-life exploits of the Burgundian hero Geoffroy de Thoisy in lifting an Egyptian blockade of that island fortress in 1444.[2] At still another point Martorell treats us to the description of a sailor's ingenious plan for setting ablaze the Genoese captain's flagship while it lies at anchor outside the harbor (Ch. 106).[3]

The purpose of this section of Martorell's novel is obviously transitional: he wants to remove his protagonist from the jousting lists and the world of hand-to-hand combat in order to prepare him for a more modern and sophisticated military era, one which will be characterized by coordinated joint land and naval assaults against castles, forts, walled cities, and the like. It is also in this section that Tirant begins to demonstrate his willingness to experiment with new weapons and modes of combat, for example the crossbow, which was the most notable advance in military technology before the development of artillery. In one memorable adventure (Ch. 106), Tirant single-handedly combines the speed and mobility of the horseman with the long-range firepower of the footsoldier's crossbow to rout a numerically superior Moorish force, killing eight and capturing ten enemy soldiers in the process.

---

[2] *Tirante el Blanco,* I, lx-lxii.

[3] For a detailed analysis of this stratagem and Martorell's meticulous description of the action, see Dámaso Alonso, "*Tirant lo Blanc,* novela moderna," *Revista Valenciana de Filología,* I (1951), 179-215; reprinted in *Primavera temprana de la literatura europea* (Madrid: Guadarrama, 1960), 201-53.

The final military action described in the section on Rhodes is the hero's memorable encounter with the brave but haughty Ricard lo Venturós, an episode which is more of a comment on the outmoded custom of chivalric oaths and vows than a study in military technology or strategy.

On the social or romantic front we witness in these chapters the courtship of Felip and Ricomana, an amorous diversion that serves to demonstrate a growing sophistication in Tirant's understanding of amatory affairs. The question of courtly behavior and formal etiquette — or rather, the complete lack of social graces in the character of the French prince that must be temporarily concealed and corrected by the sophisticated Tirant — is injected here in a fashion that would have seemed out of place during the earlier adventures in England. Tirant learns that non-military personal qualities and genteel conduct are becoming increasingly significant in matters of diplomacy and courtly protocol, to the point of equaling or even surpassing the factor of lineage and pedigreed bloodlines as the determining factor in arranging marriages between dynasties and providing for royal heirs. The contrast of Felip — of unmistakable royal descent but totally unsuitable as a courtier — with the lesser-born but elegantly mannered Tirant is the key element; the adventure at the Sicilian court is simply the final step in the hero's preparation for the encounter with his destined mate, Carmesina, at the Byzantine court.

IV. Tirant in Constantinople (Chs. 115-299)

In this, the major narrative section, we notice a virtual alternation of the love and war themes in the hero's life. Rebounding repeatedly as he does from battlefield to bedroom, Tirant naturally enters into a stage of emotional confusion that ultimately takes its toll on his desire for combat. As his enthusiasm for his military duties wanes, the romantic theme begins to dominate the action of the novel; it soon becomes obvious that the hero is spending more time wooing Carmesina at the palace than at his command post near the front.

As a military figure, Tirant is no longer portrayed as simply the bravest and most skilled of warriors; he has been transformed into the commander-in-chief of the entire Greek army, and as such assumes responsibility for the coordination of a massive land campaign in the war against the Moslem invaders. Besides being obliged to delegate responsibility among a multitude of subordinates less capable than himself, Tirant must also rely upon a measure of trickery and deceit on the field of battle to defeat what is almost always a numerically superior enemy force. The hero now finds himself engaged in a mode of combat that requires new and different skills from the ones that he employed in his earlier adventures as a knight-errant. He is required to demonstrate additional new talents as a courtier, diplomat and administrator. He succeeds militarily on all counts, but neglects to follow up his victories because of the distraction posed by the lovely Carmesina back at the capital; as a consequence, the harried Turks have time to regroup and the war is needlessly prolonged.

During the increasingly significant romantic interludes we see Martorell's hero in a new role: the neophyte Courtly Lover who tries to woo the Princess according to the precepts set down by the Provençal poets (Chs. 115-214); this is an obvious parallel to his earlier military apprenticeship first under Varoic and then at the English Court. The tangential question of clandestine marriage is presented in the parallel and contrapuntal "modern" courtship of Diafebus and Estefania, which is inserted to contrast sharply with the more traditional Tirant-Carmesina pairing. After Ch. 214, when Tirant finally realizes that the conventions of Courtly Love are no longer viable as a form of courtship, the wooing of Carmesina is entrusted to the libidinous maiden Plaerdemavida. At this point Tirant moves into the role of the timid lover who fears that any aggressiveness on his part will reap only scorn from his beloved. A further complication is introduced in a series of schemes hatched by the jealous Viuda Reposada for the purpose of alienating Carmesina from the hero; these must be combated at every turn by the vigilant Plaerdemavida.

The episodes that take place under the stewardship of Tirant's new mentor also feature a second contrasting pair of lovers against whom the reader is expected to compare the actions of the principal couple. Beginning in Ch. 248 the middle-aged Empress and the young knight Hipòlit embark upon a steamy, illicit and incestuous affair at the Imperial palace. This new, adulterous entanglement succeeds the Diafebus-Estefania relationship — which has evolved from courtship to marriage, and is consequently eliminated from the narrative as an effective model — as the active counterpoint to Tirant's courtship of Carmesina. The decision to inject this sinful liaison as a major secondary love intrigue appears to have been a late one, insofar as author Martorell was obliged here to alter radically the character of the young warrior. As Riquer has pointed out,[4] Hipòlit is originally introduced in Ch. 140 as the son of a Greek nobleman who requests and receives the order of knighthood from Tirant. By Ch. 234 he has become a Frenchman, from the very same bloodlines as Tirant, or so we are told in Ch. 238. There is still another startling reversal in his role: up until Ch. 214 Hipòlit seems destined for emotional involvement with the damsel Plaerdemavida, but as soon as she takes on the role of Tirant's romantic counsellor, he suddenly and inexplicably is launched into this adulterous liaison with the Empress (which culminates eventually in marriage, as we have already noted). Fortunately, the young maiden loses all romantic interest in him at the same time. Although some might be tempted to attribute these discrepancies to the intervention of Martorell's known collaborator, Martí Joan de Galba, I believe them to be so fundamental to the development of the plot that they could only have come from the pen of the original author. Once Martorell had removed his hero from the influence of the precepts of Courtly Love and placed him under the somewhat lascivious tutelage of Plaerdemavida, he realized the need for an illicit romance to succeed and contrast with the perfect model that he had provided earlier with Diafebus and Estefania; he also saw an opportunity to underscore the ironic denouement that he had in mind for his novel. The belated radical change in Hipòlit's character, then, would seem to be consistent — and perhaps contemporaneous — with a relatively late decision by Martorell to supply an ironic conclusion for his story.

---

[4] *Tirante el Blanco,* II, 242-43, n. 29. See also II, 291, n. 12 and V, 56, n. 14 for subsequent incongruities in detail involving young Hipòlit that appear to have escaped Martorell's authorial glance.

And so, despite the desperate attempts of the Viuda Reposada to drive apart the main lovers, and in sharp contrast to the illicit rendezvous of Hipòlit and the Empress, Tirant and Carmesina appear irreversibly destined for betrothal and marriage as the story enters Ch. 296. But the hand of fate — or rather, of the author — intervenes at this point and Tirant is carried off in his ship by an unexpected storm that deposits him shipwrecked on the North African coast, where a series of new adventures will serve to prepare him for his eventual triumphant return and reunion with Carmesina.

V. TIRANT ON THE BARBARY COAST (Chs. 299-414)

Because this section of the narrative is so different stylistically from the other parts of the novel, the African adventure is often cited as prime evidence of Galba's belated intervention in Martorell's unfinished work.[5] While I am reasonably certain that Galba's hand begins to intrude during this part of the book, I find it impossible to determine precisely which chapters or parts of the African adventure are actually Galba's. Of one thing I am positive: that the general skeleton or outline of the Barbary Coast adventure came from Martorell, because of the pivotal role that this section plays in the development of both the military and romantic themes. The hero's exile on the North African coast may or may not have been part of the original plan for *TB,* but at some point Martorell came to realize the necessity of having his protagonist spend an important block of time away from the Byzantine theatre; it is also absolutely essential that he be separated from the object of his desire long enough to undergo the final emotional maturation and psychological transformation that will

---

[5] Luis Nicolau d'Olwer, "*Tirant lo Blanc:* Examen de algunas cuestiones," *Nueva Revista de Filología Hispánica,* 15 (1961), 131-54. Here he discusses, briefly but thoroughly, the opinions of several notable critics on the Martorell-Galba authorial question. He gives particular emphasis to the views of Riquer (1947) and Corominas (1954) before adding his own opinion. All three share the conviction that Galba's intervention begins at some point during the African adventure. Each man's argument is plausible and worthy of support, but I am not prepared to accept any single theory as the definitive one.

enable him to return to her as the consummate warrior, commander, diplomat, and lover.

The Barbary chapters are occasionally dissatisfying (e.g., here Tirant seems as much interested in an evangelical calling as he is in a military one, and the episodes that treat of his proselytizing among the North African Moslems are among the most uninteresting of the book). Nonetheless, the chapters from 299 through 414 provide us with the pivotal adventures for both the military and romantic transformations. The Tirant who returns to Constantinople at the close of the novel is a more mature individual for the African experience, both as a warrior and as a lover. The key ingredient which has been absent earlier and is acquired among the Barbary Moors is that of perspective. During his exile Tirant finally learns that, despite an almost universal desire among men — especially military figures — to chisel their personal values in stone, the circumstances that determine political loyalties are highly mutable and that one's friendships and allegiances must undergo constant re-evaluation. He learns in Africa that appearances can often be deceiving; that men who are one day sworn enemies can quickly become allies, that an apparent villain may, upon a closer examination of his character, be seen in a much more positive light. A case in point would be the Ethiopian ruler Escariano, whose initial relationship with Tirant is purely confrontational but who eventually becomes the hero's comrade-in-arms and most trusted friend and ally. On the other hand, the figure of the Caudillo or Moorish Chief *(lo Cabdillo sobre los cabdillos)* gradually declines from an initially positive role to a distinctly negative one in the eyes of Tirant (and the reader). Other chameleon-like figures from the African campaign include the Albanese, who proves to be a valuable ally but whose unsettling slyness and cruelty are judged by Tirant to make him unworthy of knighthood; the King of Tlemcen, Tirant's first African protector, who is a kind but distinctly cowardly monarch and is consequently killed off early in the action; Almedíxer, a Genoese sailor (and therefore a highly suspicious character according to Tirant's experience at Rhodes) who eventually proves himself to be a trusted and valiant ally. Religion provides the one constant upon which Tirant can anchor his trust: the Christian characters are nearly always righteous, while the Moors he encounters are generally treacherous, but even the latter are capable of occasional acts of generosity and good faith — once they have been converted to the Christian faith, that is.

The Albanese is a fine example of the kind of complex personality with which Martorell's protagonist must learn to deal in Africa. When Tirant first encounters him outside the castle-city of Mount Tuber where Escariano has taken refuge, he offers the Albanese (who is at this point a slave) his freedom in return for his service as a double agent acting as Tirant's eyes and ears within the city (Ch. 311). The Albanese readily accepts the proposition — even though it entails being whipped and having his ears cut by Tirant in order to convince Escariano of his malevolence toward the Christian commander. The ruse works perfectly and the Albanese gains the complete confidence of Escariano, whose cause he thereupon betrays one night by helping Tirant's men secretly gain entrance to the city and capture the Ethiopian king (Ch. 313). The treachery and innate cruelty of the Albanese are first noted inside the city during the assault when the double-agent cold-bloodedly slits the throats of the jailer's wife and six unsuspecting comrades who have given him their trust. Tirant himself observes that the slaying of a woman constitutes a serious violation of chivalric principles (Ch. 317), a point which he will later bring up when the Albanese asks for knighthood. A short time thereafter (Ch. 319) Escariano and the Albanese exchange insults in Tirant's presence. The Ethiopian monarch denounces the Christian spy for taking a false oath of loyalty and subsequently betraying him into the enemy's hands, while the Albanese counters with the charge that Escariano's current misfortunes are a just punishment for his past transgressions in plundering the kingdom of Tlemcen, a campaign he claims was undertaken merely to satisfy the Ethiopian's lust, avarice and envy. Tirant's reaction to the aforementioned diatribes is, surprisingly, one of sympathy for Escariano, who as a royal personage should not have been subjected to such insulting remarks, in his opinion.

The final stage in the gradual disintegration of the Albanese's character takes place in Ch. 320 when the crafty and unscrupulous double-agent boldly petitions Tirant for induction into the chivalric order; he fully acknowledges that he is currently unworthy of the honor, but adds that he hopes that the new title may inspire him to the kind of courageous and noble conduct that will ultimately justify his premature elevation to that exalted rank. Tirant, recalling the Albanese's bloodthirsty conduct during the battle, his murder of the jailer's wife, and his extremely abusive diatribe against the honorable Escariano, declares him unworthy of such an honor and refuses his petition; he does, however, remember his agent's valuable and loyal service in the past and rewards him handsomely from his own pocket. The Albanese accepts the sum of fifty thousand doubloons and returns to Albania a free and wealthy man, but without a title of nobility.

If it can be said that Martorell takes care to reveal slowly and in piecemeal fashion the defects in the Albanese's character, precisely the opposite technique is used with the figure of Escariano, who gradually grows in stature with each passing chapter. He is presented initially as a hostile intruder into the affairs of the King of Tlemcen, Tirant's master and protector after his capture on the North African coast. In the course of his duties as Tlemcen's diplomatic courier, Tirant ultimately comes face-to-face with the Ethiopian invader about whom he has heard nothing but negative reports (Ch. 308). Their initial mutual distrust soon gives way to begrudging admiration and eventual friendship; from Escariano's own lips Tirant learns the real reason for the Ethiopian's ire and subsequent invasion of Tlemcen's territory: a broken promise by the King to marry his daughter Maragdina to Escariano. The Ethiopian feels that the agreement, formally executed some years before, was abrogated by Maragdina's father for internal political reasons (he attempted to placate his foremost military commander by giving Maragdina in marriage to the chieftain's son), thereby causing shame and embarrassment to Escariano. For this reason, he explains, he feels justified in mounting an invasion whose sole purpose is to claim the prize that is rightfully his and bring Maragdina to Ethiopia as his bride.

The gradual reconciliation that is achieved between these two exemplary military figures, one Christian and one Moorish, culminates in the conversion of Escariano to Christianity and his elevation to the role of Tirant's staunchest ally and most dependable comrade-in-arms. They become in fact like brothers, mirror images of one another and practically indistinguishable as to their military prowess and leadership abilities. Only the color of their skin is different.

There is, however, one important area in which the Ethiopian clearly outshines his Christian counterpart: the matter of courtship and the pursuit of his intended bride. The timid Tirant can learn much from the example of the bold and aggressive Escariano; his black brother will serve as the model for the "new" Tirant who will return to Constantinople and finally succeed in bedding and taking as his fiancée the fair Carmesina — a goal which he has been singularly *un*successful in achieving during his first sojourn at the Greek court.

In many ways the Tirant who reappears on the Byzantine front toward the close of the novel is a much older and wiser individual than the one who disappeared so abruptly in Ch. 299; the lessons he has learned in Barbary have made a profound impression on his character. As a warrior and leader of men he has learned to be patient with subordinates and more conscious of political/diplomatic complexities in relations with both his allies and his enemies. He has also acquired valuable experience in making assaults against walled fortresses (as well as in defending against the same sort of attack). Even more importantly, he has learned to make use of strategic information supplied by double agents and other intelligence sources to complement his modest firepower, a factor which has occasionally allowed him to overcome some serious disadvantages in both manpower and technology. It should also be remembered that in the course of the prolonged Barbary campaign Martorell's hero adds a totally new dimension to his character: that of the evangelist and proselytizer who manages to convert Moors to Christianity by the thousands, even hundreds of thousands. And to close the case, we must mention the tutoring he has received from Escariano that will make him a more aggressive suitor, a lover who will move boldly to achieve his romantic desires. When viewed in the light of all of the above, the North African adventure can easily be seen as a pivotal one for both of Martorell's principal themes.

VI. THE RETURN TO CONSTANTINOPLE: TRIUMPH AND DEATH
(Chs. 415-87)

When Tirant finally returns to the Byzantine theatre after an absence of several years, he appears as a hardened veteran of many campaigns, an experienced field commander at the helm of a formidable array of land and naval forces. The hero engages the Turks just outside the capital city and soundly defeats them there with the aid of an ingenious battle plan: his fleet feints boldly up the coast in a move designed to draw the enemy away from a strategic area on the other side of the peninsula near the river; his armada then doubles back under cover of darkness and lands troops on the shore at a point from which the infantry can easliy march overland and seize the river bank, thereby cutting the Turks off from the capital. Tirant's daring maneuver and masterful coordination of this combined land-and-sea assault is absolute proof of his newly honed leadership skills.

Martorell's hero is equally triumphant on the romantic front; with the aid of Plaerdemavida (now bearing the title Queen of Fez and Bougie), he finally succeeds in consummating with Carmesina the secret wedding vows they exchanged earlier in the palace garden. Consummation is followed almost immediately by a formal betrothal ceremony — a combination of events which in the eyes of the Church in Martorell's time would have constituted a valid marriage bond at that point. With the subsequent naming of Tirant as "Cèsar de l'Imperi," he has become an official member of the Imperial family and heir apparent to the crown as the Princess' legal consort.

Although it is impossible to ascertain what may have been Martorell's original intention regarding the denouement of his story, it would seem that at some late point he decided to inject a strongly ironic note in the final chapters. And so, at the precise moment when it appears that all of Tirant's hopes and aspirations are about to be fulfilled, at the hour of his greatest triumph when he seems virtually invincible, he is suddenly and inexplicably cut down by a fatal attack of appendicitis. A most exemplary and heroic life thus concludes on a supremely ironic and unheroic note. The irony continues with the deaths immediately thereafter of the old Emperor and Carmesina, respectively. This strange combination of circumstances paves the way for Hipòlit to ascend to the throne by virtue of being Tirant's legal heir as well as through his subsequent marriage to the newly widowed Empress. This most disquieting turn of events at the close of the action serves only to underscore the didactic nature of Martorell's plan for *TB*: the novel is intended to trace the evolution of its hero and protagonist toward perfection as both a warrior and as a lover. To have him suddenly struck down at the very peak of his military and romantic success therefore allows the reader to retain the image of Tirant in full bloom and at the height of his powers; it gives us pause to reflect upon the virtues that have been displayed by this most perfect of military heroes and courtly lovers.

Martorell's decision to reinforce the didactic content of his novel with an ironic denouement was an extremely fortuitous one. It is doubtful that any more efficacious ending could have been devised for this story. The only alternative — to close with a Tirant grown old, fat and complacent at the side of his beloved Carmesina — would have served only to undermine the principal lesson Martorell wished to teach in his novel: that complacency leads inevitably to corruption and decay. Joanot Martorell was firmly convinced that such self-satisfaction had been the cause of the decline and degeneration of Christian military might in the Mediterranean and ultimately of the fall of Constantinople in 1453, an event which, as we said earlier, was the principal inspiration for Martorell's book. In a similar manner, the alarming decline in social mores, as evidenced by the well-known abuses connected with the practice of clandestine marriage (with Martorell's sister Damiata as one notable victim), was the result of a lax, complacent social attitude within Christendom. It was Martorell's intention to expose these weaknesses and to suggest some practical remedies.

* * *

Before I bring to a close this study of *TB*, there are two ancillary issues that can and should be addressed; the first of these is the question of Martí Joan de Galba's intervention in the writing and/or preparation for printing of the original manuscript. As we can see from the colophon that follows Ch. 487,

> *Aquí feneix lo llibre del valerós e estrenu cavaller Tirant lo Blanc, príncep e Cèsar de l'Imperi grec de Constantinoble, lo qual fon traduït d'anglès en llengua portuguesa, e aprés en vulgar llengua valenciana, per lo magnífic e virtuós cavaller Mossèn Joanot Martorell, lo qual, per mort sua, no en pogué acabar de traduir sinó les tres parts. La quarta part, que és la fi del llibre, és estada traduïda, a pregàries de la noble senyora Dona Isabel de Lloris, per lo magnífic cavaller Mossèn Martí Joan de Galba; e si defalt hi serà trobat, vol sia atribuït a la sua ignoràncìa; al qual Nostre Senyor Jesucrist, per la sua immensa bondat, vulla donar, en premi de sos treballs, la glòria de paradís. E protesta que si en lo dit llibre haurà posades algunes coses que no sien catòliques, que no les vol haver dites, ans les remet a correcció de la santa catòlica Església.*
>
> FON ACABADA D'EMPREMTAR LA PRESENT OBRA EN LA CIUTAT DE VALÈNCIA, A 20 DEL MES DE NOEMBRE DE L'ANY DE LA NATIVITAT DE NOSTRE SENYOR DÉU JESUCRIST 1490. [6]

the "translation" (but more likely, the actual composition) of the fourth and final part of the novel is attributed to Galba. But since there is no division of the work into parts in the 1490 edition, the precise contribution of Galba, who, like Martorell before him, also passed away before the printing could be completed, remains a mystery.

---

[6] "Thus concludes the book about the brave and outstanding knight Tirant lo Blanch, Prince and Caesar of the Greek Empire of Constantinople, which was translated from English to Portuguese, and later to popular Valencian by the great and virtuous knight, Lord Joanot Martorell, who, because of his intervening death, could translate only three of the parts. The fourth one, which is the end of the book, has been translated at the request of the noble lady Isabel de Lloris by the illustrious Lord Martí Joan de Galba. And if some defect should be discovered in it, it should be attributed to his ignorance, and may Our Lord Jesus Christ in His great goodness grant him the glory of Paradise as a reward for his efforts. He further states that if there are some things in this book that are not Catholic, they are unintentional; he hereby submits it in advance for correction by the Holy Catholic Church.

"The printing of the present work was completed in the city of Valencia, the twentieth day of November of the year 1490 after the nativity of Our Lord God Jesus Christ."

Logically, it would appear that Chs. 415-78, which deal with Tirant's return to Constantinople and his subsequent death, should be attributed to the second author. Stylistically, only certain portions of the North African adventure — especially those involving Plaerdemavida, whose personality is debased to such an extent that she no longer resembles the sprightly damsel of the earlier episodes — seem to betray the hand of a different author.[7] Early critics — Martínez y Martínez (1916), Vaeth (1918) and Givanel Mas (1921-22) — have proposed that Galba's participation was limited to the preparation and correction of Martorell's original manuscript for the printer, plus the composition of rubrics and chapter headings. On the other hand, Riquer (1947) and Corominas (1954) have argued more recently for a progressive intervention of Galba in Martorell's unfinished original draft. They propose that Galba finished off some chapters, amplified others (especially toward the close of the novel), and performed the final editorial work on the finished manuscript. Unfortunately, these two critics do not agree as to which of the sections or chapters belong to the second author.[8] Where they *do* agree is in attributing the ironic denouement to Galba, which I find difficult to accept.

Joanot Martorell was virtually a walking encyclopedia of medieval customs, conventions, rites, ceremonies and rituals. He carefully displays in his novel a vast knowledge of the various dueling customs of the Middle Ages, including several versions of the letter of challenge. He is likewise knowledgeable regarding modes of combat, the conventions of Courtly Love, and many ceremonies of social significance (weddings, baptisms, the conferring of knighthood, the defrocking of delinquent knights, etc.). And according to Riquer, Martorell depicted them with amazing realism and fidelity to detail. As a final note we should add that Tirant's creator was also an expert in the matter of military strategy — both land and naval maneuvers — and an accurate chronicler of

---

[7] See Entwistle, "*Tirant lo Blanc* and the Social Order of the End of the 15th Century," *Estudis Romànics,* 2 (1949-50), 149-64; also Nicolau d'Olwer, "*Tirant lo Blanc:* Examen de algunas cuestiones," *Nueva Revista de Filología Hispánica,* 15 (1961), 131-54.

[8] See Nicolau d'Olwer's 1961 article in *NRFH* for a summary of Corominas' and Riquer's respective views.

the various advances that had taken place in military technology in the course of the previous few centuries.

On the other hand, Galba's knowledge, background and personal interests are unknown or imprecise. I find it quite plausible that he may have retouched a few parts of Martorell's original and prepared the manuscript for publication. He may also have expanded some of Martorell's briefer chapters or added a few of his own — which, by the way, I believe to be the case with the adventures of Plaerdemavida in Africa. Even this, however, cannot be demonstrated conclusively, despite Riquer's effort to do so in his 1974 Castilian edition.

The essential question here has to do with the design and execution of the plan for the novel, for which I believe Joanot Martorell is almost totally responsible. Even the ironic conclusion is logically attributable to the original author. It should be remembered that one of the models for Martorell's hero was the Hungarian Johannes Hunyadi, whose untimely and unheroic demise as the victim of the plague occurred only a few short weeks after his glorious victory over the Turks at Belgrade (1456). Consequently, a similar pedestrian death for his hero was probably a part of Martorell's plan from the very beginning. The only ironic aspect that definitely appears to have been a late insertion is the adulterous and incestuous romance involving the Empress and her young paramour, Hipòlit; it commences at a rather late point (Ch. 248) and is reprised at the very end of the story (Chs. 479-87) simply to provide a final bitter note. Hipòlit's scandalous conduct not only goes unpunished, but he is actually rewarded by the fates with an undeserved elevation, through marriage, to the role of heir and successor to the Imperial crown, a prize that eluded the grasp of the much more deserving Tirant. But even this heaping of irony upon irony at the close of the novel seems logically consistent with the original plan of the initial and principal author, and does *not* necessarily point toward any belated intervention on the part of his literary executor.

The second and final consideration I would like to offer is Cervantes' reaction to *TB;* let us ponder, as so many others have done, the famous words of the Priest in Chapter Six of the 1605 *Quixote* regarding the Castilian version, *Tirante el Blanco:*

—¡Válame Dios! — dijo el cura, dando una gran voz. —¡Que aquí esté Tirante el Blanco! Dádmele acá, compadre; que hago cuenta que he hallado en él un tesoro de contento y una mina de pasatiempos. Aquí está don Quirieleisón de Montalbán, valeroso caballero, y su hermano Tomás de Montalbán, y el caballero Fonseca, con la batalla que el valiente de Tirante hizo con el alano, y las agudezas de la doncella Placerdemivida, con los amores y embustes de la viuda Reposada, y la señora Emperatriz, enamorada de Hipólito, su escudero. Dígoos verdad, señor compadre, que, por su estilo, es éste el mejor libro del mundo: aquí comen los caballeros, y duermen y mueren en sus camas, y hacen testamento antes de su muerte, con estas cosas de que todos los demás libros deste género carecen. Con todo eso, os digo que merecía el que le compuso, pues no hizo tantas necedades de industria, que le echaran a galeras por todos los días de su vida. Llevadle a casa y leedle, y veréis que es verdad cuanto dél os he dicho.[9]

Leaving aside the enigmatic penultimate sentence that critics have been unable to explain away or decipher satisfactorily for over 150 years, an examination of some of the specific references Cervantes makes to Martorell's text can lead us to some interesting speculations, particularly if we compare the cited episodes to similar adventures in Ariosto's *Orlando Furioso*. The enormous brothers Tomàs and Kirieleison de Montalbán (Multalbà) and the oft-cited tooth-to-tooth battle of Tirant and the mastiff are reminiscent of the many battles Ariosto's chivalric figures engage in with giants and beasts; the reference to the clever utterances of Plaerdemavida recalls the many erotic episodes of the *Furioso,* especially the double-entendre use of military imagery and terminology to describe sexual encounters. Mentioning the jealous schemes *(embustes)* of the evil Viuda Reposada puts her in the company of Ariosto's own deceitful character, Polinesso; the reference to the liaison of the Empress with young Hipòlit is reminiscent again of Ariostan themes of adultery and incest. Only the naming of the knight Fonseca, who appears only once — and insignificantly — in *TB* (Ch. 132), fails to conform to this pattern. Martín de Riquer

---

[9] Miguel de Cervantes, *Don Quijote de la Mancha,* ed. Martín de Riquer, 2 vols. (Barcelona: Juventud, 1969), I, 72.

has offered an interesting theory regarding the unexpected mention of Fonseca's name in the *Quixote:* the name Fonseca appears on the penultimate line of the second column of folio 88 v. of the 1511 Castilian translation of Martorell's novel (which is generally assumed to be the version of *TB* read by Cervantes); while composing the Priest's comments about the book during the library scene of the *Quixote,* the Spanish novelist may have wished to add a reference to one more episode, opened the book and selected at random Fonseca's name from the bottom of the folio. [10]

Ariosto's *Furioso* has often been cited by critics as a possible major influence on Cervantes and his masterpiece; the correspondence of these cited episodes from *TB* to similar elements in the popular Italian romance are probably more than a mere coincidence. Cervantes may indeed have considered the Catalan novel to be similar in kind to the Ariostan masterpiece. I am inclined to believe that the great Spanish novelist held both works in the same high esteem, but an investigation of this matter must necessarily fall outside the scope of the present study. For the moment I am content to leave this issue for others to resolve. Or, as Cervantes attempted to say at the close of *Don Quixote,* Part One (but botched the job),

Forse altri canterà con miglior plettro.

---

[10] *Tirante el Blanco,* II, 189, n. 12. Cervantes' use of the 1511 Castilian edition of *TB* may also explain why Cervantes appears to be ignorant of the identity of the book's author(s); the 1511 edition lists no author's name.

Chapter VI

SOME LITERARY CONSIDERATIONS:
TIRANT LO BLANCH, PRECURSOR OF THE
MODERN NOVEL?

Cervantes' encomium in *Don Quixote,* Part One, notwithstanding, the best and most influential analysis of *TB* as a "modern" work of fiction to date has been Peruvian novelist Mario Vargas Llosa's oft-published *carta de batalla* in defense of Martorell's masterpiece. [1] In my opinion, no one has ever stated more forcefully the case for *TB* as a precursor of the modern novel than the Peruvian novelist-critic did in 1969. Since that date, almost every evaluation of the literary merits of Martorell's book has, to some degree, been based upon Vargas Llosa's watershed essay. [2]

The judgments I am about to make here are likewise, I must confess, largely derivative of Vargas Llosa's most original treatise. I plan to present a brief recapitulation of the major points he made in his 1969 article, then proceed with expansions of my

---

[1] Written in 1968, the *carta de batalla* has appeared in various publications and in a variety of languages. I am aware of the following: "A Challenge on Behalf of *Tirant lo Blanc,*" *Research Studies* (Olympia: Washington State University), 37 (1968?), 1-16; "Carta de batalla por *Tirant lo Blanc,*" Prologue to the J. F. Vidal Jové edition of *TB* (Madrid: Alianza, 1969), I, 9-41; "Carta de batalla por *Tirant lo Blanc,*" *Revista de Occidente,* 70 (Jan. 1969), 1-21; *Lletra de batalla per Tirant lo Blanc* (Barcelona: Edicions 62, 1976). All citations in my text are taken from the Prologue to the Vidal Jové edition of *TB*.

[2] The best example I can cite of this phenomenon is Arthur Terry, "Character and Role in *Tirant lo Blanc,*" in *Essays on Narrative Fiction in the Iberian Peninsula in Honour of Frank Pierce,* ed. R. B. Tate (Oxford: Dolphin, 1982), 177-95.

own, based upon the findings contained in the preceding chapters of this study. From time to time I will find it necessary to disagree with the Peruvian analyst, but on the whole I find myself in strong accord with his very sound and sensible critical views. Toward the close of my essay I will attempt to integrate *TB* — or at least certain sections of it — with a scheme proposed by still another critic regarding the evolution of the *novela sentimental* during the fifteenth and sixteenth centuries.

* * *

Vargas Llosa's principal reason for praising so highly Martorell's narrative achievement is *not* merely the oft-cited realistic tone of *TB*. The Peruvian critic readily admits that the Catalan novel contains a number of very *un*realistic elements. He points instead to the fact that author Martorell, while remaining practically invisible throughout, manages to anticipate the techniques of such "modern" writers as Balzac, Flaubert, and Faulkner in the role of what Vargas Llosa calls "suplantadores de Dios," authors who play God by creating a universe of their own, a world with an existence that is apparently independent of the control or influence of any outside force — including the author's.

One of the major elements of *TB*'s "modernity" is the strong focus the author places on sexual themes and erotic episodes. But can we really call it an erotic novel? I believe I have demonstrated convincingly in Chapter III above that there is indeed a valid — didactic, actually — reason for the numerous sexual adventures Martorell has seen fit to scatter at intervals through his novel; they are not presented simply to titillate the reader, although they certainly do achieve that result. In these erotic episodes Vargas Llosa considers Martorell a "neutral" figure, an unbiased observer and objective commentator on the fundamental conflict that is presented between the chaste and refined "amor tímido" demanded by the precepts of Courtly Love and the more worldly bourgeois notion of carnal "amor vicioso" that is advocated by Plaerdemavida. As the Peruvian writer views it, Martorell's narrative technique was to present both arguments dispassionately and let the reader decide for himself which of the two was superior.

I would strongly disagree, of course. It is true that Martorell's tendency is to allow both sides of any issue to be fairly represented in his narrative; even the nefarious and loathsome Duke of Macedonia is permitted to speak his piece directly and without interruption or contradiction. But I have shown throughout this study that on most political, social or religious issues the discerning reader can eventually discover where Martorell's personal sentiments lie. Unfortunately, the author's penchant for clever understatement and the sly ironic twist often makes it difficult for a casual reader to grasp the "tilt" that Martorell provides in his text. I find Martorell strongly in favor of Plaerdemavida's "amor vicioso" — but not without at the same time advocating certain practical legal precaution (e.g., Estefania's *albarà*) to guard against abuse.

Similarly, I would part company with Vargas Llosa on the issue of Martorell's right to be called a "disinterested novelist." I have already said a sufficient amount about the Valencian writer's personal biases and how he went about injecting them into his narrative. I would, nonetheless, agree with the Peruvian novelist's high estimation of Martorell's "modern" technique of seeming to disappear from his own narrative (except for those relatively rare occasions when he deliberately chooses to intrude into the action). All in all, I hold Martorell in probably even loftier esteem than does Vargas Llosa. The pose of equanimity that Martorell affects in his novel has evidently convinced even so sophisticated a reader as the celebrated writer. This, I feel, constitutes the highest tribute that can be offered to the Valencian's technical genius as a narrator and the manner in which he was able to blend both aesthetic and didactic elements in his text.

Still another feature of *TB* that has shown strong appeal to nineteenth-and twentieth-century readers is Martorell's sharp portrayal of basic human psychology. The Catalan novel exhibits subtleties of characterization that cannot be found in most of the prose fiction of its time. To begin with, the protagonist in *TB* is considerably more complex than the stereotyped one-dimensional heroes we find in the chivalric romances. The reader can actually observe Martorell's protagonist develop from an awkward and shy adolescent into a forceful and self-confident adult; he matures both professionally (from squire to knight-errant, and eventually to the rank of a full-fledged general in command of a combined infantry and naval force) and emotionally (as a suitor who gradually and painfully learns to woo and win the heart of his chosen mate). As Vargas Llosa points out, the psychological depth of Tirant and the other major characters is never forced; their slow and gradual development always seems quite natural. The only exception to this is Martorell's rigid portrayal of Tirant's Moslem adversaries; rarely can they match their Christian counterparts in dignity and generosity, and when such a spiritually righteous Moslem can be found, he/she invariably elects to convert to the Christian faith.

I distinguish three basic levels of psychological development within the panorama of characters that Martorell rolls before us. First there are the simple stereotypes: the Viuda Reposada is the jealous woman scorned and bound for vengeance; Felip is cast in the traditional comic role of the tightwad; the Duke of Macedonia epitomizes all the arrogance and treachery one would normally associate with the figure of a vile traitor and murderer; Hipòlit is the essence of ambition, a selfish social-climber who will seize any opportunity to advance his social rank. At this level Martorell's book is practically indistinguishable from any of the chivalric works of the period.

The second group, with which Martorell's book begins to set itself apart from the rest of the genre, consists of characters with a slightly more complex psychological make-up that causes them to be perceived first one way, then another, as the author requires. Actually, these personalities exhibit very slight psychological mutation in and of themselves; what is altered is merely the perspective from which the author chooses to present them to the reader. The Cabdillo and the Albanese, to cite two examples from the North African adventure, are first presented as positive and/or sympathetically drawn characters who befriend the hero at a low point in his life. In the course of the Barbary campaign, however, both Tirant and the reader soon begin to see them in a new light as additional layers of each man's true personality come to the forefront. They are eventually disposed of — brutally in the case of the Cabdillo and by means of a sharp reprimand and curt dismissal for the Albanese — but only after they have exhausted their usefulness to the author. Conversely, the dark-skinned Ethiopian monarch Escariano is initially presented as something akin to the Devil himself, if one were to believe the rumors that have been circulating about his previous conduct. Personal contact between Tirant and his black adversary — first on the diplomatic front, then later when Escariano has been made Tirant's prisoner — ultimately convinces the hero of the Ethiopian's great personal dignity, and the two warriors end up being the closest of friends and firm military allies. In this same category I would place the figure of the middle-aged Greek Empress who suddenly initiates an adulterous relationship with the young knight Hipòlit. It should be noted, however, that the development of her character does not follow perfectly the pattern of the three previous cases because she is not perceived as moving from a positive to a negative mode or vice-versa. In her case, the grieving Empress simply undergoes a fundamental psychological transformation about halfway through the novel. This sudden change in her personality is highly plausible, however, if one takes into account the circumstance of her having recently lost her only son as a war casualty, and it has the beneficial effect of carrying her from the periphery of the action to center stage for a brief interlude. Her good/bad status in the reader's eyes is not affected much at all; she will remain a positive figure in the novel right up to the moment of her peaceful and natural death in the final chapters. What makes her more interesting than the stereotypical figures I place in the first category is the fact that the incestuous overtones of her passion for the young knight — who, it must be recalled, bears a strong physical resemblance to her lost son — are revealed at a relatively late stage, and that they give her character a totally unique added dimension.

The highest level of psychological complexity in *TB* is that at which a gradual but fundamental change of personality can be observed in a single character in the course of several hundred chapters — a truly rare occurrence in pre-Renaissance fiction. Within this category I place only Tirant, Carmesina and the salacious Plaerdemavida. Tirant, of course, is the character in whom we would logically expect to find such complex development. I need not recapitulate the changes I documented earlier in Chapters II and III regarding the hero's development both as a military leader and as a lover. In the case of Carmesina, she is required to undergo a psychological transformation only in the second of these two areas: her conservative outlook on courtship and the hoary precepts of Courtly Love.

The third case is the most interesting of all — at least for twentieth-century tastes. The figure of the sprightly damsel Plaerdemavida is arguably the most successfully drawn character in the entire novel and the one which has tickled the fancy of more readers and critics than any other. She makes her initial appearance relatively late in the novel (Ch. 139, more than twenty chapters after the hero's arrival in Constantinople) and has little or no function until Ch. 163, when she provides us with her amusing account of the bedroom rendezvous (the *bodes sordes*) of Tirant-Carmesina and Diafebus-Estefania. From this point forward she assumes an evermore important role as the go-between in Tirant's courtship of the Princess, an arrangement that provides her with ample opportunity to exhibit the delightfully lascivious side of her personality. Furthermore, she is an energetic and humorous bundle of self-contradiction: although as Tirant's counsellor she is the most outspoken and enthusiastic proponent of early and frequent pre-marital sexual contact, she is actually quite prudish regarding her own social/sexual conduct. An early flirtation with Hipòlit generates absolutely no physical contact of any kind between them; and her courtship and eventual marriage to Tirant's cousin, Lord Agramunt, is most chastely conducted. She is a character whose theoretical reach far exceeds her practical grasp. (There also is one slight hint of a possible lesbian attraction on her part toward the Princess, but there is no subsequent action to confirm it.) The only real blemish I can find in her character is the literary lobotomy she seems to undergo during the African adventure (roughly Chs. 350-83), when she suddenly becomes a long-winded bore. Several critics have opined that this curious transformation betrays the intervention of the less-skillful hand of Martí Joan de Galba, Martorell's friend and collaborator who prepared the manuscript for printing and added an unspecified "fourth part" to the original. I find such arguments very persuasive; in fact, those unfortunate chapters dealing with Plaerdemavida's wanderings on the Barbary Coast are virtually the only chapters I am willing to accept at this time as definitely Galba's work, and I do so simply because they are at such variance with the portrait of the lively and witty damsel presented earlier in the chapters that we know were penned by Martorell. Characterization such as we find in her is extremely rare in pre-Renaissance works and becomes a hallmark of narrative fiction only after the appearance of *Don Quixote*. On this point, then, *TB* might well be considered a precursor of Cervantes' masterpiece.

Still another thorny problem that Vargas Llosa addresses in his essay is that of the frequent examples of literary piracy and plagiarism found in *TB*. As I pointed out in the first chapter of this study, Joanot Martorell was a master plagiarist. His was a true gift for organizing and integrating materials that would at first glance seem incongruous or incompatible, then forging them into a new artistic whole; he could skillfully blend elements of his own invention with "foreign" material he had borrowed — often on a large scale — from other writers. And he knew how to alloy the two in such a way that the casual reader would be unable to distinguish between them. Contemporary literary figures such as Enrique de Villena and Joan Roiç de Corella are simply two of the more notable sources of "borrowed" material to be found in *TB*. As the Peruvian writer observes at one point, "esos plagios confirman su genio" (p. 22).

Unfortunately, modern criticism no longer recognizes such plagiaristic talents as a sign of genius. But within the context of medieval literary practice wherein such techniques were commonly employed and universally approved, Martorell should be viewed as a truly outstanding author of his time, one who could take total command of materials provided by others and use them to fortify and enhance his own literary creation, producing in the end a hybrid text of startling originality. It is this remarkable but outmoded talent that earlier critics have failed or refused to recognize in the author of *TB*. Martorell makes use of this gift, to give just one example, in his utilization of historical data. Several scholars have noted Martorell's liberal borrowing of data about the real-life exploits of Roger de Flor in the Balkans (as recorded in Muntaner's *Crónica*) to provide the background for Tirant's fictional adventures at the Byzantine Court. But at the same time Martorell also employs a great deal of pseudo-historical material (e.g., a purely imaginary Arab invasion of the British Isles that takes place in the first 28 chapters) that has an equally "realistic" ring to it. Episodes such as these are, from the standpoint of narrative verisimilitude, virtually indistinguishable from the verifiably historical events portrayed in the book, e.g., Geoffroy de Thoisy's heroic efforts in breaking the Egyptian siege of Rhodes in 1444, which is fictionally reenacted (with Tirant in the role of Thoisy) in Chs. 98-107 of Martorell's masterpiece. The Valencian author's genius for combining disparate historical and fictional elements and then forging them into a plausible and convincing "realistic" hybrid is again demonstrated in the clever hoax he perpetrates regarding the identity of the subject of his book's Dedication, as I demonstrated earlier in Chapter I. The final product is a unique work of narrative fiction that captures, as Vargas Llosa puts it, "la realidad total de su tiempo" (p. 25).

A major portion of the Peruvian critic's 1969 article is devoted to an examination and explanation of Martorell's peculiar narrative strategy in *TB*. Within the same medieval work we find oral and written monologues of great rhetorical value balanced by some of the wittiest and most entertaining colloquial dialogues found anywhere. The novel features elaborate descriptions of complex battle strategies together with spirited accounts of romantic interludes that exhibit considerable erotic charm. The author provides us with skillful outlines of dastardly plots and cruel deceptions, with frequent and detailed descriptions of heavy battlefield carnage, but also with outrageously comic scenes that rival those which Cervantes will write a century-and-a-half later.

Vargas Llosa makes a particularly important contribution when he signals as a primary characteristic of Martorell's style the fluctuation of "cráteres activos" and "tiempos muertos" throughout *TB* — a phenomenon, he is quick to point out, that bears no relation whatsoever to the chapter divisions, which seem to have been made after the author's death. Martorell's technique for alternating highly-charged episodes of tremendous narrative energy with slower-paced interludes when practically no action occurs is at once exhilarating and maddening for the modern-day reader. Although Martorell's injection of wordy speeches and letters probably would have found considerable favor among his fifteenth-century audience, the technique quickly wears thin with the modern public.[3]

Vargas Llosa analyzes at some length what he considers the two most outstanding examples of Martorell's "craters of activity" technique: 1) the moment when Tirant first lays eyes on the beautiful Carmesina (Chs. 116-19), and 2) the famous seduction scene of the *bodes sordes* (Ch. 163) at Malveí castle, narrated by Plaerdemavida in "flashback" sequence. Rather than attempt to summarize or re-state all the points that the Peruvian author-critic makes in his discussion of these two scenes, I will simply point out and describe the four basic narrative levels he discerns in Martorell's narrative style:

a) the Rhetorical Level: this consists principally of oral and written discourses delivered at irregularly spaced intervals throughout the book. These are — to the modern mind, at least — the sections of least interest, although, as I said earlier, the fifteenth-century audience probably would have welcomed and praised them as a display of the author's verbal virtuosity. These weighty passages tend to bog down the action because nothing is allowed to occur while the reader is obliged to plow through this pregnant prose. For the specialist, however, these sections can be of considerable interest, insofar as they are an accurate reflection of various medieval customs, traditions and rhetorical conventions. Only a literary archeologist could be attracted today to a lengthy discourse on the nobility of the chivalric warrior, or to one on the visceral bond that theoretically unites a monarch with his subjects, or to another touching on the finer points of courtship, etc., etc.

As Vargas Llosa notes, here the tendency is toward the monologue, to superficial expository utterances that tell us virtually nothing about the innermost sentiments or the fundamental

---

[3] It makes one long for an abridged version of *TB* that would eliminate the "dead spots" and link all the exciting episodes that take place either on the battlefield or in the bedroom. But such an edition, I fear, would simply overpower the reader. The most difficult task for the editor of such a text would be to select and retain the inactive interludes that actually contribute to maintaining the flow of the narrative and promoting character development. It is a task that I would not relish having set before me.

personal values of the speaker/writer; the exercise clearly tends to be more conventional than personal. Even the formal letters of challenge and the oral *desafíos,* as we saw in Chapter IV, are often more ceremonial exercises than reflections of real personal outrage. They are characteristically long-winded, at times flowery, at others erudite, but almost always mechanical and cold in nature. What these rhetorical passages accurately reflect are the firmly established religious, social, and moral conventions of fifteenth-century Christendom. From an archeological or sociological standpoint, they have much to say; as literature, they contain little of interest for the modern reader.

b) the Objective Level: this consists of the purely external description of reality by the omniscient narrator; everything here is reduced to visual and auditory phenomena. Martorell is very adept at presenting the sights and sounds of the fifteenth-century world — what Vargas Llosa calls "realidad sensorial compacta" (p. 32) — and this is the predominant narrative level in his novel.

c) the Subjective Level: this represents an upward shifting of gears as Martorell's authorial glance moves from purely external reality to the higher dimension of the secret thoughts and emotions of the characters. In these moments the reader is suddenly made privy to the innermost hopes and fears of some important character — usually Tirant. This passing to a higher form of reality in the narrative is barely perceptible to the average reader; Martorell moves from the objective to the subjective plane with scarcely any observable change on the surface. It is to this kind of smooth transition that Vargas Llosa attributes the distinctly "modern" flavor of Martorell's style.

d) the Symbolic or Mythical Level: this is a less-frequently employed technique in *TB,* but one which the author handles adeptly when he elects to use it. Injecting symbolic parallels to reinforce the effect of certain elements in his story raises the narrative to its highest state, as in the description of the alcove of famous lovers at the Byzantine palace, the unexpected appearance of Morgana and King Arthur at the Imperial Court, and the adventure of Espèrcius on the island.

The real merit of Martorell's narrative style, according to Vargas Llosa, does not lie in the employment of any single level of description, but rather in the dynamic interaction that results from his ingenious combination of these four planes, a rare display of technical mastery for a fifteenth-century writer. Martorell's style is able to absorb and combine the most significant conventions, acts, sentiments, and symbols of his age, then reconstitute them in an original work of fiction from which the vitality of medieval society literally bursts forth. From so many diverse elements the author is able to produce, almost miraculously, a new and virtually perfect literary unity.

The secret of Martorell's narrative technique lies in a tandem of procedures that Vargas Llosa has named 1) *la muda o salto cualitativo* and 2) *los vasos comunicantes*. The former is a device for separating and distinguishing the different planes of reality within the narrative; the latter is a technique for reuniting and integrating them to produce a single, smooth narrative flow. When these techniques are handled well, the narration passes from one level to another so subtly that only the trained eye of a critic can detect the change. What the casual or innocent reader notices are simply the resultant movement, ambiguity, depth, and animation of the episode in question.

Vargas Llosa concedes that the *muda* or *salto* from plane to plane of reality is also frequent in the other books of chivalry, especially when "reality" passes from the historical to the marvelous plane (or, to look at it another way, from the rational to the irrational level). But, he adds, no other work of that genre utilizes this procedure as effectively as *TB*. In Martorell's work there is frequently no outward sign given in the text to indicate that a substitution has been made; in some instances the signal is given only at a belated point, after the reader has become totally immersed in the new material and is unable to reject this new, unannounced dimension of reality. We normally associate this particular strategy with writers of fantastic works (e.g., Kafka and Cortázar, who need to make us accept as normal events and situations which can only be described as nightmarish or highly improbable). What Vargas Llosa is pleased — and perhaps surprised — to discover is that a medieval writer like Martorell (ca.

1460) demonstrates the very same sort of flexibility in the organization of his material.

In his analysis of the celebrated *bodes sordes* episode (Ch. 163), Vargas Llosa points to Martorell's disruption of the normal chronological ordering of events as an anticipation of modern storytelling techniques. The critic describes how Martorell teases the reader by having the action jump forward and back among three distinct time frames: we move from the light-hearted preliminaries of the nocturnal rendezvous of the lovers (A), to the bitter recriminations of the morning after (C), and then back in time as Plaerdemavida recounts her "dream," a flashback sequence (B) in which the reader is belatedly given the titillating details of Estefania's deflowering the night before.

The Peruvian writer also draws our attention to the subtle change in the narration's point of view that Martorell carries out in the course of this episode. The preliminaries are described in the third-person objective mode by the omniscient narrator. But the action leaps forward then to the following day and suddenly back again, at which time the remainder of the story is recounted, not by the original objective narrator, but in a subjective first-person account delivered by one of the novel's characters. Almost imperceptibly, Martorell has transformed the nature of this adventure from that of an unbiased, straightforward account to a more complex and sophisticated story-within-the-story format. The simple narrative structure used at the beginning has, by the time we reach the end, been replaced by something quite different; at the close of the story we find an audience composed of some of the actual participants being obliged to listen to a third party's eyewitness account of their clandestine — or so they thought — sexual activities the night before. This *caja china* effect, as Vargas Llosa calls it, is at least as old as the *1001 Arabian Nights,* but has also become one of the hallmarks of modern fiction (Conrad, Faulkner, et al.). To be sure, Martorell uses this technique most successfully and inventively in the *bodes sordes* episode, but he employs it also at several other points in his novel, e.g., Diafebus' account to the hermit Varoic of Tirant's heroic exploits at the English Court, and the story told by the French legates about the clever Genoese plan to capture the fortress at Rhodes.

Martorell's great gift was an ability to cross temporal zones, to shift from one plane of reality to another, to combine apparently incompatible narrative elements (e.g., the historical with the fantastic, the brutal with the erotic), to inject humor or irony where the reader might least expect it — without any rupture of continuity or loss of verisimilitude. Vargas Llosa describes the creator of *TB* as an ambitious writer who utilized narrative techniques that would not become frequent in the novel for several centuries. But all this would be of merely anecdotal interest if he had not, in the process, written so fine a work as *TB*. Or as the Peruvian critic says toward the close of his article, "No son esta ambición y estas técnicas las que dan grandeza a esta creación, es esta creación la que da grandeza a esa ambición y a esas técnicas" (p. 41).

* * *

Before bringing this chapter to a close, I would like to offer a few additional thoughts concerning the relationship of *TB* to a genre with which it is rarely compared, the sentimental novel. To begin, I would refer my readers to a recent (1982) article by Julio Rodríguez-Puértolas in which he comments incisively and at length on the evolution of the fifteenth-century *novela sentimental* away from the traditional aristocratic values of the moribund medieval society of the 1400s and toward the new bourgeois ideas that came into vogue with the Renaissance. [4] Specifically, the critic analyzes and explains the changes that took place in the sentimental genre during the years 1430-1514, roughly the same period during which Martorell wrote and Galba edited *TB*. The article traces a gradual movement toward intimacy, subjectivity and individualism in the portrayal of protagonists in these novels. He points out, for example, that the early heroes of this genre found themselves caught between the musty aristocratic courtship conventions based on the spiritual precepts of Courtly Love on the one hand, and the sexual vitality inherent in the new, materialistic social values

---

[4] "Sentimentalismo 'burgués' y amor cortés. La novela del siglo xv," in *Essays on Narrative Fiction in the Iberian Peninsula in Honour of Frank Pierce*, ed. R. B. Tate (Oxford: Dolphin, 1982), 121-39.

of the burgeoning middle class on the other. The high-born characters in these novels, bound as they are to the laws and rules of the Code of Courtly Love, are almost invariably doomed to failure. As lovers they seem unable or unwilling to break free of the traditional social restraints that frustrate their amorous intentions; and those who actually dare to circumvent these impediments generally come to an unpleasant — often disastrous — end, a fate not unlike that which will soon await the transgressors of the Honor Code in the later Golden Age Spanish theater.

Starting with the *Siervo libre de Amor* (ca. 1430-40) and taking us through the 1514 publication of *Penitencia de Amor,* Rodríguez-Puértolas points to the central problem posed in the sentimental novel: the uncertainty that the lover experiences regarding which set of ideological principles he should obey, the decaying social values of the old nobility or the emerging new morality of the bourgeoisie. The commentator cites several examples from the genre in which the feudal and bourgeois views of life are contrasted. Particular mention is made of two novels by Juan de Flores, *Grisel y Mirabella* and *Grimalte y Gradissa,* both written between 1480 and 1485 and published in 1495, which Rodríguez-Puértolas feels signal the critical period when the newer system of values began to gain the upper hand. By the time Pedro Manuel de Urrea published his *Penitencia de Amor* in 1514, the conventions of Courtly Love had clearly declined to the point of being only a faint echo and faded shadow of their formerly imposing presence.

Rodríguez-Puértolas posits a progressive growth in popularity, over several decades, of middle-class ideological elements as the prime factor in the conversion of the originally aristocratic *novela sentimental* into a bourgeois genre. Beginning with the novels of Juan de Flores, the protagonists begin to find new solutions to the old "non-conforming individual vs. oppressive feudal society" problem; they embrace a new, sensual kind of courtship that is both free of formal restrictions and steeped in humanistic social values. By the early 1500s, he claims, the sentimental novel had actually been converted into an anti-feudal genre.

I find it ironic that in his catalogue of novels, each of which he claims represents one stage of the sentimental novel's evolution, Rodríguez-Puértolas fails to mention another fictional work from the same period that portrays in one continuous narrative thread the entire process he describes. That work, of course, is Joanot Martorell's *TB*. As I pointed out in Chapter III earlier, Tirant begins his courtship of Carmesina by attempting to adhere strictly to the frustrating rules and conventions of Courtly Love, but with a notable lack of success. When it becomes painfully evident that the creaky system of courtship designed by the Provençal poets will not deliver what he covets (the hand of Carmesina in marriage), Tirant quickly and smoothly alters his battle plan; he abandons the old ways and enlists the aid of a counsellor whose modern, bourgeois notion of courtship (including prompt carnal gratification) shows greater potential.

If Flores' *Grisel y Mirabella* features a corps of feminist reformers who strive to do away with the restrictive old feudal traditions in favor of a sensual, pleasure-seeking philosophy of courship, *TB* in turn offers the influence of Plaerdemavida who counsels the same kind of radical, materialistic approach to finding a mate. *Grimalte y Gradissa,* the second of Flores' novels mentioned in the article, presents a contrasting pair of suitors who are at opposite poles in their approach to courtship. Grimalte accepts unquestioningly the platonic approach demanded by the conventions of Courtly Love, while his counterpart, Pamphilo, is an avid practitioner of the sensual bourgeois style. As might be expected from the extreme positions they take, both fail to win the heart of their respective ladies. Martorell, on the other hand, presents a more measured and moderate case for the "new morality" in his novel; the reasonable accommodations reached first by Diafebus and Estefania, then by Hipòlit and the Empress, and finally by Tirant and Carmesina invariably produce sexually satisfying courtships and felicitous marital unions.

Rodríguez-Puértolas rightly observes that the figure of Pamphilo is merely a symbol of the kind of dehumanization to which certain bourgeois postures, if allowed to run unbridled, can lead. Martorell's Plaerdemavida, conversely, comes across as a relatively reasonable spokesperson for the sensual elements of bourgeois courtship — and in the process she emerges as one of the most realistically drawn characters in the book.

It is my opinion that Rodríguez-Puértolas excluded *TB* from his survey of sentimental novels simply because Martorell's work has always been catalogued as part of the chivalric genre. A sufficient amount of evidence has been presented in this study with regard to the two principal themes of Martorell's novel to justify re-classifying *TB* as both a *novela sentimental* and a *novela caballeresca*. It may in fact be the *only* novel of its time to represent faithfully all the evolutionary stages through which medieval courtship rituals actually passed during the tumultuous fifteenth century.

In closing, then, let me reiterate my contention that Martorell's *TB* can no longer be blithely ignored or pushed off to one side as some sort of curious anomaly. The book must be seriously considered by anyone who wishes to examine the process through which the medieval romance was converted into the modern novel. For all the reasons outlined in this chapter, but especially because of Martorell's skillful employment of what are now considered modern novelistic techniques and his accurate portrayal of military and social changes in the fifteenth century, *TB* should now be viewed as one of the precursors of *Don Quixote* and the modern novel.

BIBLIOGRAPHY

A) EDITIONS OF *TIRANT LO BLANCH* CONSULTED:

IN CATALAN:

Libre del valerós e strenu cavaller Tirant lo Blanch. Valencia: Nicolau Spindeler, 1490. I was able to peruse the copies currently held by the Biblioteca Provincial de Valencia and the Hispanic Society of America in New York. I did not need to consult the only other extant copy of this edition, that of the British Museum in London.

Libre del valerós e strenu cavaller Tirant lo Blanch. Barcelona: Diego de Gumiel, 1497. I consulted the partial copy housed at the Biblioteca de Catalunya in Barcelona and the complete surviving text at New York's Hispanic Society of America.

Riquer, Martín de, ed. *Tirant lo Blanc*. Barcelona: Selecta, 1947.

———, ed. *Tirant lo Blanc i altres escrits de Joanot Martorell*. Barcelona: Ariel, 1979.

IN CASTILIAN:

Los cinco libros del esforçado e invencible cavallero Tirante el Blanco de Roca Salada, cavallero de la Garrotera. Valladolid: Diego de Gumiel, 1511. Reproduced with introduction and notes by Martín de Riquer, Clásicos Castellanos, 5 vols. Madrid: Espasa-Calpe, 1974.

Vidal Jové, J. F., trans. *Tirant lo Blanc*. 2 vols. Madrid: Alianza, 1969. Prologue ("Carta de batalla") by Mario Vargas Llosa.

B) WORKS OF GENERAL INTEREST:

Dunlop, John Colin. *History of Prose Fiction*. London: Longman, 1814. Revised and edited by Henry Wilson. London: G. Bell, 1888; New York: AHS Press, 1969.

Durán, Armando. *Estructura y técnicas de la novela sentimental y caballeresca*. Madrid: Gredos, 1973.

Menéndez y Pelayo, Marcelino. *Orígenes de la novela*. Vol. 1. Madrid: Bailly-Ballière, 1905-15. Reprinted in Edición Nacional, 2nd ed., Vol. XIII. Madrid: Consejo Superior de Investigaciones Científicas, 1961.

Milá y Fontanals, Manuel. *Estudios sobre historia, lengua y literatura de Cataluña*. Vol. III of *Obras completas*. 6 vols. Barcelona: Verdaguer, 1889-99.
Warren, Frederick Morris. *A History of the Novel Previous to the Seventeenth Century*. New York: Holt, 1895.

C) *TIRANT LO BLANCH* AND *DON QUIXOTE*:

Arnold, H. H. "The Most Difficult Passage of *Don Quijote*." *Modern Language Notes*, 50 (1935), 182-85.
Aylward, Edward T. "The Influence of *Tirant lo Blanch* on the *Quijote*." Diss. Princeton 1974.
Bandera, Cesáreo. "Cervantes frente a *Don Quijote*. Violenta simetría entre la realidad y la ficción." *MLN*, 89 (1974), 159-72. Reproduced in *Mimesis conflictiva. Ficción literaria y violenta en Cervantes y Calderón*. Madrid: Gredos, 1975, pp. 39-44.
Bates, Margaret. "Cervantes' Criticism of *Tirant lo Blanch*." *Hispanic Review*, 21 (1953), 142-44.
———. "Cervantes and Martorell." *Hispanic Review*, 35 (1967), 365-66.
Centeno, Augusto. "Sobre el pasaje del *Quijote* referente al *Tirant lo Blanch*." *Modern Language Notes*, 50 (1935), 375-78.
Díaz-Valenzuela, Octavio. "Sobre el pasaje más oscuro del *Quijote*." *Hispania*, 16 (1933), 149-53.
Eisenberg, Daniel. "Pero Pérez the Priest and His Comment on *Tirant lo Blanch*." *MLN*, 88 (1973), 321-30.
Escribano Sánchez, Federico. "El sentido cervantino del ataque contra los libros de caballería." *Anales Cervantinos*, 5 (1955-56), 19-40.
Givanel i Mas, Joan. "El *Tirant lo Blanch* i *Don Quijote de la Mancha*." Barcelona: Casa de Caritat, 1922.
Impiwaara, Heikki. "La portentosa memoria de Cervantes." *Neuphilologische Mitteilungen*, 37 (1936), 42-45.
McCready, Warren T. "Cervantes and the Caballero Fonseca." *MLN*, 83 (1958), 33-35.
Mendizábal, Rufo. "Más notas para el *Quijote*." *Revista de Filología Española*, 12 (1925), 180.
Montoliu, Manuel de. "El juicio de Cervantes sobre el *Tirant lo Blanch*." *Boletín de la Real Academia Española*, 29 (1949), 263-77.
Palacín, G. B. "El pasaje más oscuro del *Quijote*." *Duquesne Hispanic Review*, 3 (1964), 1-18.
Riley, Edward C. *Cervantes' Theory of the Novel*. Oxford: Clarendon Press, 1962.
Riquer, Martín de. "Cervantes y la caballeresca." In *Summa Cervantina*. Eds. Juan B. Avalle-Arce and Edward C. Riley. London: Tamesis, 1973, pp. 273-92.
———. "'Echar a galeras' y el pasaje más oscuro del *Quijote*." *Revista de Filología Española*, 27 (1943), 82-86.
Rubens, E. F. "Sobre el capítulo VI de la primera parte del *Quijote*." *Cuadernos del Sur Bahía Blanca: Universidad Nacional del Sur, Instituto de Humanidades*, N. D. (1959), 35-37, n. 13.
Sansone, Giuseppe E. "Ancora del giudizio di Cervantes sul *Tirant lo Blanch*." *Studi Mediolatini e Volgari*, 8 (1960), 235-53.

Sanvisenti, Bernardo. "Il passo più oscuro del *Chisciotte*." *Revista de Filología Española*, 9 (1922), 58-62.
Sola-Solé, Josep M. "El *Tirant* i el *Quixot*." In *Estudis de llengua i literatures catalanes oferts a Ramon Aramon i Serra en el seu setantè aniversari*. Barcelona: Curial, 1980, I, 543-52.
Torres-Alcalá, Antoni. *El realismo de* Tirant lo Blanch *y su influencia en el* Quijote. Barcelona: Puvill, 1979.

D) ON *TIRANT LO BLANCH:*

Alonso, Dámaso. "El realismo libre y vitalista del *Tirant-lo-Blanc:* Un ejemplo." *Coloquio*, 7 (1972), 5-11.
———. "*Tirant lo Blanch*, novela moderna." *Revista Valenciana de Filología*, I (1951), 179-215. Reproduced in *Primavera temprana de la literatura europea*. Madrid: Guadarrama, 1960, pp. 201-53.
Avalle-Arce, Juan B. "Para las fuentes de *Tirant lo Blanc*." In *Temas Hispánicos Medievales*. Madrid: Gredos, 1974, 233-61.
Beltrán Llavador, Rafael. "*Tirant lo Blanc*, evolución y revuelta de la narración de caballerías." Diss. Universidad de Valencia 1981. Forthcoming as: Tirant lo Blanc, *evolució i revolta de la narració de cavalleries*. Valencia: Institució Alfons el Magnànim.
Boehne, Patricia. *Dream and Fantasy in Fourteenth- and Fifteenth-Century Catalan Prose*. Barcelona: Hispam, 1975.
Bohigas, Pere, ed. "Guillem de Varoic." In *Tractats de Cavalleria:* Vol. 57 of the series "Els Nostres Clàssics." Barcelona: Barcino, 1947.
———. "La Matière de Bretagne en Catalogne." *Bulletin Bibliographique de la Société Internationale Arthurienne*, 13 (1961), 92-94.
Bonilla y San Martín, Adolfo. "Las novelas catalanas de caballerías y *Tirant lo Blanch*. In *Primer Congrés Internacional de la Llengua Catalana*. Barcelona: 1908, pp. 577-83.
Bonsoms y Sicart, Isidoro. "La edición príncipe de *Tirant lo Blanch*. Cotejo de los tres ejemplares impresos en Valencia, únicos conservados hoy día." *Discursos leídos en la recepción pública de don Isidoro Bonsoms y Sicart el día 9 de mayo de 1907*. Barcelona: Tip. La Académica, de Serra Hermanos y Russell, 1907, pp. 9-63.
Bosch, Siegfried. "La batalla a 'ús e costum de França' en el *Tirant lo Blanch*." *Estudis Romànics*, 3 (1951-52), 99-101.
———. "Les fonts orientals del *Tirant lo Blanch*." *Estudis Romànics*, 2 (1949-50), 1-50.
Brummer, Rudolf. "Die Episode von König Artus im *Tirant lo Blanc*." *Estudis Romànics*, 10 (1962), 283-90.
Colón, Germán. "Premiers échos de l'Ordre de la Jarretière." *Zeitschrift für Romanische Philologie*, 81 (1965), 441-53.
Corominas, Joan. "Sobre l'estil i manera de Martí J. de Galba i el de Joanot Martorell." *Homenatge a Carles Riba*. Barcelona: 1954, 168-84.
Dauster, Frank. "Pantaleón and Tirant: Points of Contact." *Hispanic Review*, 48 (1980), 269-85.
Entwistle, William J. "Observacions sobre la dedicatòria i primera part del *Tirant lo Blanch*." *Revista de Catalunya*, 7 (1927), 381-98.
———. "*Tirant lo Blanch* and the Social Order of the End of the Fifteenth Century." *Estudis Romànics*, 2 (1949-50), 149-64.

Fanés, Félix. "Ací jau *Tirant lo Blanc*...." *Tele/express*. 11 Dec. 1974.
Gili y Gaya, Samuel. *Interpretació moderna de* Tirant lo Blanc. Lleida (Lérida): Institut d'Estudis Llerdenses, 1969.
———. "Notas sobre Johanot Martorell." *Revista de Filología Española*, 24 (1937), 204-08.
———. "Nous aspectes del *Tirant lo Blanc*." *Pont Blau*, 7 (1959), 46-50.
———. "Noves recerques sobre *Tirant lo Blanc*." *Estudis Romànics*, I (1947-48), 135-47.
Givanel i Mas, Joan. "Les edicions gòtiques del *Tirant lo Blanch* en la Biblioteca de Catalunya." *Butlletí de la Biblioteca de Catalunya*, 3 (1916), 58-72.
———. "Estudio crítico de la novela caballeresca *Tirant lo Blanch*." *Archivo de Investigaciones Históricas*, I, 213-48, 319-48; II, 392-445, 477-513; Madrid, 1911. Reproduced as *La novela caballeresca española: Estudio crítico de* Tirant lo Blanch. Madrid: V. Suárez, 1912.
Goertz, Wolf. "Zur Frage der Einheit des *Tirant lo Blanc*." *Romanistisches Jahrbuch*, 18 (1967), 249-67.
Goldberg, Harriet. "Clothing in *Tirant lo Blanc*: Evidence of 'realismo vitalista' or of a New Unreality," *Hispanic Review*, 52 (1984), 379-92.
Guillén, Julio F. "Un golpe de mano en el siglo xv." *Revista General de Marina*, 174 (1968), 651-58.
———. *Lo marinero en el* Tirant lo Blanc. Madrid: Instituto Histórico de la Marina, 1969.
Hatzfeld, Helmut. "La Décadence de l'amour courtois dans le *Saintré*, *Revista de Archivos, Bibliotecas y Museos*, 37 (1917), 239-69.
Hatzfeld, Helmut. "La décadence de l'amour courtois dans le *Saintré*, l'*Amadís* et le *Tirant lo Blanc*." In *Mélanges de littérature: Du moyen-âge au XXe siècle*. Paris: École Normale Supérieure de Jeunes Filles, 1978, I, 339-50.
Ivars, Andreu. "Ausías March y Joanot Martorell." *Erudición Ibero-Ultramarina*, I (1930), 68-82; 173-206.
———. "Estatge de Joanot Martorell a Londres." *Anales del Centro de Cultura Valenciana*, 2 (1929), 54-62.
Knowlton, Edgar G., Jr. "Lewis' *The Monk* and *Tirant lo Blanch*." *Notes and Queries*. New Series, 30 (1983), 64-65.
Marinesco, Constantín. "Du nouveau sur *Tirant lo Blanch*." *Estudis Romànics*, 4 (1953-54), 137-204. Later issued as "Nuevas notas sobre *Tirant lo Blanch*." *Boletín de la Real Academia de la Historia*, 138 (1956), 287-305.
———. "Nouvelles recherches sur *Tirant lo Blanch*." *Boletín de la Real Academia de Buenas Letras de Barcelona*, 28 (1959-60), 363.
———. "Nouvelles recherches sur *Tirant lo Blanch*." In *Estudis de llengua i literatures catalanes oferts a Ramon Aramon i Serra en el seu setantè aniversari*. Barcelona: Curial, 1980, II, 402-24.
Martínez y Martínez, Francisco. *Martín Juan de Galba, coautor del* Tirant lo Blanch. Valencia: Vives Mora, 1916.
McNerney, Kathleen. Tirant lo Blanc *Revisited: A Critical Study*. Ann Arbor: Fifteenth-century Symposium, 1983.
Miquel i Planes, Ramón. "Bibliografía del *Tirant lo Blanch*." *Bibliofilia*, I (1911-14), 455-61.
Miralles, Carles. " 'Mas no les obres.' Remarques sobre la narració i la concepció de l'amor en el *Tirant lo Blanc*." In *Estudis de llengua i*

literatures catalanes oferts a Ramon Aramon i Serra en el seu setantè aniversari. Barcelona: Curial, 1980, II, 395-413.
Molas, Joaquim. "El cas *Tirant*." In *Una cultura en crisi*. Barcelona: Edicions 62, 1971, pp. 28-35.
Moliné i Brasés, Ernest. "Addició a la 'Letra de reyals costums' del Petrarca." *Anuari de l'Institut d'Estudis Catalans*, 2 (1908), 619-20.
———. "La 'Letra de reyals costums' del Petrarca." *Anuari de l'Institut d'Estudis Catalans*, I (1907), 345-51.
Moll, Francesc de B. "Els refranys del *Tirant lo Blanch*." *Bolletí del Diccionari de la Llengua Catalana*, 15 (1933), 169-72.
———. "Rudiments de versificació en el *Tirant lo Blanch*." *Bolletí del Diccionari de la Llengua Catalana*, 16 (1934), 179-82.
Montoliu, Manuel de. *Un escorç en la poesia i la novel·lística dels segles XIV i XV*. Barcelona: Alpha, 1961.
Navarro, Josep. "Una interpretació hispanoamericana del *Tirant lo Blanc*." In *Estudis de llengua i literatures catalanes oferts a Ramon Aramon i Serra en el seu setantè aniversari*. Barcelona: Curial, 1980, II, pp. 435-44.
Nicolau i d'Olwer, Lluís. "Al marge de *Tirant lo Blanc*." In *Paisatges de la nostra història: Assaigs i notes de literatura catalana*. Barcelona: 1929, pp. 189-94.
———. "L'Art dans la vie sociale de la Catalogne, d'après les romans du XVe siècle." In *La peinture catalane à la fin du moyen-âge*. Paris: Presses Universitaires de France, 1933, pp. 119-35.
———. "Un Témoignage catalan du siège de Rhodes en 1444." *Estudis Universitaris Catalans*, 12 (1927), 376-87.
———. "*Tirant lo Blanc*: Examen de algunas cuestiones," *Nueva Revista de Filología Hispánica*, 15 (1961), 131-54.
Pierce, Frank. "The Role of Sex in the *Tirant lo Blanc*." *Estudis Romànics*, 10 (1962), 291-300.
Riquer, Martín de. "L'Art militar al *Tirant lo Blanc*." In *In memoriam Carles Riba*. Barcelona: Ariel, 1973, pp. 325-38.
———. "Nuevas contribuciones a las fuentes del *Tirant lo Blanc*." In *Conferencias desarrolladas con motivo del IV Centenario del nacimiento de Miguel de Cervantes*. Barcelona: Biblioteca Central, 1949, pp. 9-30.
———. "Un nuevo ejemplar del *Tirant lo Blanc* de Valladolid, de 1511." In *Miscellánea Barcinonensia*, año XIV, 42 (1975), 7-15.
———. Prologue to his edition of *Tirant lo Blanc*. 2 vols. Barcelona: Seix Barral, 1970.
———. "Relaciones entre la literatura renacentista castellana y la catalana en la Edad Media." *Escorial*, 2 (1941), 31-49.
——— and Mario Vargas Llosa. *El combate imaginario: las cartas de batalla de Joanot Martorell*. Barcelona: Barral, 1972.
Roubaud, Sylvia. "Chevalier contre chien: l'étrange duel du *Tirant lo Blanc*." In *Mélanges de la Casa de Velázquez*. Madrid: 1970; 6, pp. 131-59.
Rubió i Balaguer, Jordi. "Els plagis del *Tirant lo Blanc*." In *De l'Etat Mitjana al Renaixement: Figures literàries de Catalunya i València*. Barcelona: Aymà, 1948, pp. 74-77.
Rubió i Lluch, Antoni. "Discurso de contestación." *Discursos leídos en la recepción pública de D. Isidoro Bonshoms Sicart el día 9 de mayo de 1907*. Barcelona: Tip. La Académica, de Serra Hermanos y Russell, 1907, pp. 141-70.

Salvador, Vicent. "Les formes rituals al *Tirant lo Blanc*. Algunes reflexions semiòtiques." *L'Espill*, 12 (1981), 43-52.
Serís, Homero. "La reaparición del *Tirant lo Blanc* de Barcelona de 1497; primera descripción bibliográfica completa." *Homenaje ofrecido a Menéndez Pidal*. Madrid: Hernando, 1925; 3, 57-76.
Southey, Robert. "Tirante el Blanco." In *Omniana*, ed. Robert Gittings. Carbondale: Southern Illinois Press, 1969, pp. 275-80.
Tate, Robert B. "Joanot Martorell in England." *Estudis Romànics*, 10 (1962), 277-81.
Terry, Arthur. "Character and Role in *Tirant lo Blanc*." In *Essays on Narrative Fiction in the Iberian Peninsula in Honour of Frank Pierce*. Ed. R. B. Tate. Oxford: Dolphin, 1982, pp. 177-95.
Vaeth, Joseph A. *Tirant lo Blanch: A Study of its Authorship, Principal Sources and Historical Setting*. Studies in Romance Philology and Literature. New York: Columbia University, 1918; reprint New York: AMS Press, 1966.
Valesio, Paolo. "Genealogy of a Staged Scene (*Orlando Furioso*, V)." *Yale Italian Studies*, New Series I (1980), 5-31.
Vargas Llosa, Mario. "Carta de batalla por *Tirant lo Blanc*." In the J. F. Vidal Jové edition of *Tirant lo Blanc*. Madrid: Alianza, 1969; I, 9-41.
———. *Lletre de Batalla per Tirant lo Blanc*. Barcelona: Edicions 62, 1976.
Yates, Alan. "*Tirant lo Blanc:* the Ambiguous Hero." In *Hispanic Studies in Honour of Frank Pierce Presented by Former and Present Members of the Department of Hispanic Studies in the University of Sheffield*. Sheffield: Dept. of Hispanic Studies, Univ. of Sheffield, 1980, pp. 181-98.

E) RELATED STUDIES:

Ashmole, Elias. *The Institution, Laws and Ceremonies of the Most Noble Order of the Garter*. London: J. Macock, 1672.
Belenguer Cebrià, Ernest. *València en la crisi del segle XV*. Barcelona: Edicions 62, 1976.
Bohigas, Pere. "Orígenes de los libros de caballería." In *Historia general de las literaturas hispánicas*. Barcelona: Barna, 1949, 3, pp. 521-41.
Coleman, Alexander. "The Transfiguration of the Chivalric Novel." *World Literature Today*, 52 (1978), 24-30.
Green, James Ray, Jr. "La forma de la ficción caballeresca del siglo XVI." In *Actas del sexto congreso internacional de hispanistas*. Toronto: University of Toronto, 1980, pp. 353-55.
Huizinga, Johan. *The Waning of the Middle Ages*. London: E. Arnold, 1924; reprint 1963.
Keightley, Ronald G. "Muntaner and the Catalan Grand Company." *Revista canadiense de estudios hispánicos*, 4 (1979), 37-58.
Lida de Malkiel, María Rosa. "Arthurian Literature in Spain and Portugal." In *Arthurian Literature in the Middle Ages*. Ed. Roger S. Loomis. Oxford: Clarendon Press, 1959, pp. 406-18.
———. *La idea de la fama en la Edad Media castellana*. Mexico: Fondo de Cultura Económico, 1952.
Moncada, Francisco de. *Expedición de los catalanes y aragoneses contra turcos y griegos*. Madrid: Espasa-Calpe, 1941.

Montoliú, Manuel de. *Les quatre grans cròniques.* Barcelona: Alpha, 1959.
Muntaner, Ramon. *Chronica, o descripció dels fets, e hazanyes del inclyt rey don Jaume Primer Rey d'Aragó, de Mallorques e de Valencia, Compte de Barcelona e de Muntpeller, e de molts de sos descendents.* Valencia: Vda. de Joan Mey Flandro, 1558.
―――. *The Chronicle of Muntaner.* Trans. Lady Goodenough. 2 vols. Hakluyt Society, 1920-21; reprint Weisbaden: Kraus, 1967.
―――. *Crónica.* Trans. J. F. Vidal Jové. Introduction by Joan Fuster. Madrid: Alianza, 1970.
―――. *L'expedició dels catalans a orient.* Barcelona: Barcino, 1951.
Nicolau i d'Olwer, Lluís. *L'expansió de Catalunya en la mediterrània oriental.* Barcelona: Barcino, 1926.
Riquer, Martín de. *L'Arnès del cavaller: armes i armadures catalanes medievals.* Barcelona: Ariel, 1968.
―――. *Caballeros andantes españoles.* Madrid: Espasa-Calpe, 1967.
―――. "Evolución estilística de la prosa catalana medieval." *Miscellánea Barcinonensia,* año XVII, 49 (1978), 7-19.
―――. *Lletres de Batalla.* 2 vols. Barcelona: Barcino, 1963.
―――. *Vida caballeresca en la España del siglo XV.* Madrid: Gráficas Marina, 1965.
Rubió i Balaguer, Jordi. *La cultura catalana del renaixement a la decadència.* Barcelona: Edicions 62, 1964.
―――. "Sobre els orígens de l'humanisme a Catalunya." *Bulletin of Spanish Studies,* 24 (1947), 88-99.
Rubió i Lluch, Antoni. *El renacimiento clásico en la literatura catalana.* Barcelona: Jepus Roviralta, 1889.
Ruiz de Conde, Justina. *El amor y el matrimonio secreto en los libros de caballerías.* Madrid: Aguilar, 1948.
Vendrell y Moll, Francisca. "La corte literaria de Alfonso V de Aragón." *Boletín de la Real Academia Española,* 19 (1932), 85-100, 388-405, 468-84, 584-607, 733-47; 20 (1933), 69-92.
Vinaver, Eugène. *The Rise of Romance.* Oxford: Clarendon Press, 1971.

NORTH CAROLINA STUDIES IN THE ROMANCE LANGUAGES AND LITERATURES

I.S.B.N. Prefix 0-88438

Recent Titles

LE VAIN SIECLE GUERPIR. A Literary Approach to Sainthood through Old French Hagiography of the Twelfth Century, by Phyllis Johnson and Brigitte Cazelles. 1979. (No. 205). *-9205-X.*

THE POETRY OF CHANGE: A STUDY OF THE SURREALIST WORKS OF BENJAMIN PÉRET, by Julia Field Costich. 1979. (No. 206). *-9206-8.*

NARRATIVE PERSPECTIVE IN THE POST-CIVIL WAR NOVELS OF FRANCISCO AYALA "MUERTES DE PERRO" AND "EL FONDO DEL VASO", by Maryellen Bieder. 1979. (No. 207). *-9207-6.*

RABELAIS: HOMO LOGOS, by Alice Fiola Berry. 1979. (No. 208). *-9208-4.*

"DUEÑAS" AND "DONCELLAS": A STUDY OF THE "DOÑA RODRÍGUEZ" EPISODE IN "DON QUIJOTE", by Conchita Herdman Marianella. 1979. (No. 209). *-9209-2.*

PIERRE BOAISTUAU'S "HISTOIRES TRAGIQUES": A STUDY OF NARRATIVE FORM AND TRAGIC VISION, by Richard A. Carr. 1979. (No. 210). *-9210-6.*

REALITY AND EXPRESSION IN THE POETRY OF CARLOS PELLICER, by George Melnykovich. 1979. (No. 211). *-9211-4.*

MEDIEVAL MAN, HIS UNDERSTANDING OF HIMSELF, HIS SOCIETY, AND THE WORLD, by Urban T. Holmes, Jr. 1980. (No. 212). *-9212-2.*

MÉMOIRES SUR LA LIBRAIRIE ET SUR LA LIBERTÉ DE LA PRESSE, introduction and notes by Graham E. Rodmell. 1979. (No. 213). *-9213-0.*

THE FICTIONS OF THE SELF. THE EARLY WORKS OF MAURICE BARRES, by Gordon Shenton. 1979. (No. 214). *-9214-9.*

CECCO ANGIOLIERI. A STUDY, by Gifford P. Orwen. 1979. (No. 215). *-9215-7.*

THE INSTRUCTIONS OF SAINT LOUIS: A CRITICAL TEXT, by David O'Connell. 1979. (No. 216). *-9216-5.*

ARTFUL ELOQUENCE, JEAN LEMAIRE DE BELGES AND THE RHETORICAL TRADITION, by Michael F. O. Jenkins. 1980. (No. 217). *-9217-3.*

A CONCORDANCE TO MARIVAUX'S COMEDIES IN PROSE, edited by Donald C. Spinelli. 1979. (No. 218). 4 volumes, *-9218-1* (set); *-9219-X* (v. 1); *-9220-3* (v. 2); *-9221-1* (v. 3); *-9222-X* (v. 4.)

ABYSMAL GAMES IN THE NOVELS OF SAMUEL BECKETT, by Angela B. Moorjani. 1982. (No. 219). *-9223-8.*

GERMAIN NOUVEAU DIT HUMILIS: ÉTUDE BIOGRAPHIQUE, par Alexandre L. Amprimoz. 1983. (No. 220). *-9224-6.*

THE "VIE DE SAINT ALEXIS" IN THE TWELFTH AND THIRTEENTH CENTURIES: AN EDITION AND COMMENTARY, by Alison Goddard Elliot. 1983. (No. 221). *-9225-4.*

THE BROKEN ANGEL: MYTH AND METHOD IN VALÉRY, by Ursula Franklin. 1984. (No. 222). *-9226-2.*

READING VOLTAIRE'S "CONTES": A SEMIOTICS OF PHILOSOPHICAL NARRATION, by Carol Sherman. 1985. (No. 223). *-9227-0.*

THE STATUS OF THE READING SUBJECT IN THE "LIBRO DE BUEN AMOR", by Marina Scordilis Brownlee. 1985. (No. 224). *-9228-9.*

MARTORELL'S "TIRANT LO BLANCH": A PROGRAM FOR MILITARY AND SOCIAL REFORM IN FIFTEENTH-CENTURY CHRISTENDOM, by Edward T. Aylward. 1985. (No. 225). *-9229-7.*

When ordering please cite the *ISBN Prefix* plus the last four digits for each title.

Send orders to: University of North Carolina Press
　　　　　　　　　Chapel Hill
　　　　　　　　　North Carolina 27514
　　　　　　　　　U. S. A.

The Department of Romance Studies Digital Arts and Collaboration Lab at the University of North Carolina at Chapel Hill is proud to support the digitization of the North Carolina Studies in the Romance Languages and Literatures series.

www.ingramcontent.com/pod-product-compliance
Lightning Source LLC
Chambersburg PA
CBHW022018220426
43663CB00007B/1122